AF395935

What should I say about Seoul?

Editorial Letter

What should we say about Seoul? When we started this book we wanted to create an alternative tourist guide to the city. We took photos, talked to local designers, and tasted the Korean cuisine. Back at home, we became painfully aware that our impressions weren't so alternative after all. We had fallen into the trap of documenting and viewing Seoul through a typical western lens—thereby reproducing a stereotype. This was a humbling discovery about ourselves.

So, where to go from here? Ditch the whole project or start anew? We decided to double down on subjectivity. But instead of just portraying our subjective viewpoint, we asked others to include theirs as well. This way, the book gives a glimpse into South Korean society that is not so common after all.

By no means is the book all-encompassing. We focused on the works and experiences of designers because that is what we could relate to the most considering we are design students ourselves.

Some of the insights into the Seoul work experience appear grim at places. We think this was in part colored by the ongoing pandemic that forced people to cut down on social interactions. Despite the work conditions, the designers we spoke to where overall happy with the work they did.

We also included the experiences of Korean-German designers in the book and through that we noticed that there is really no reason to think of Germany as a country that "has it figured out." The modern workplace can be a very mixed bag at times and bad working conditions plague the creative industry worldwide. Speaking about these experiences allows us to feel less isolated and work towards change—so it is not all doom and gloom. Over all, we encountered many instances of motivation and inspiration in the interviews.

The interviews also gifted us with the title for the book. When formulating answers to our questions the interviewees often used the phrase "뭐라고 하지?" (molago haji—"What should I say?"). This grasping for words expressed our own uncertainty over formulating something definitive about Seoul so we found it to be a perfect fit for the book's title.

So, what should we say about Seoul? Nothing conclusive, but a lot that makes you want to know more.

David Wiesner, Omid Fröhlich, Youjin Kim
Editorial Staff

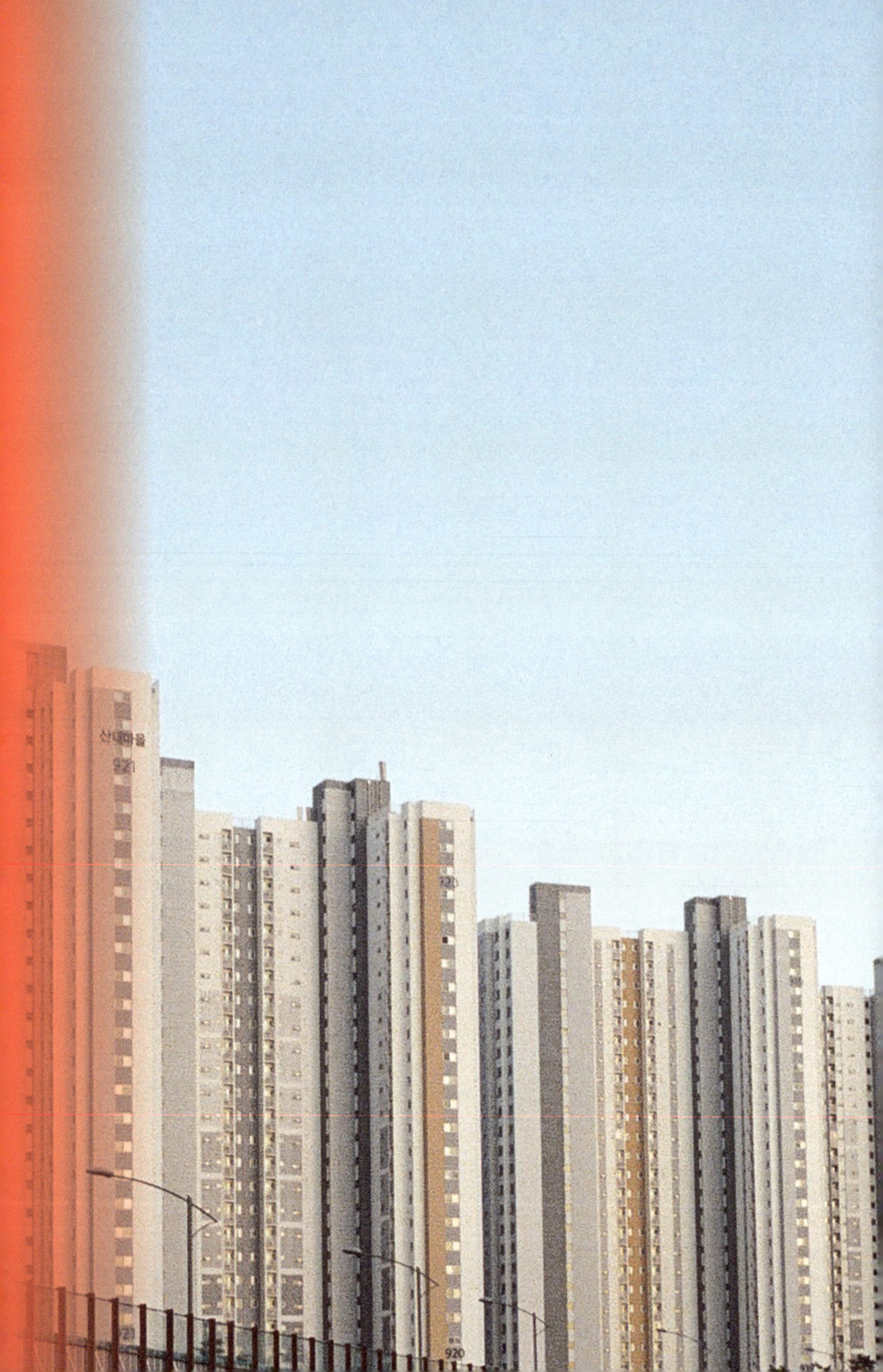

산내마을
920
920

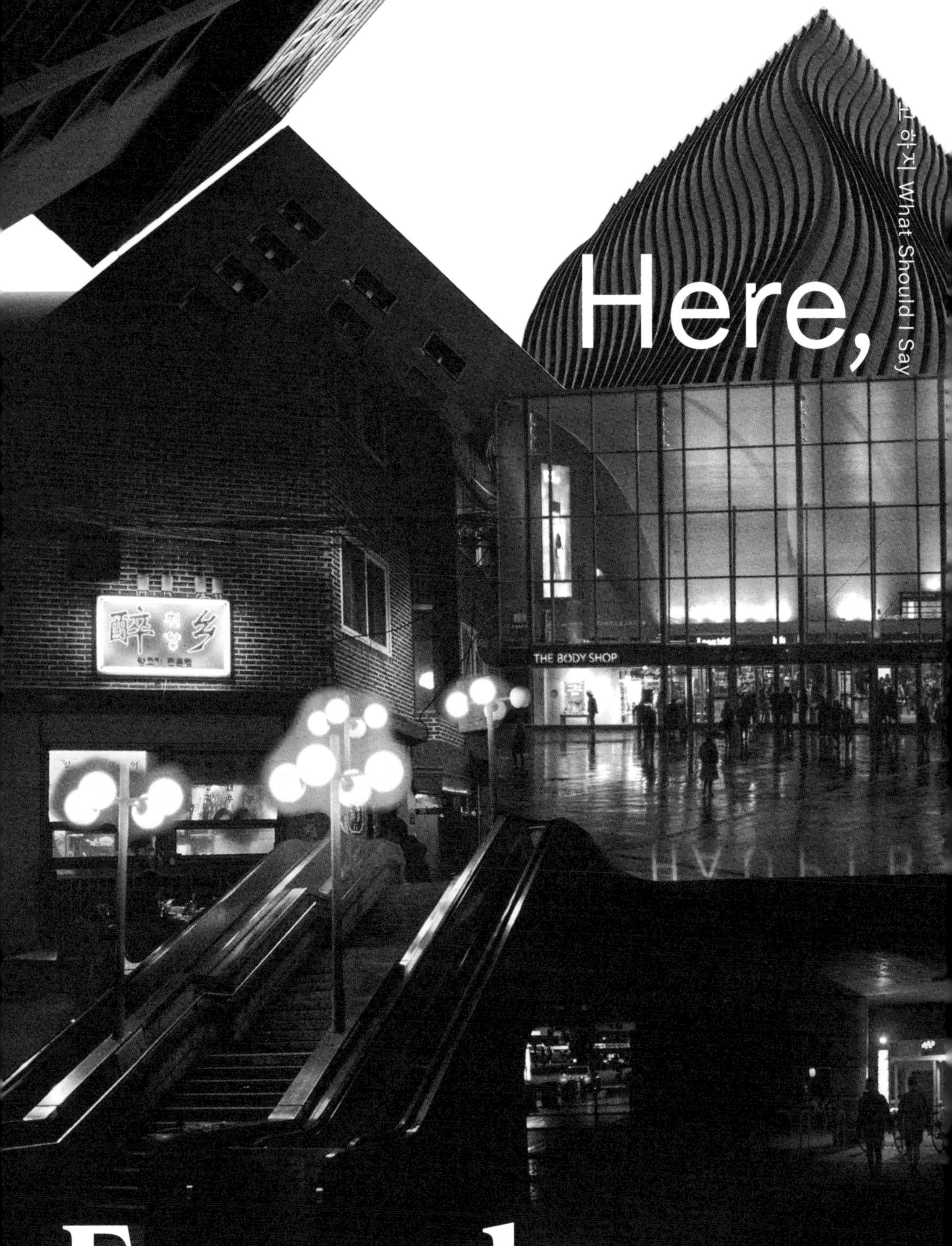
Here,
Everywhere
THE BODY SHOP
醉多

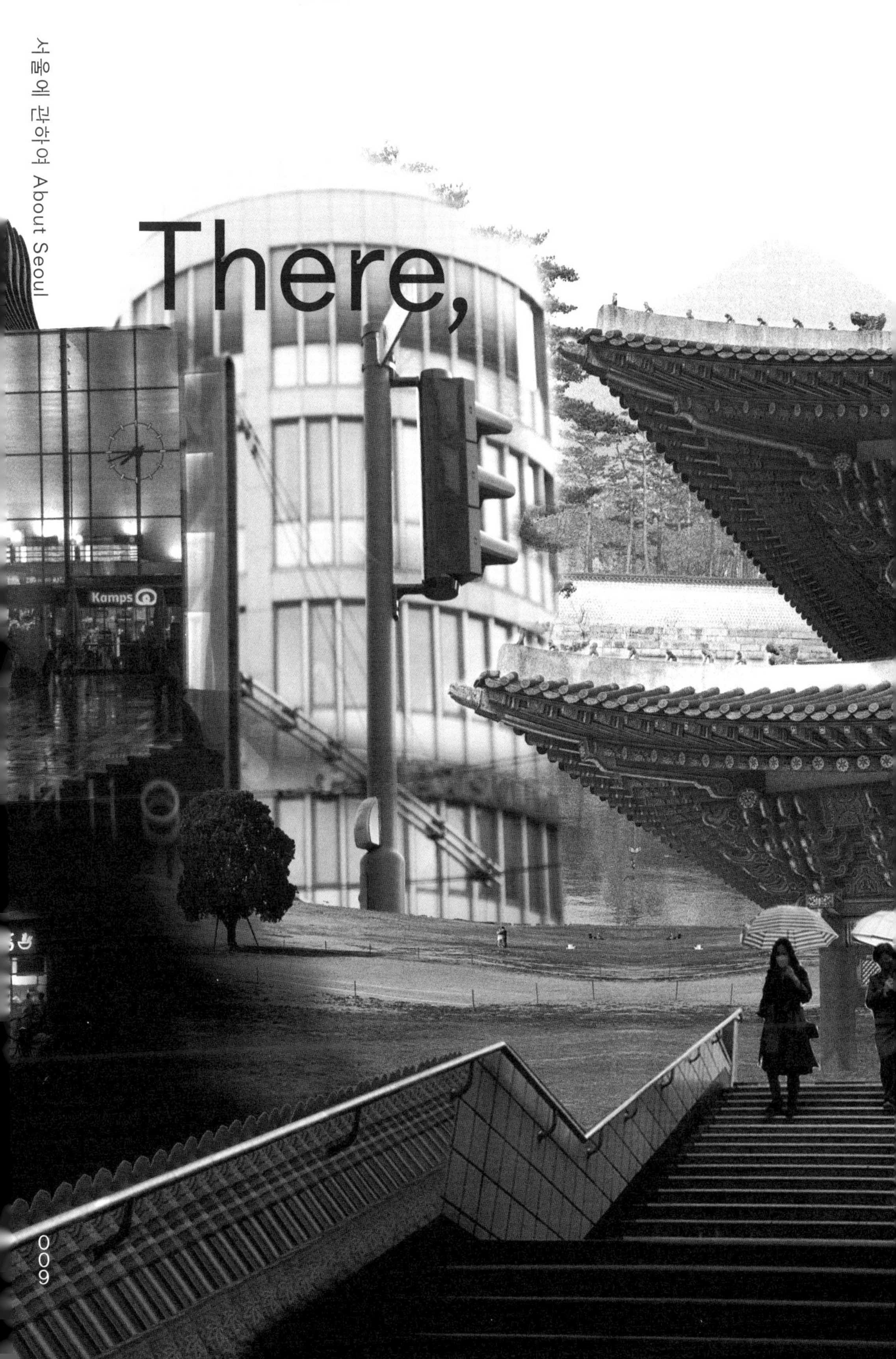
There,

Pictures: Omid Fröhlich & David Wiesner

There is often an expectation that things
have to be oh-so-different in another
country. But in a globalized world there are
a lot of structural similarities all across the
world. Without diminishing each countries
unique features we wanted to challenge
our own assumption on the foreign other
by pairing pictures of scenes that bear
similarity, but were taken at different cities
(namely Seoul and Cologne).

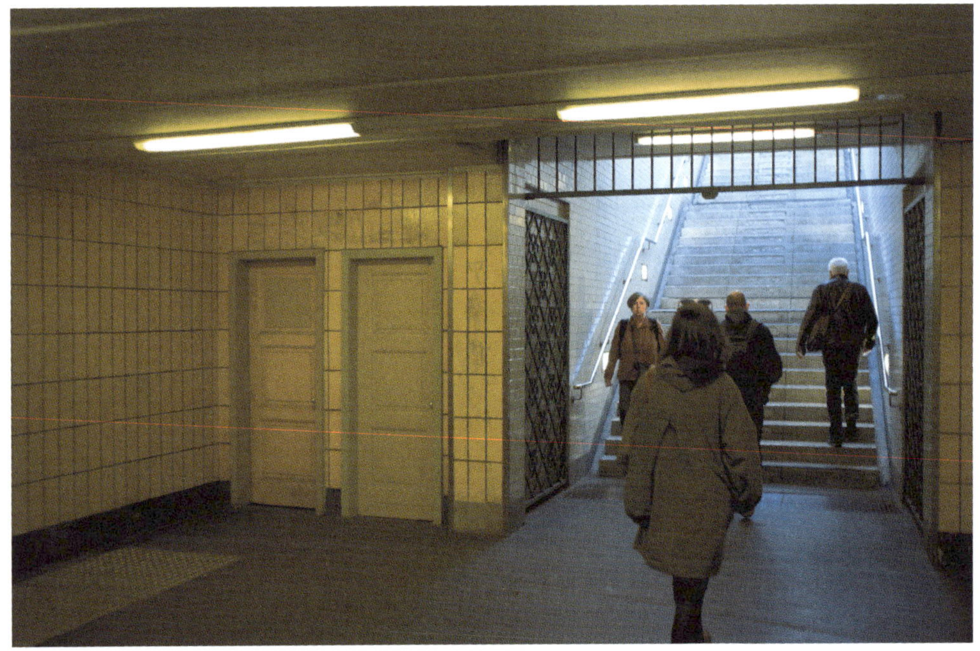

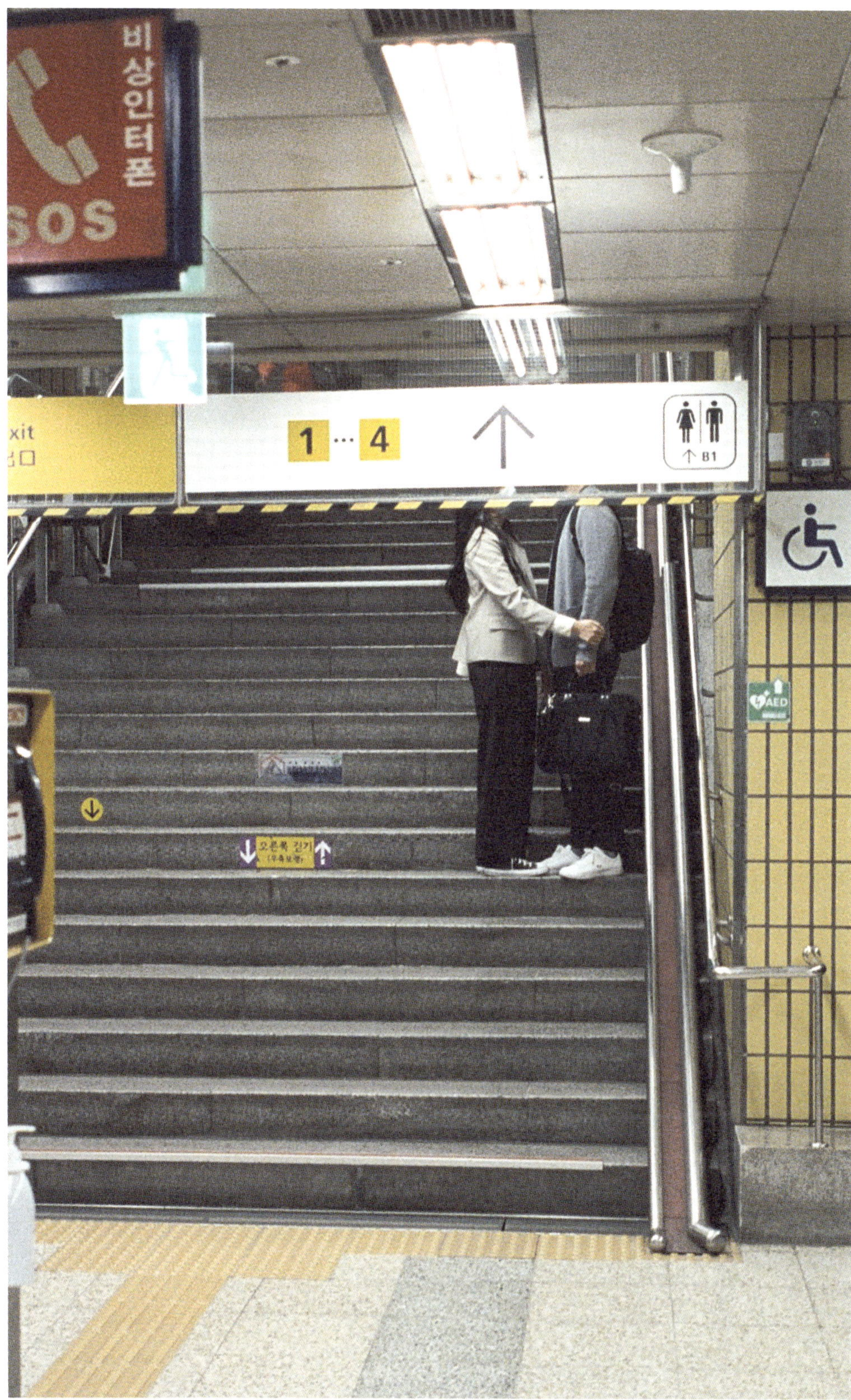
SOS
비상인터폰
비상인터폰
xit
出口
1 … 4
B1
오른쪽 걷기
(우측보행)
AED

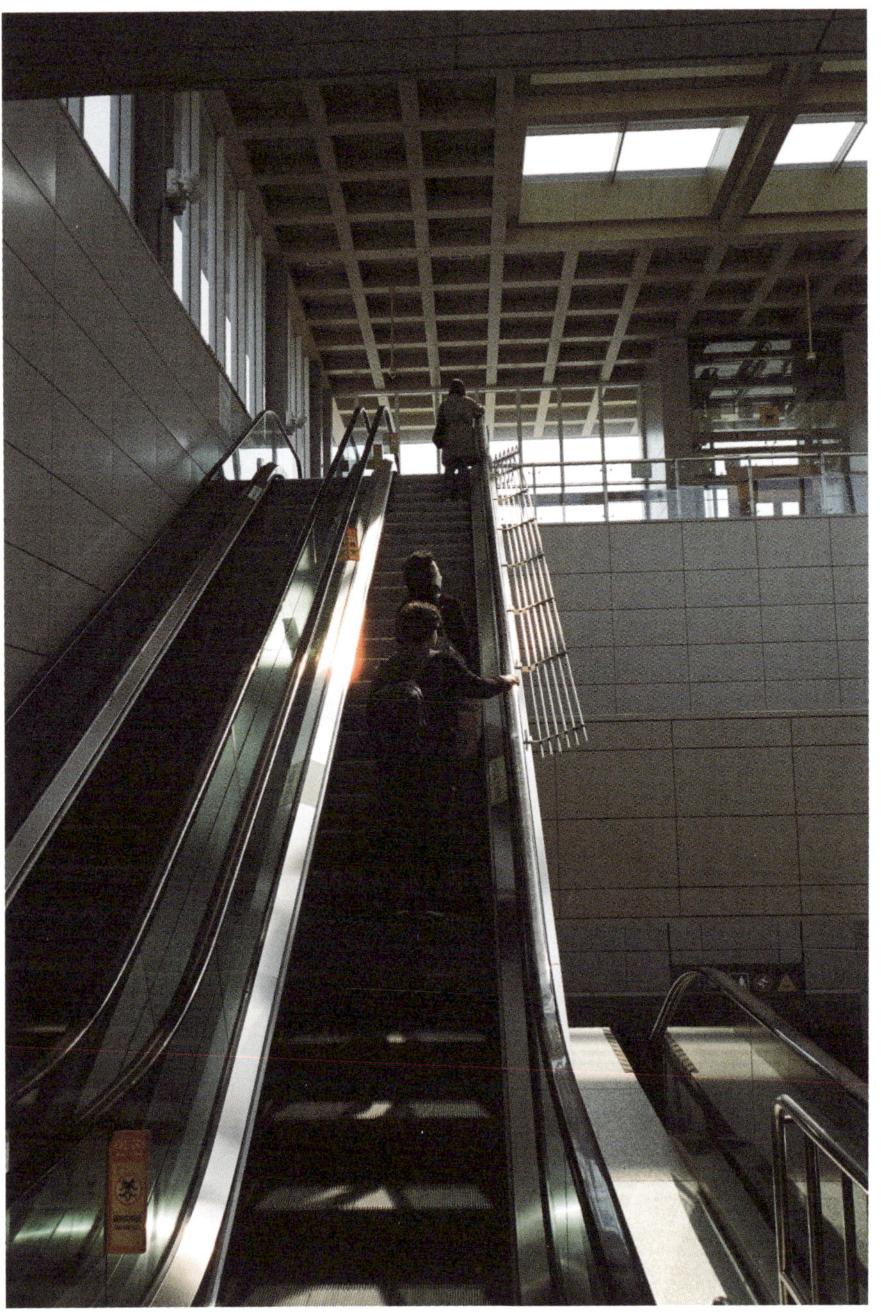

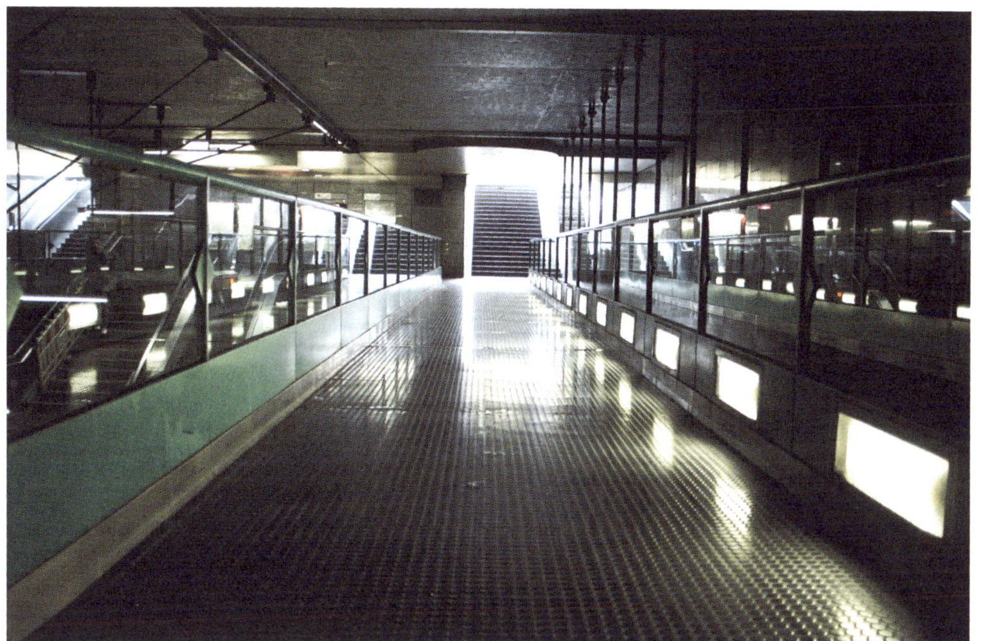

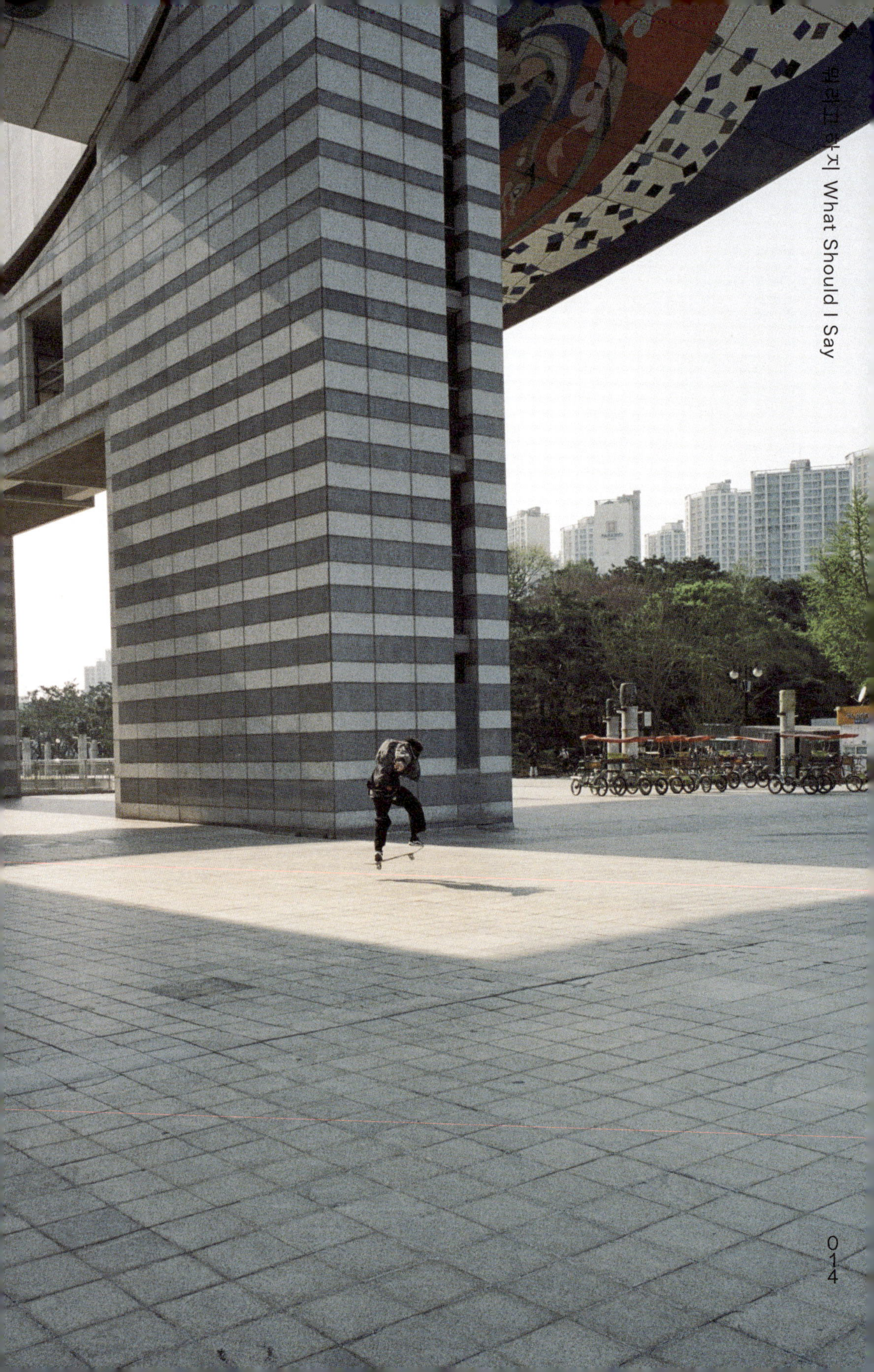

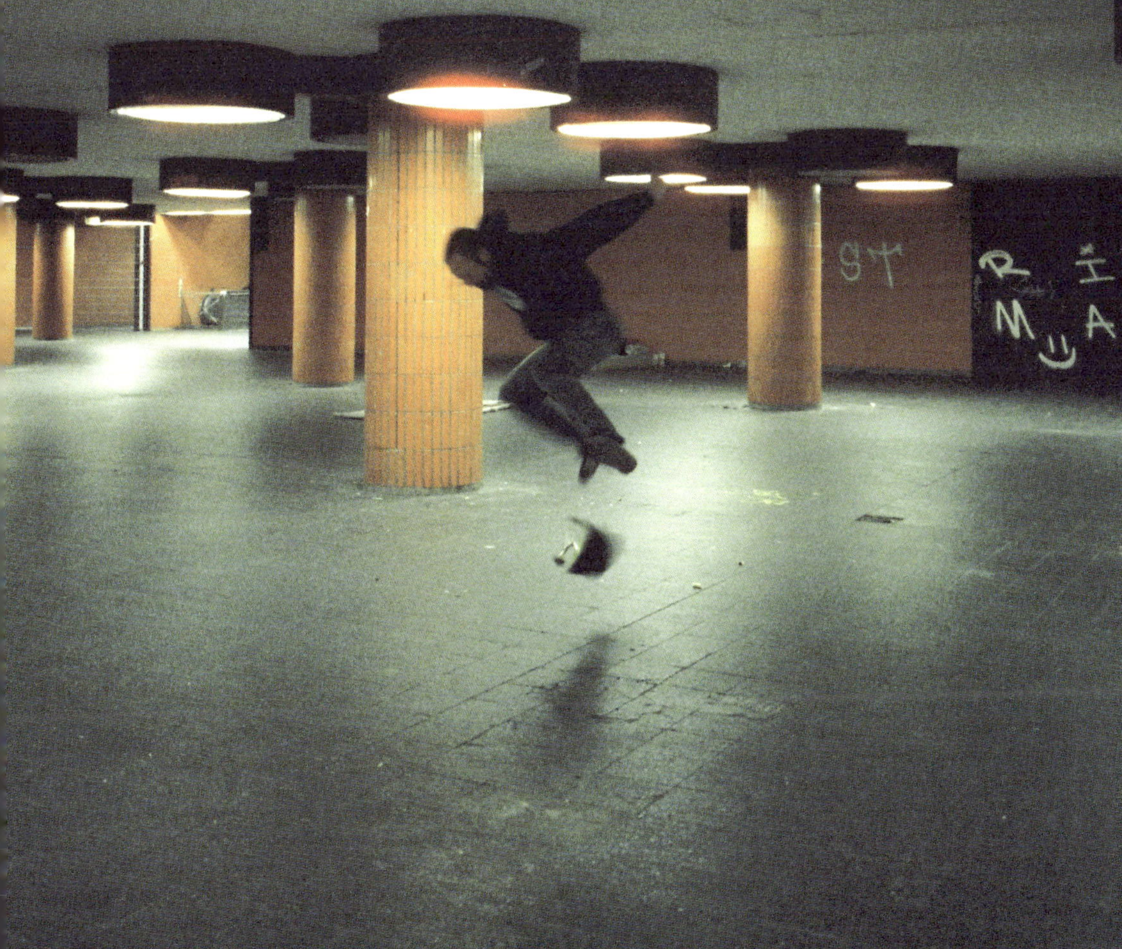
ST
R
M
A

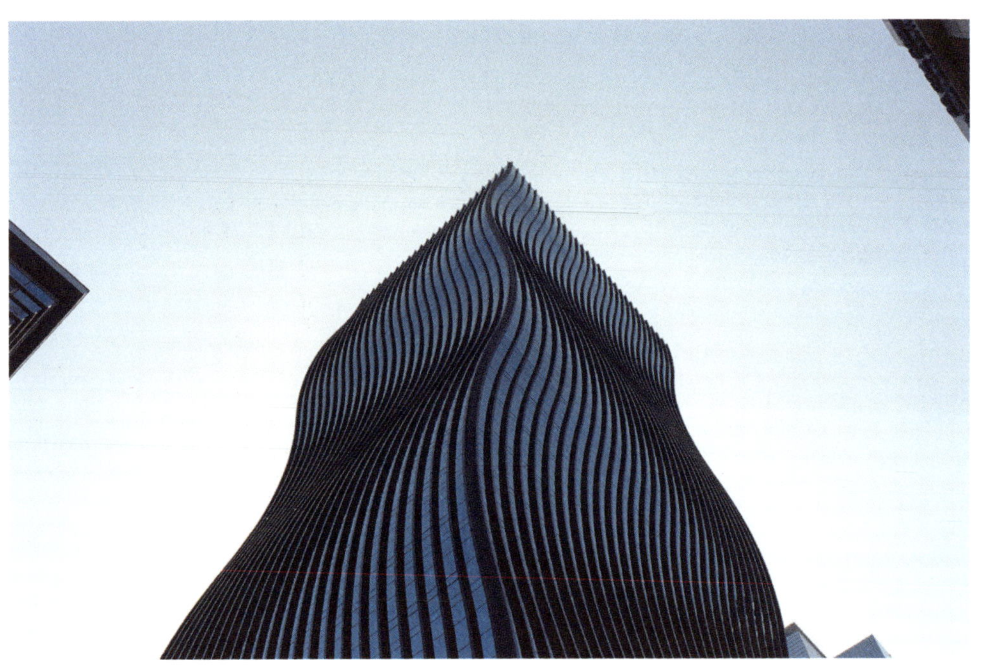

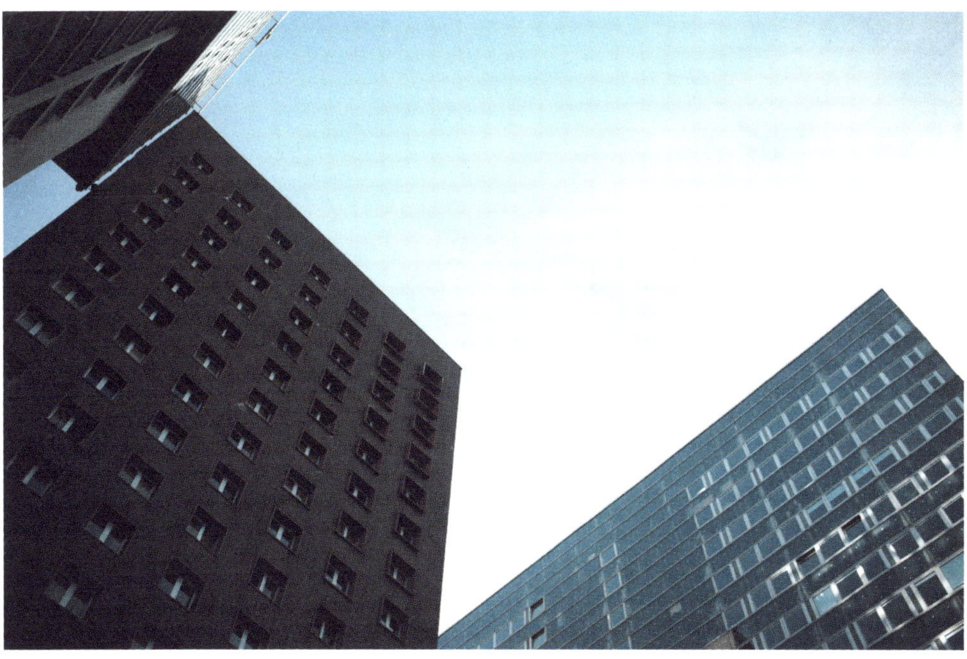

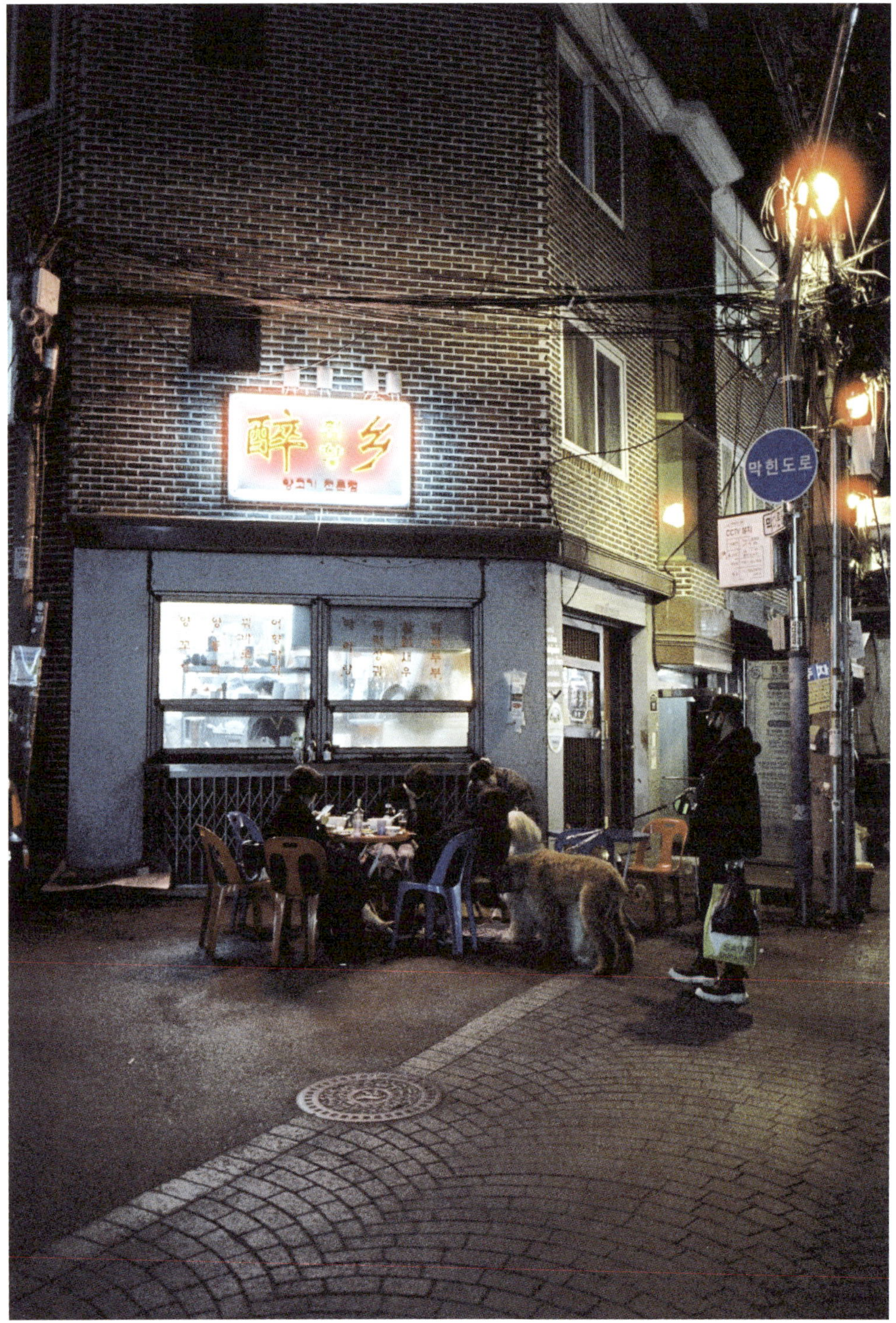

醉
막힌도로

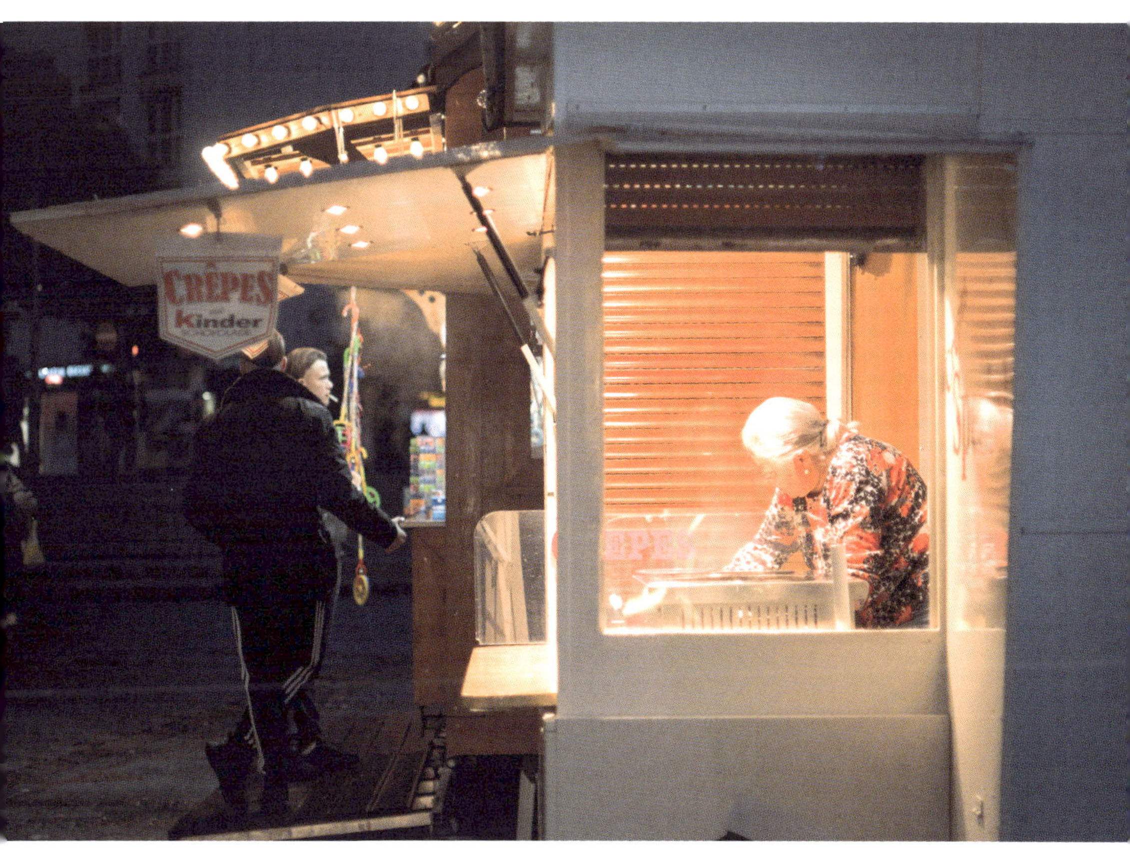

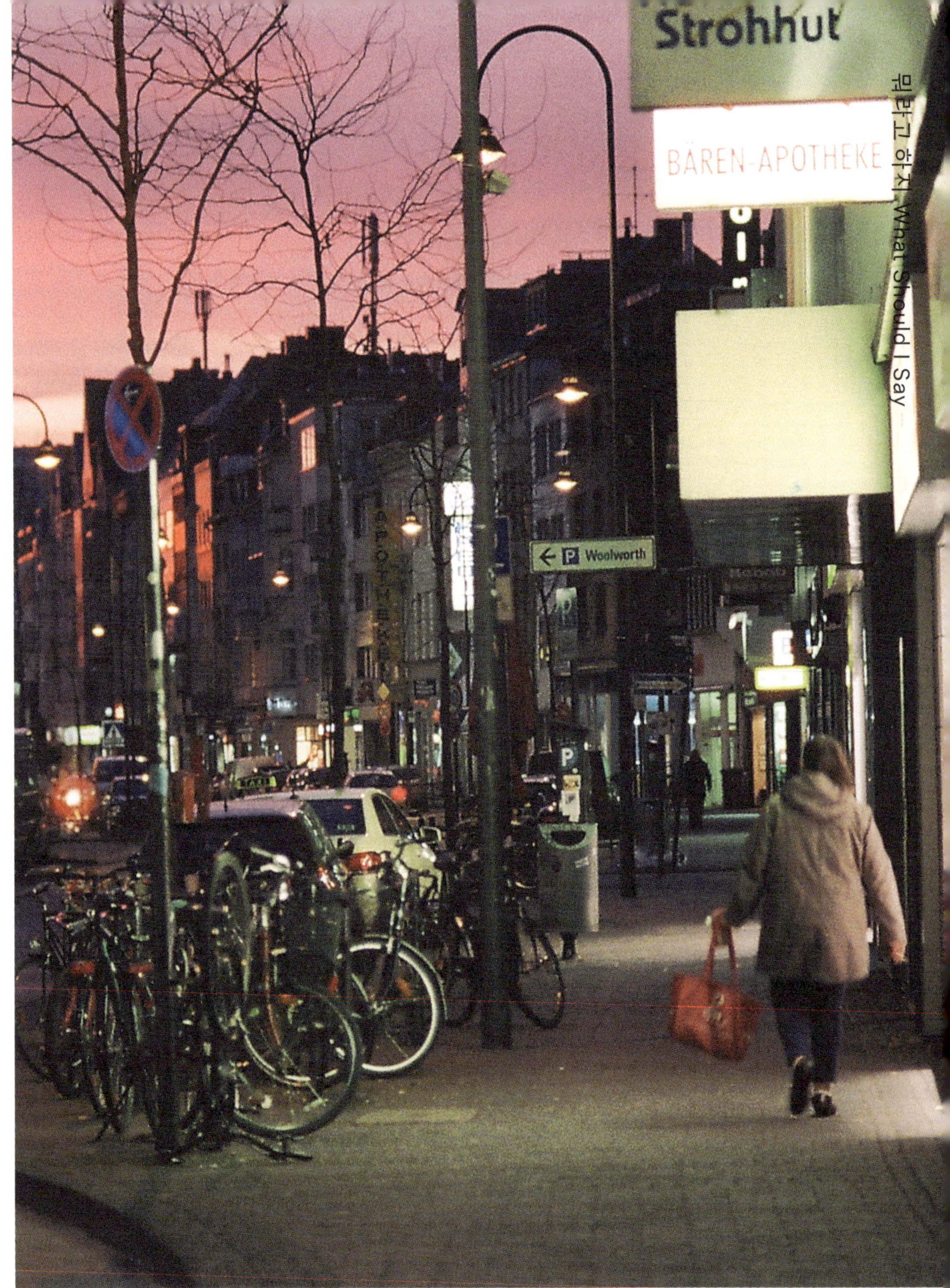

Strohhut
BÄREN-APOTHEKE
← P Woolworth

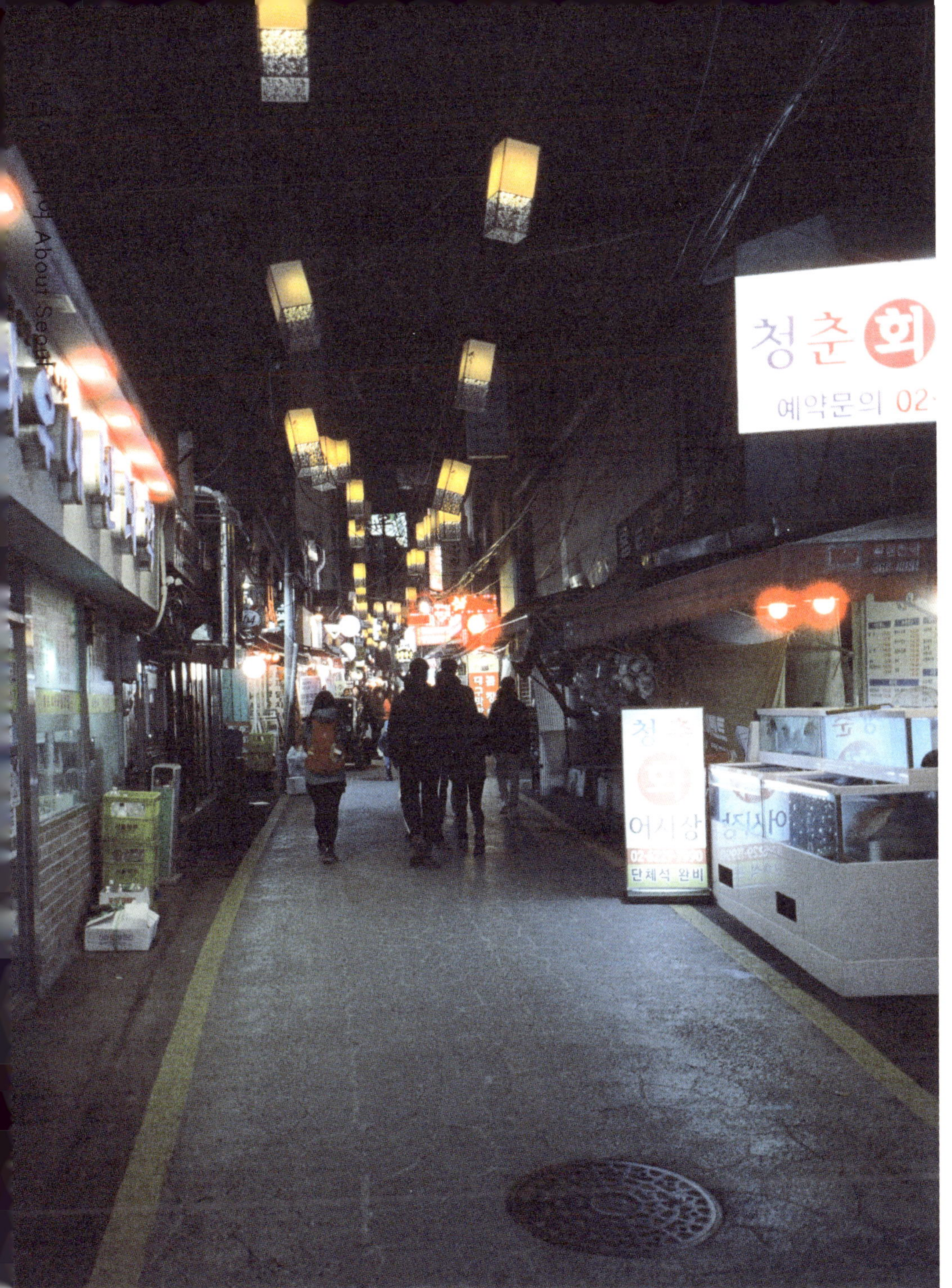

청춘회
예약문의 02
청춘
어시장
단체석 완비

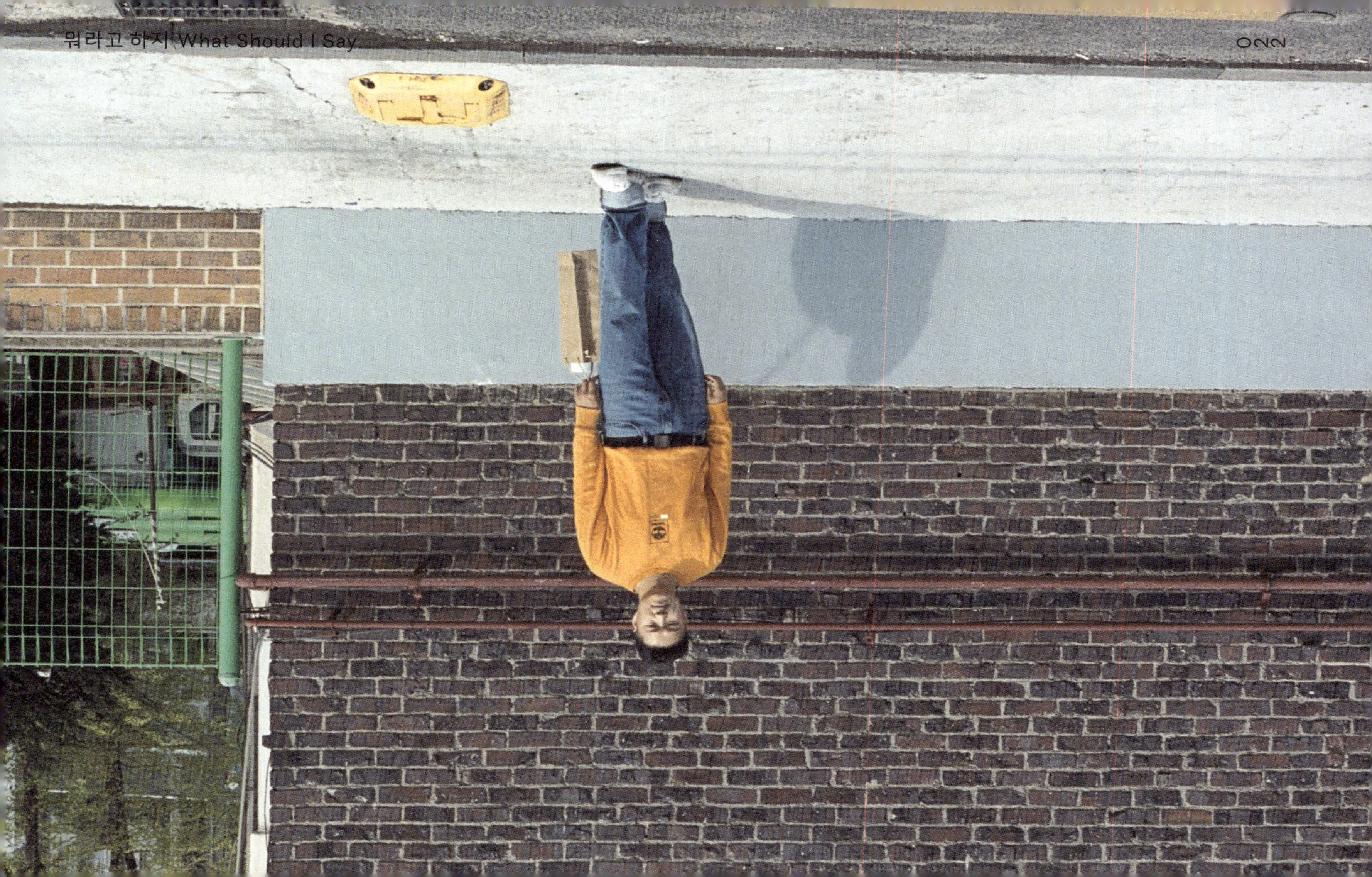

Hi, I'm Pakdo — Graphic Designer

Interview with Pakdo Interview | Pictures: Omid Fröhlich

Can you tell us a bit about yourself? Sure, my name is Pakdo, I am 26 years old and I work as a graphic designer.

How do you go about when starting a new design project? In my opinion, it is of great significance to stay in conversation with the clients. That's the only way to get a grasp on what they really want. From there I can figure out how to translate their requirements into a graphic representation. Some designers just submit their final designs without nailing the briefing first. This approach is prone to leading to disappointment on the client's site—including reworking the design. I simply don't want to do that extra work when I thought to have finished a project.

What do you think makes working as a self-employed designer distinct?

Compared to someone working as an employed designer you have to take care of many different areas. You are not just a designer. When you run your own studio you have to be a CEO, you have to take care of consulting as well as finances.

Is there anything you want to do as a designer in the future?

I think I would like to be part of the graphic design studio 'Everyday Practice.' They are a Seoul-based studio that is constantly experimenting with various design methods—which I like very much. If you're interested, they also showcase their work on Instagram.

Is there someone who inspired you lately?

Helmut Schmid, a famous typographer from Austria. I got to know him because he was a professor at our university. He was part of the 'Swiss Style' movement and his knowledge of grids and typography is still amazing to me today. It's also baffling to see how he created expressive designs only using letters.

Well, since I studied Design, I had really no other choice than to become a designer. In the beginning it was very difficult. I was always questioning myself and doubting my work. I thought nobody wanted my Design.

I am really proud to create the design for this year's 'Pride Parade' in Seoul. Being part of the community myself, it feels great that I can contribute to the parade. The biggest obstacles I face in my design process are grids and typography. This is possibly why I get so much inspiration from my former teacher. Looking at

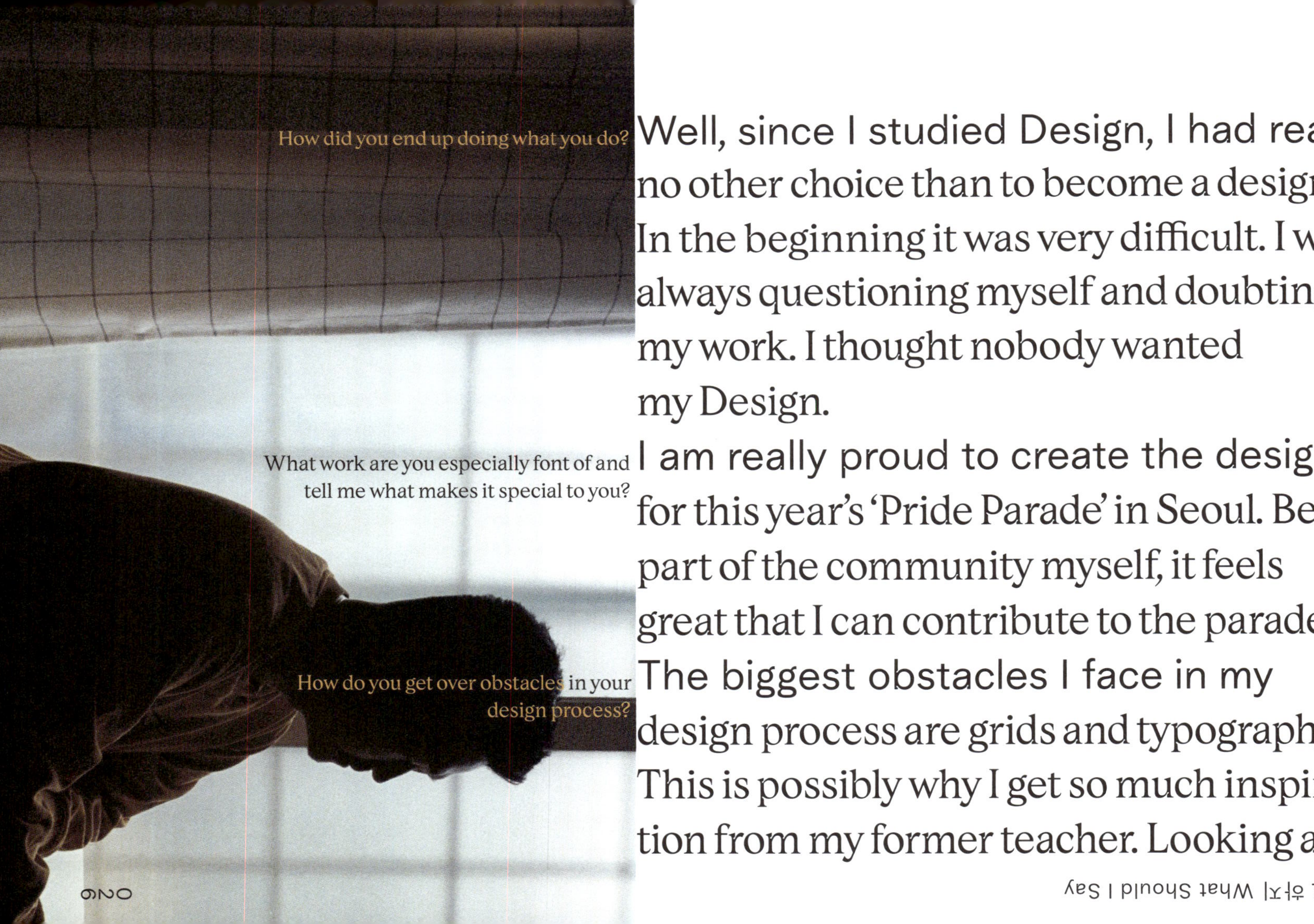

the work of other designers allows me to see my own designs from a new perspective and inspire me to explore new ideas.

What do you do for relaxation?

I like to go out with my boyfriend. We visit new restaurants or just walk around the city together. The whole city is made up of restaurants—you know, because everyone loves good food in Korea. So it's really nice to discover new restaurants and cafés.

What is your biggest concern these days?

Living with my boyfriend in a small apartment is not easy. I also am worried about politics a lot.

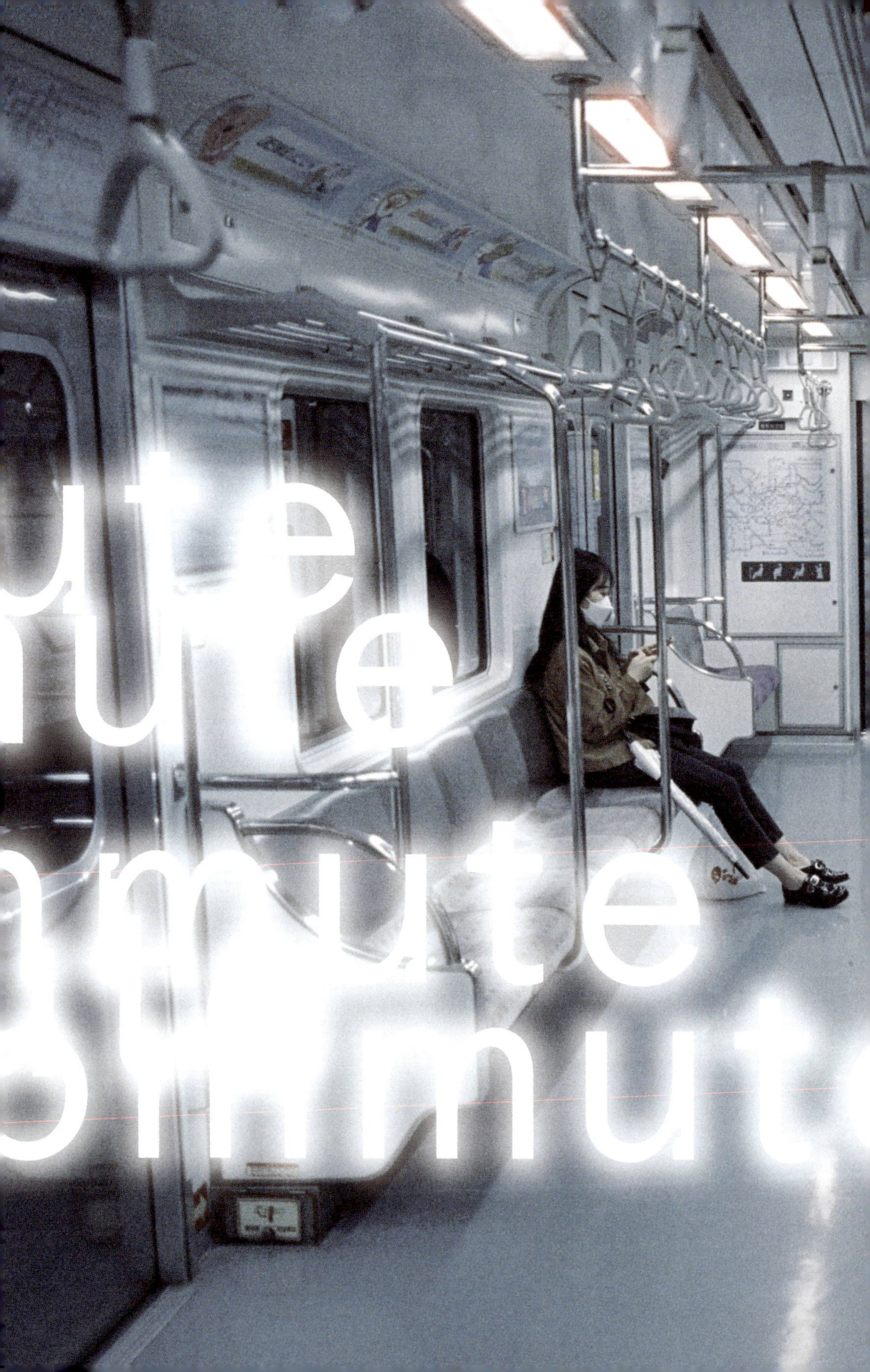
ute
mute
mute
mute
mute

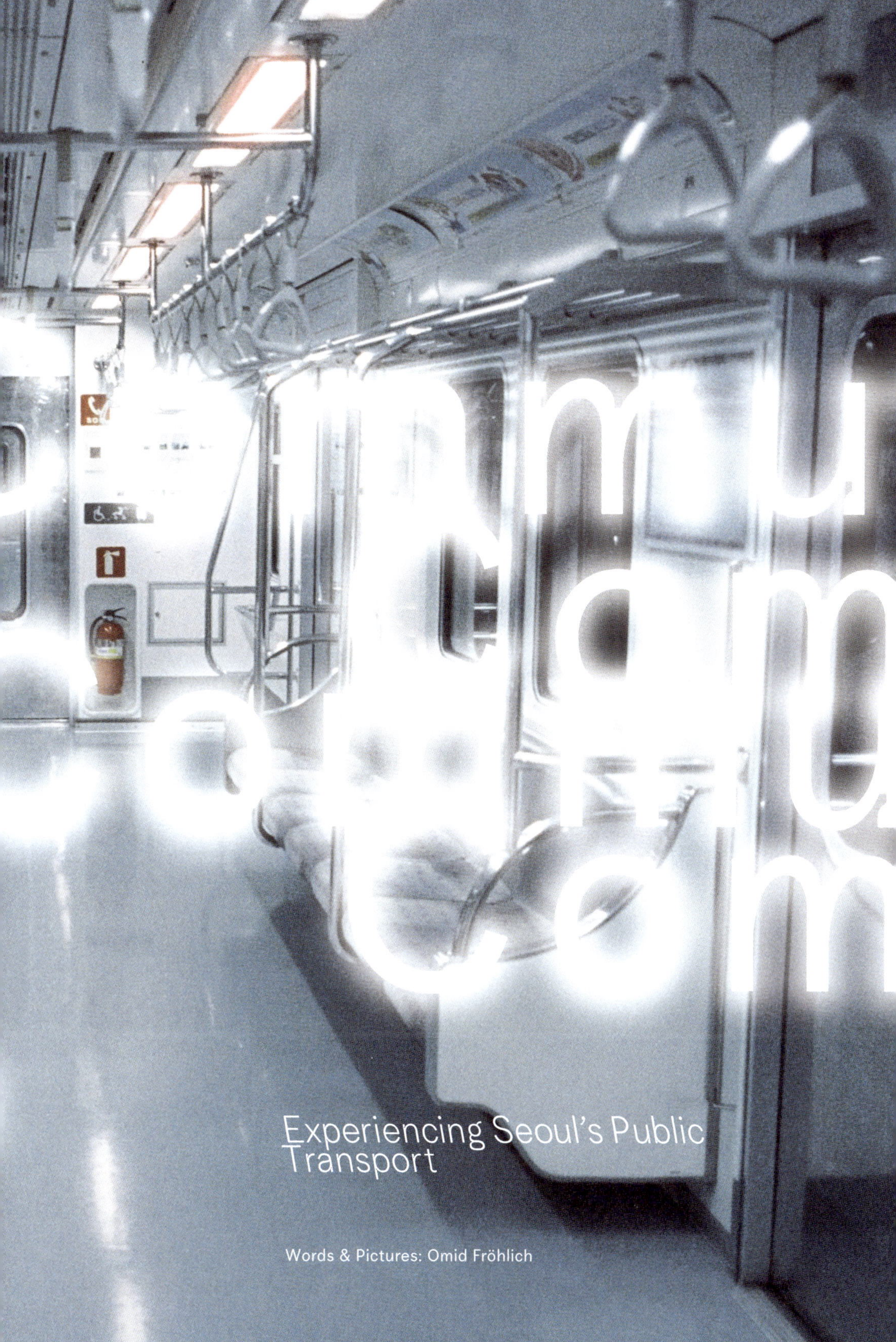
Experiencing Seoul's Public Transport
Words & Pictures: Omid Fröhlich

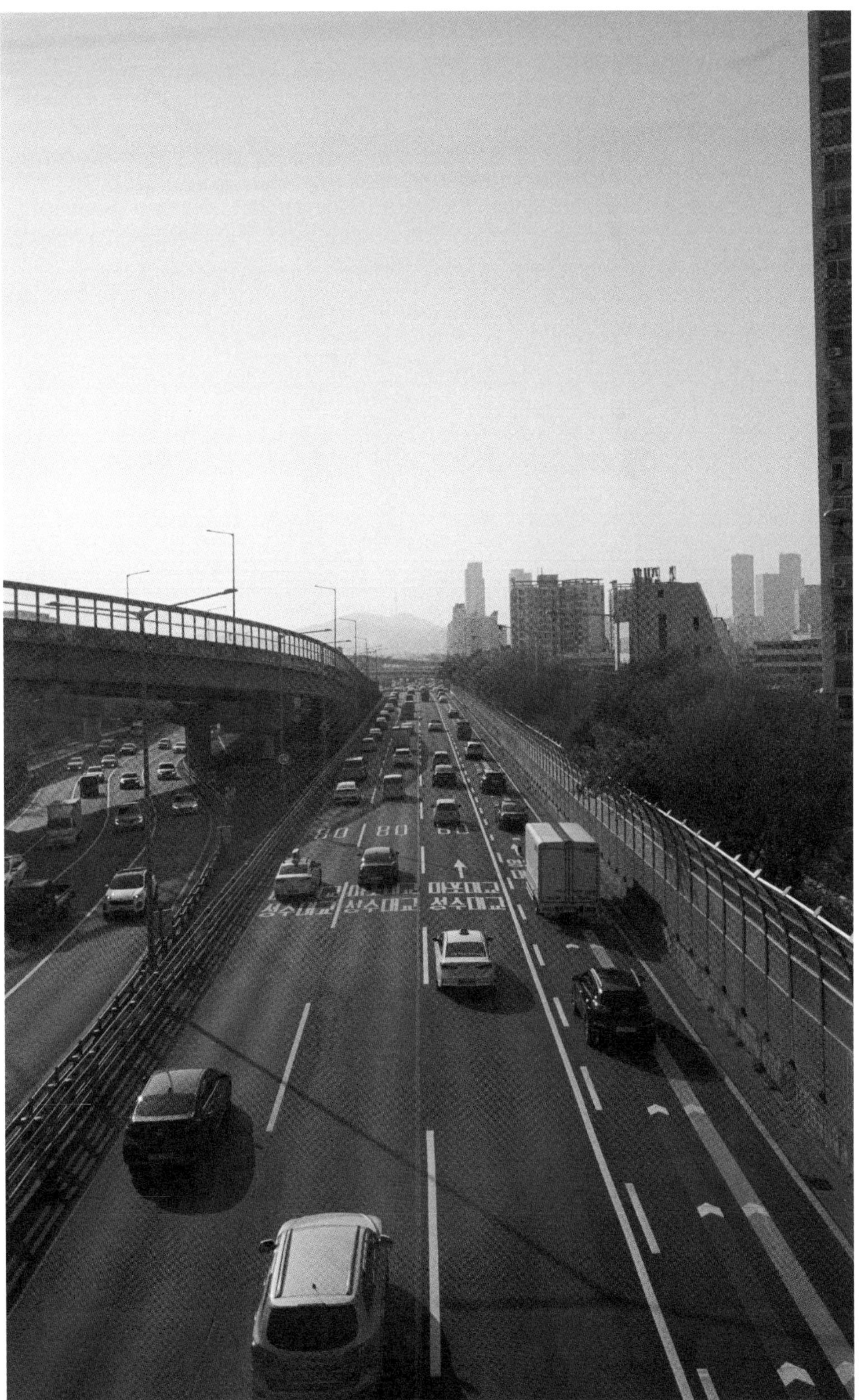

Seoul, the capital and largest city in South Korea
accounts for only 0.6 % of the country's total
land mass, yet it is home to around 19 % of Korea's
population. This concentration on one city brings
with it a high demand for public transport.

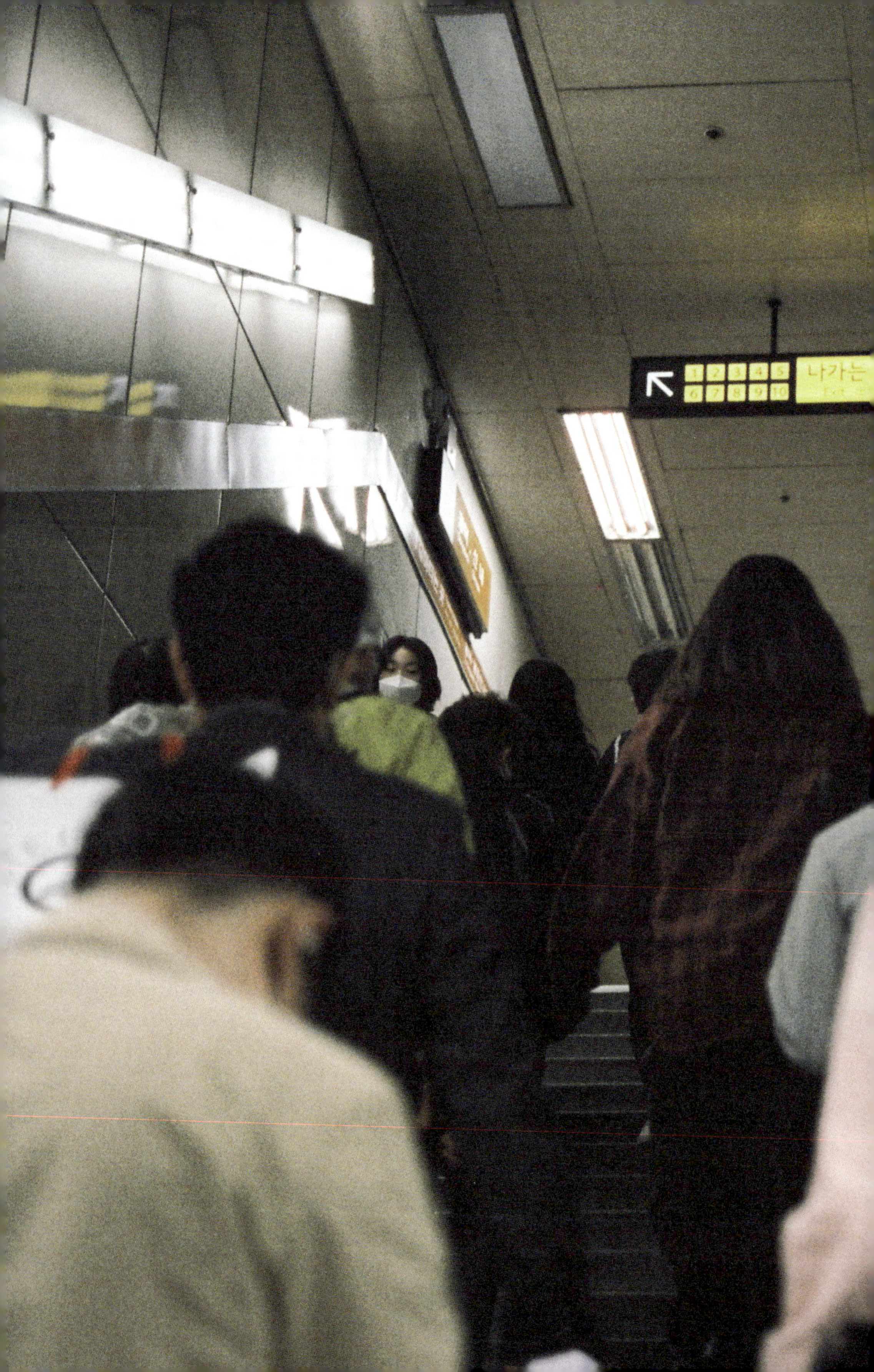
1 2 3 4 5
6 7 8 9 10
나가는

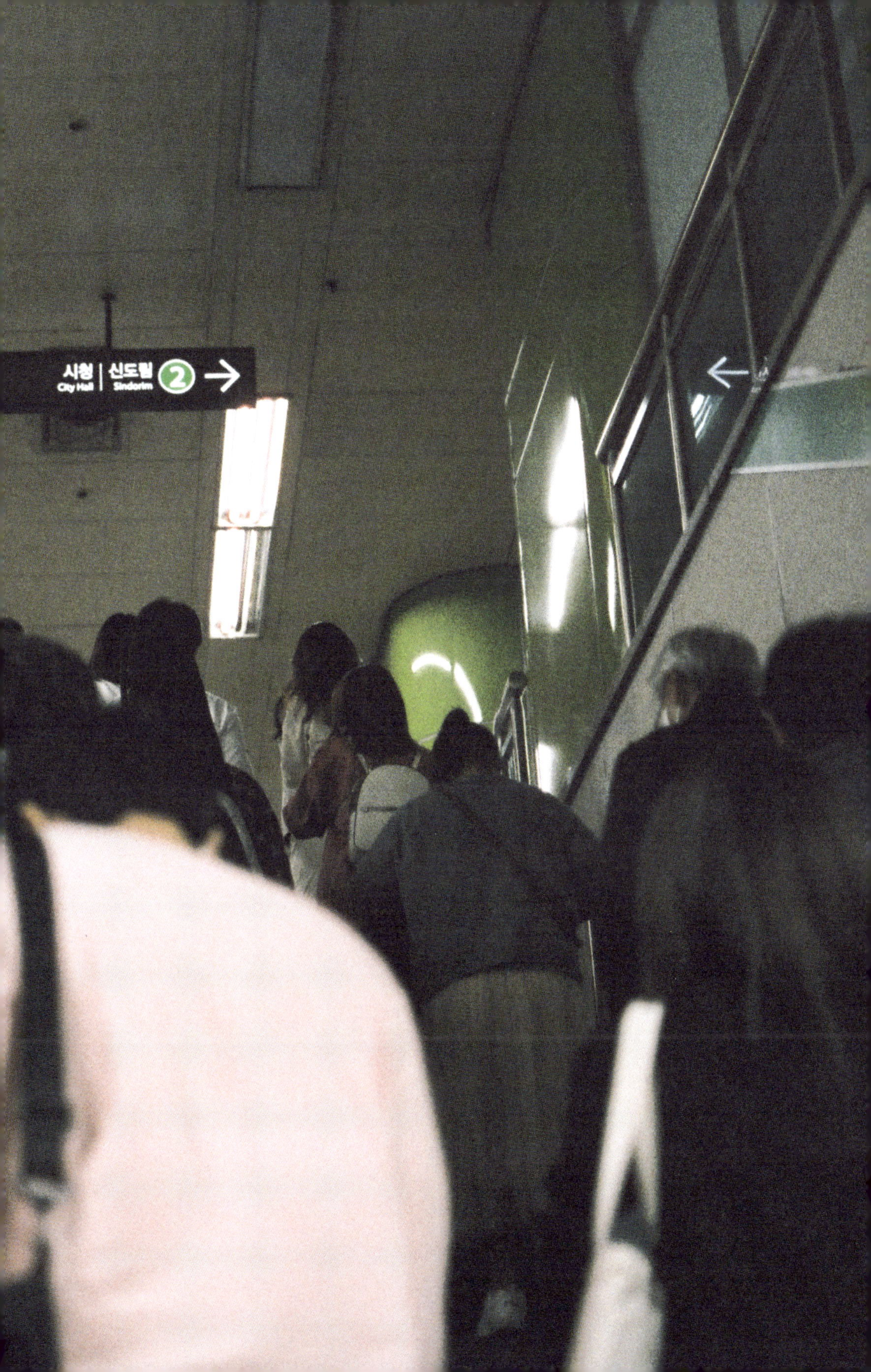
시청
City Hall
신도림
Sindorim
②
→
←

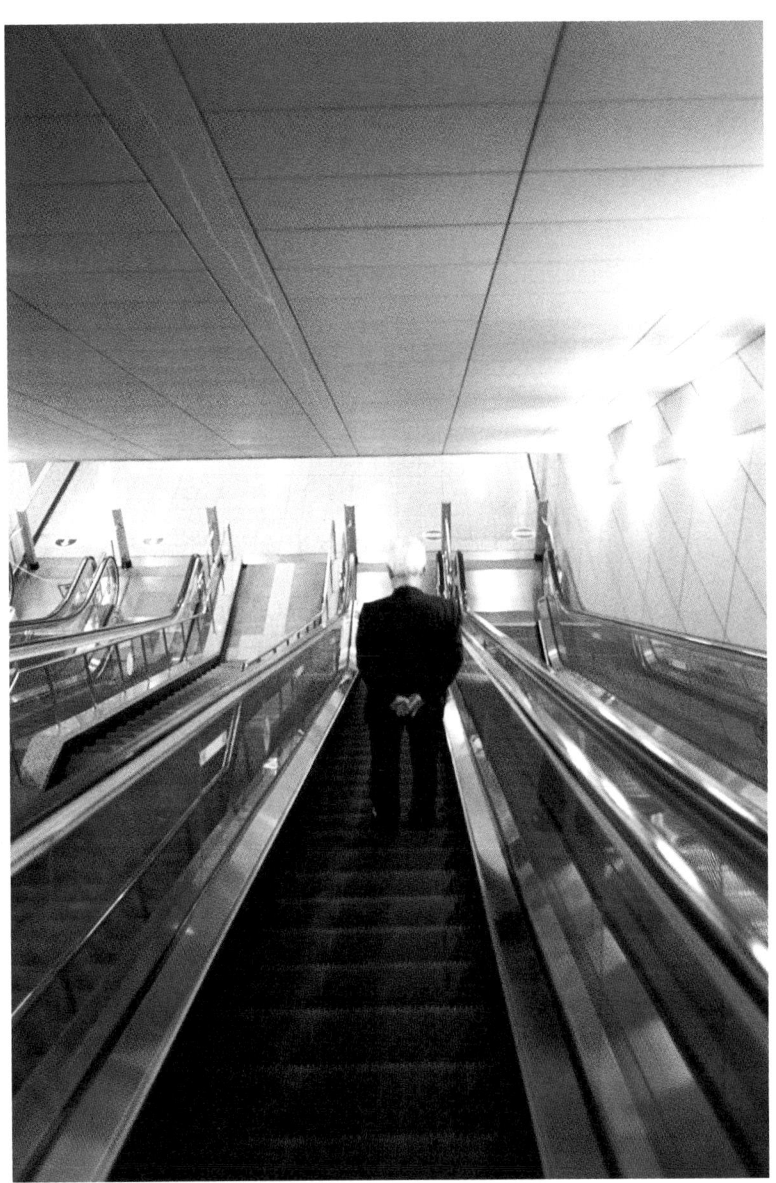

You enter the station and dive into a world that is cut off from time and space —— it feels like a second world underground.

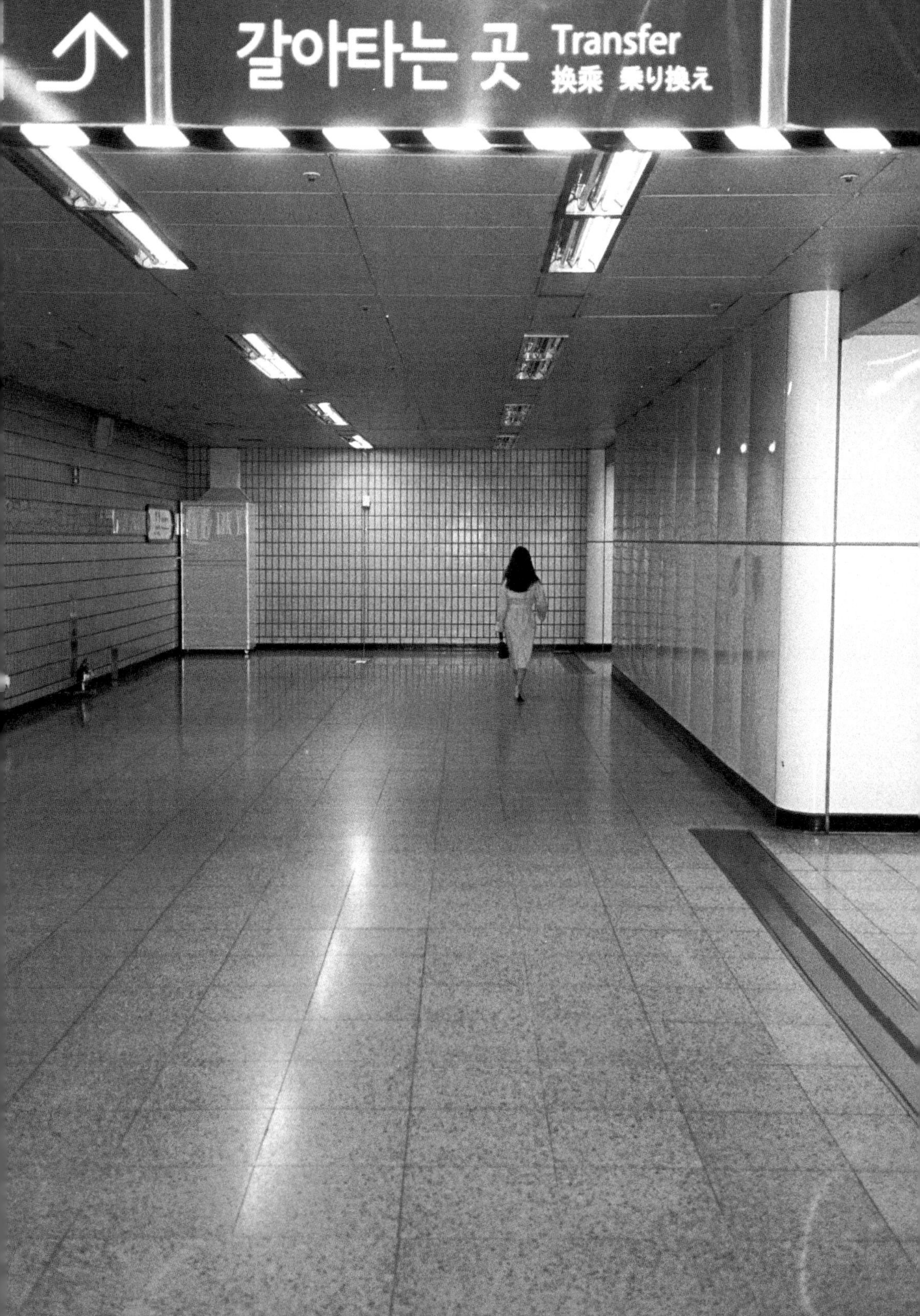
갈아타는 곳 Transfer
換乘 乗り換え
갈아타는 곳 Transfer
換乘 乗り換え

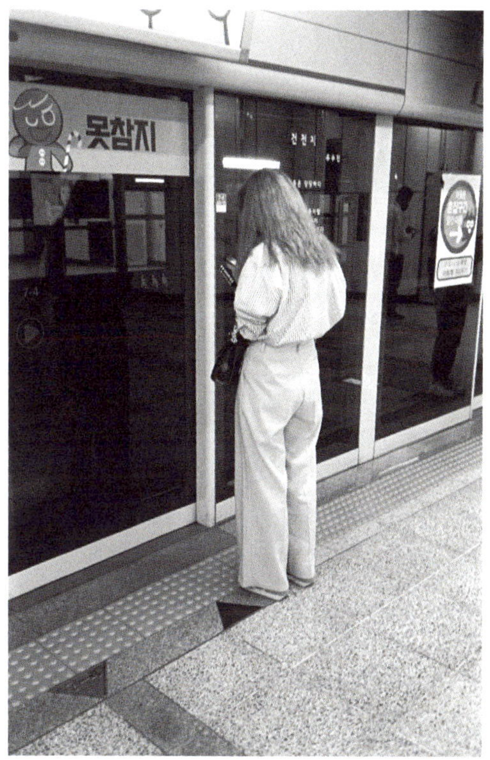

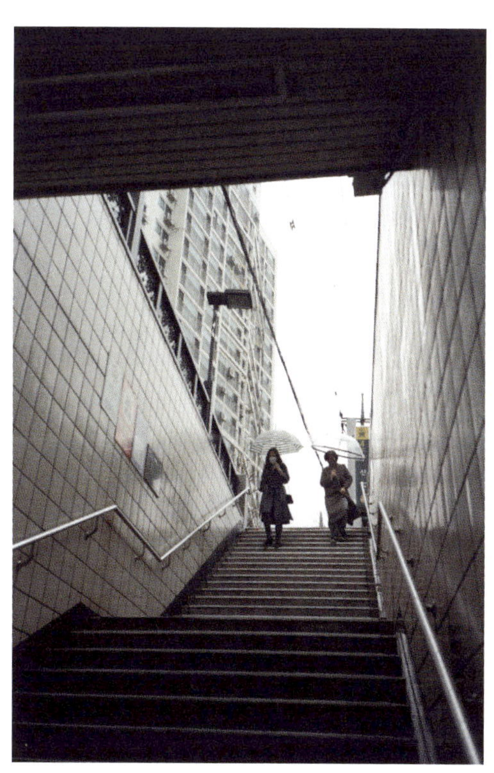

With millions of commuters daily, the Seoul Metropolitan Subway is one of the busiest metro systems in the world.

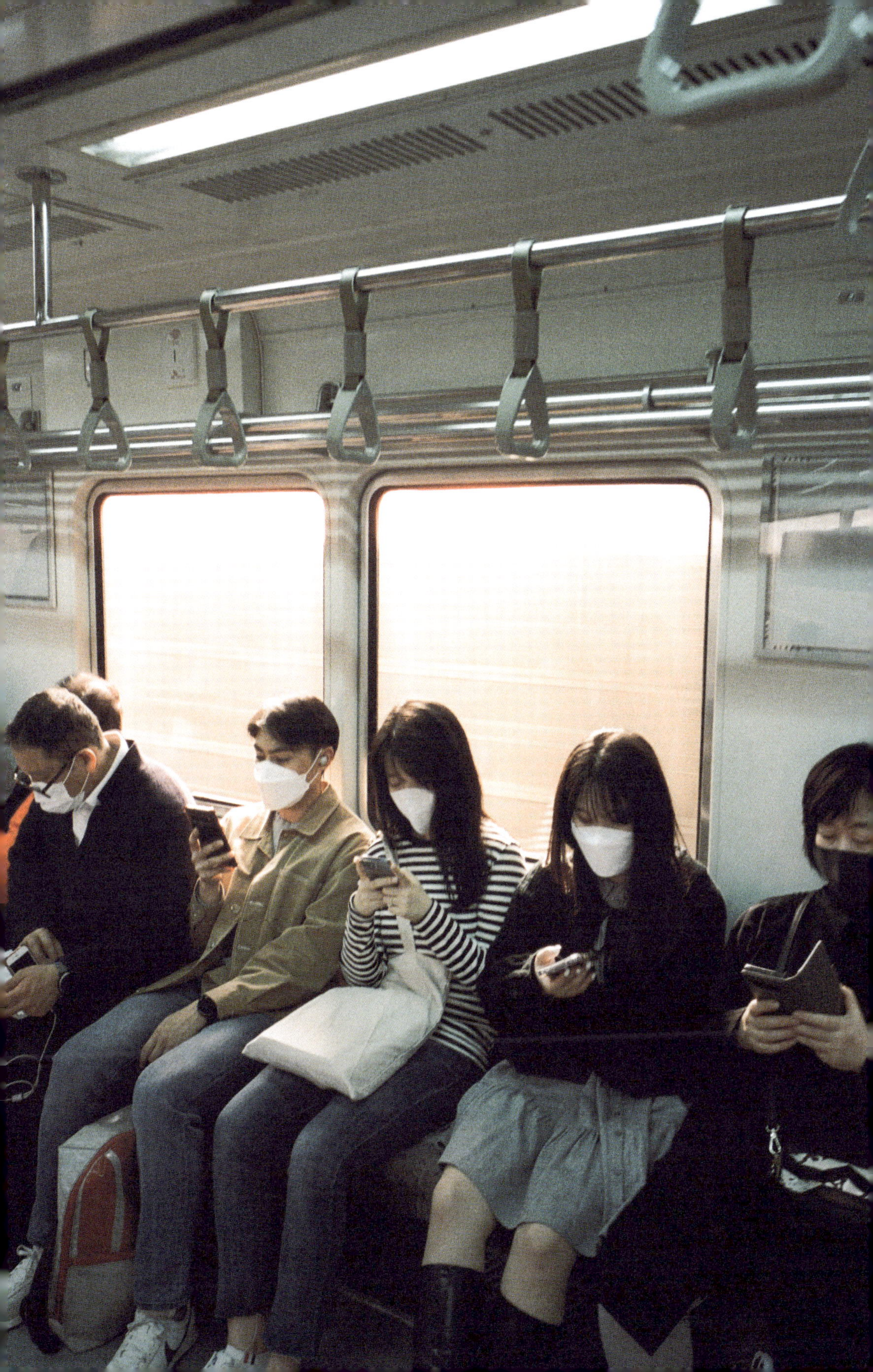

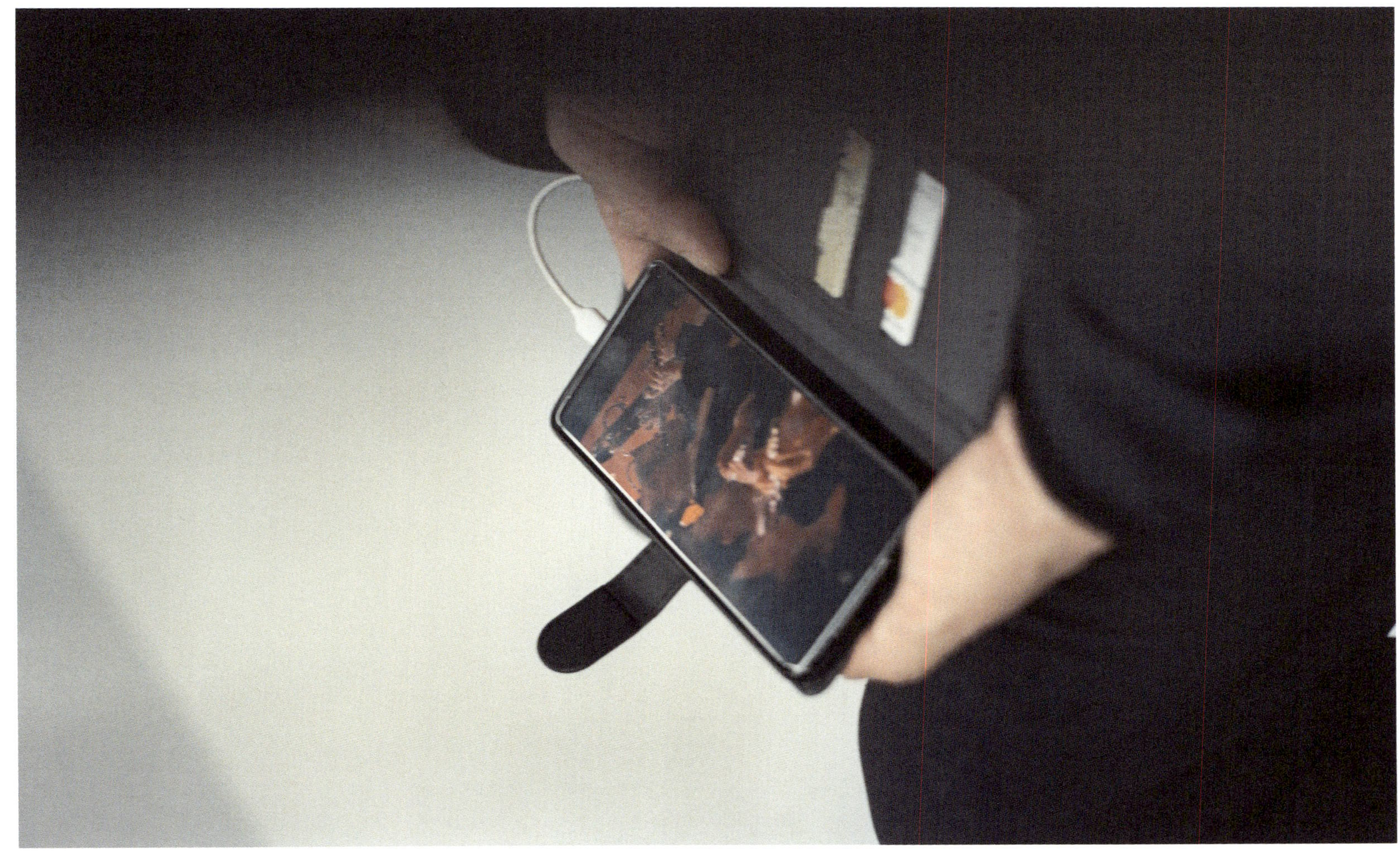

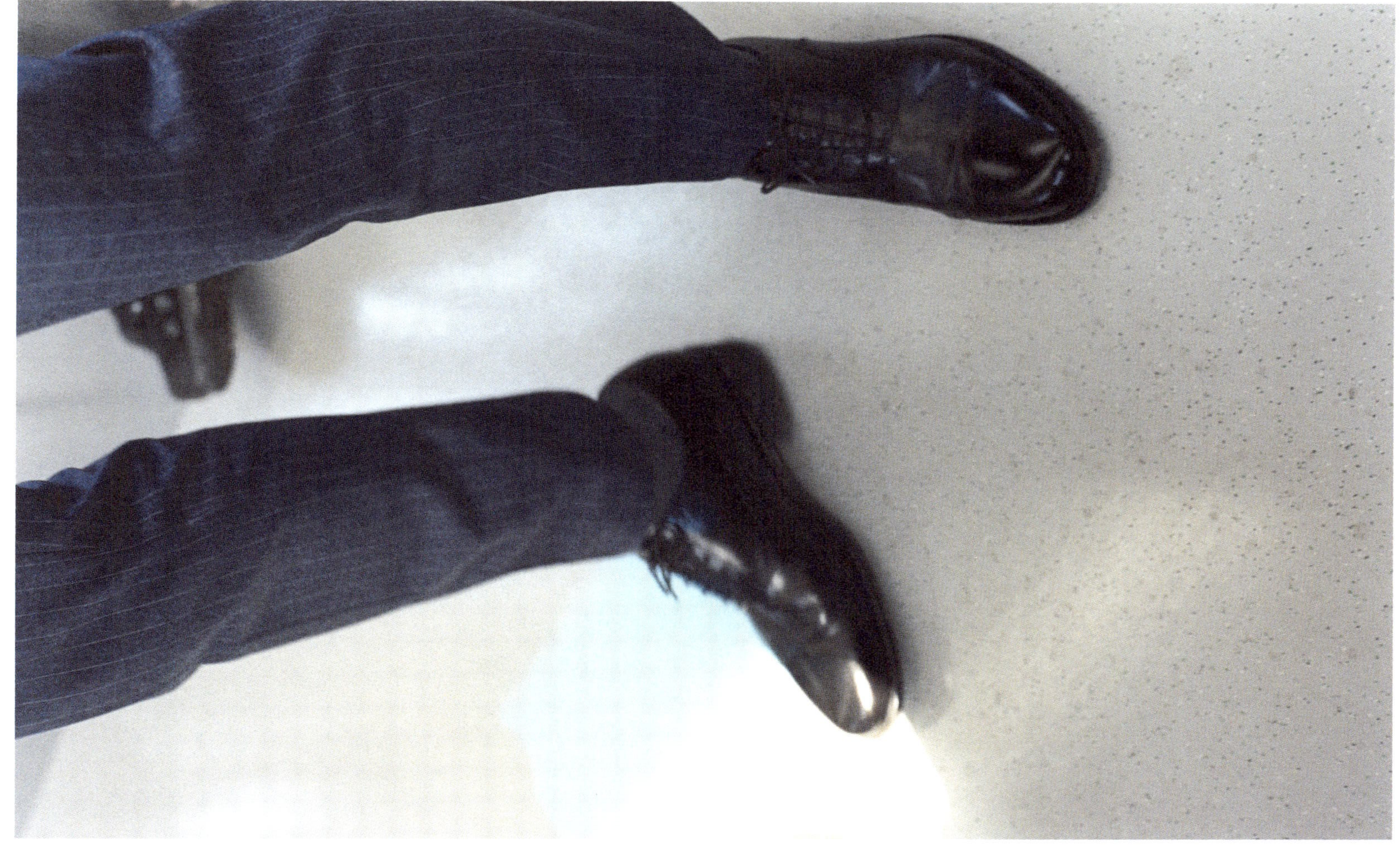

I hear the announcements. I check
my phone every three seconds
to see if I already missed the station.
People stand up, sit down, enter,
and exit. I leave the train and submerge
in a stream of commuters——
swarming out to reach their connection
or exit the station.

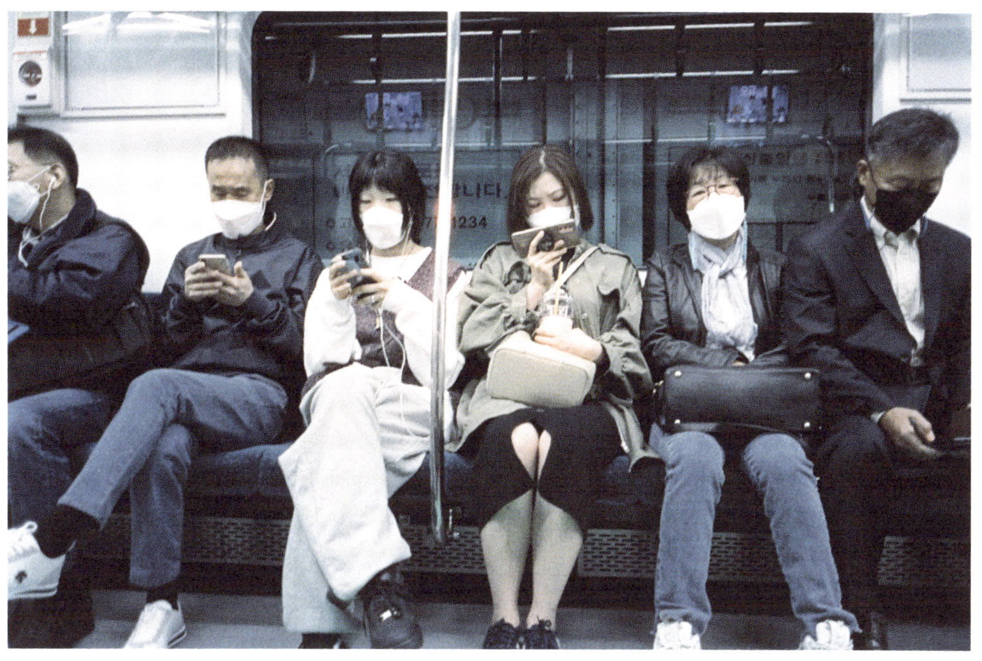

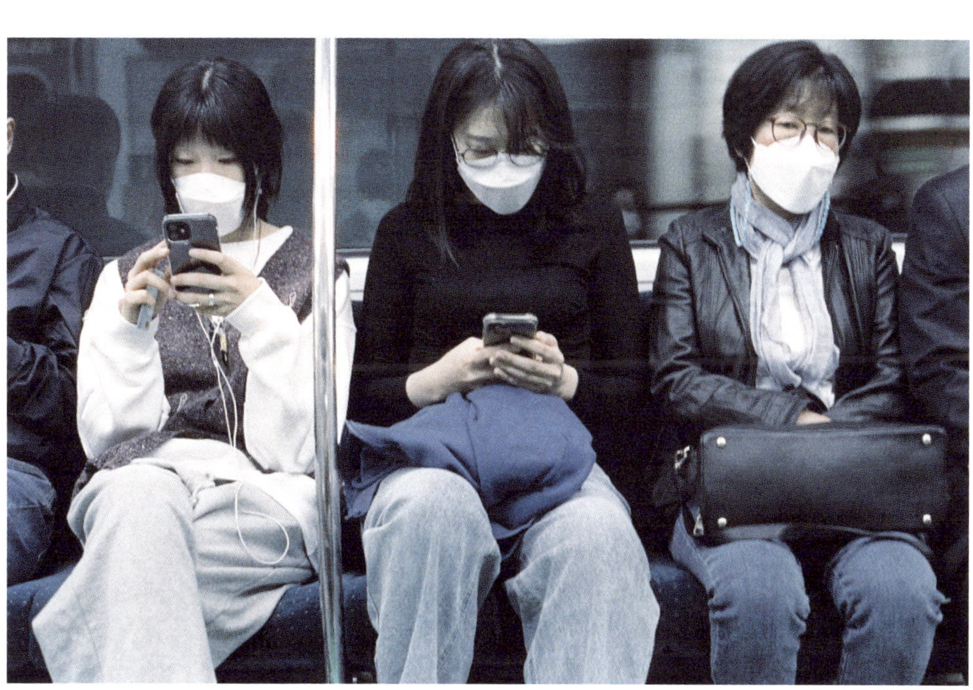

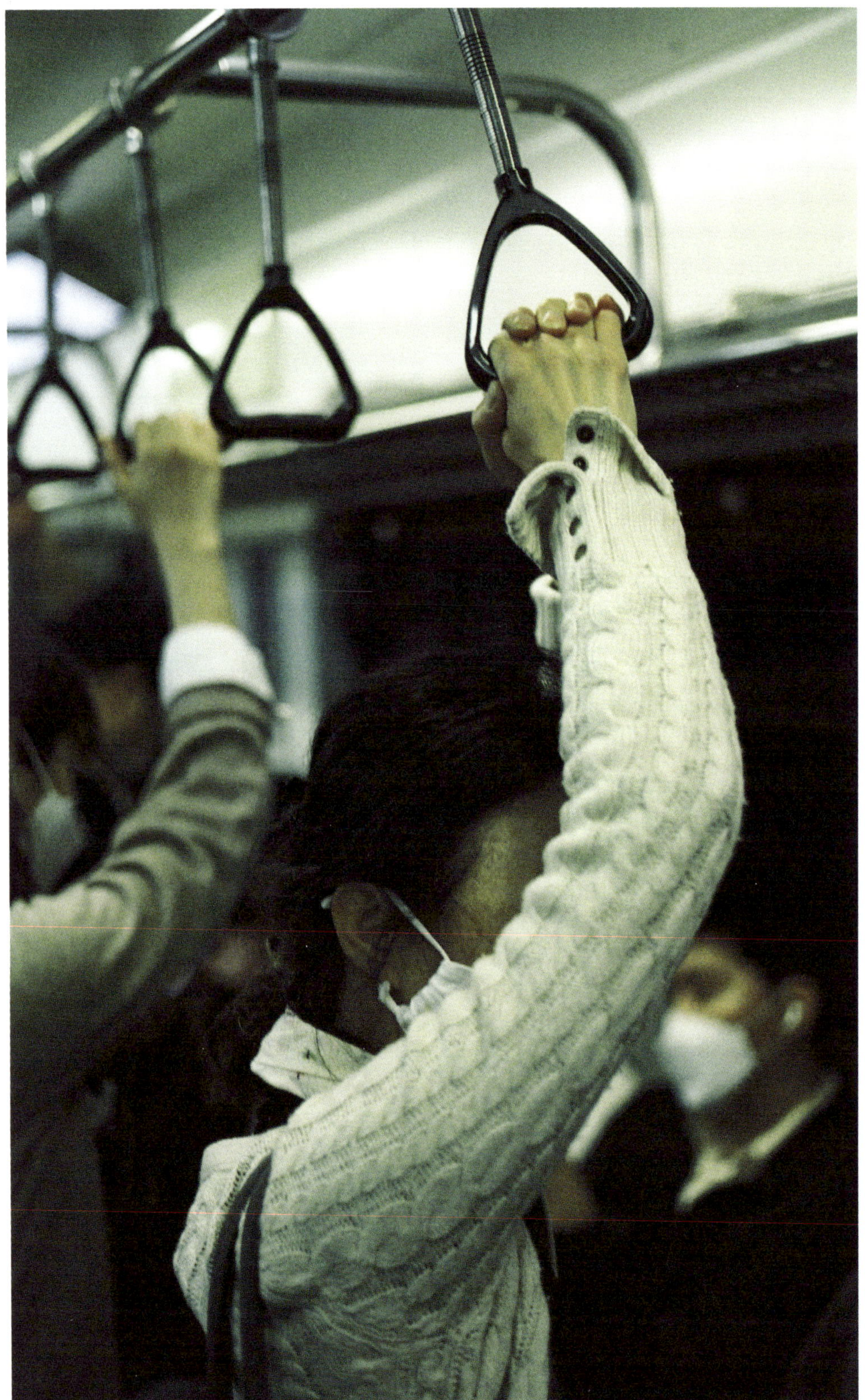

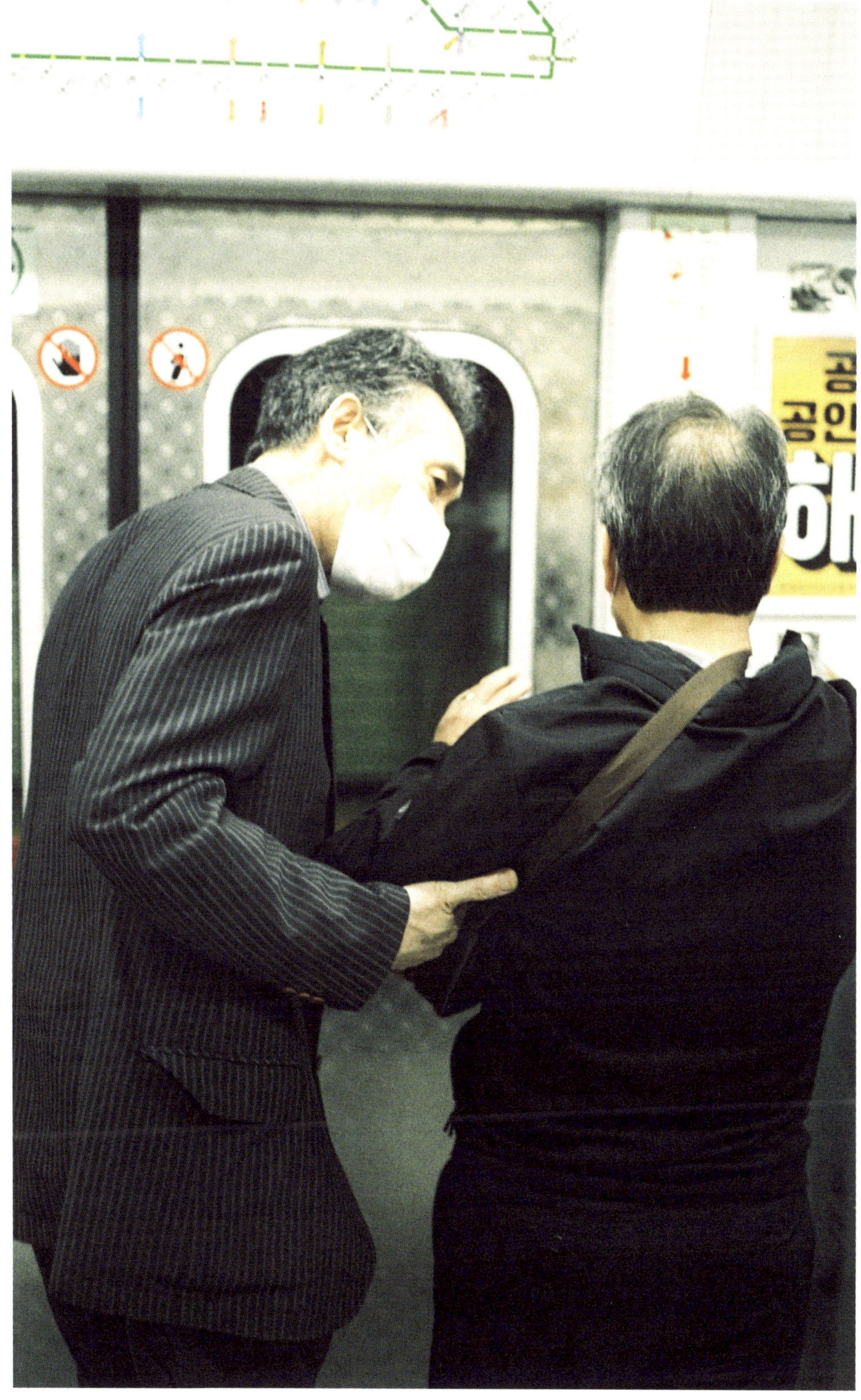

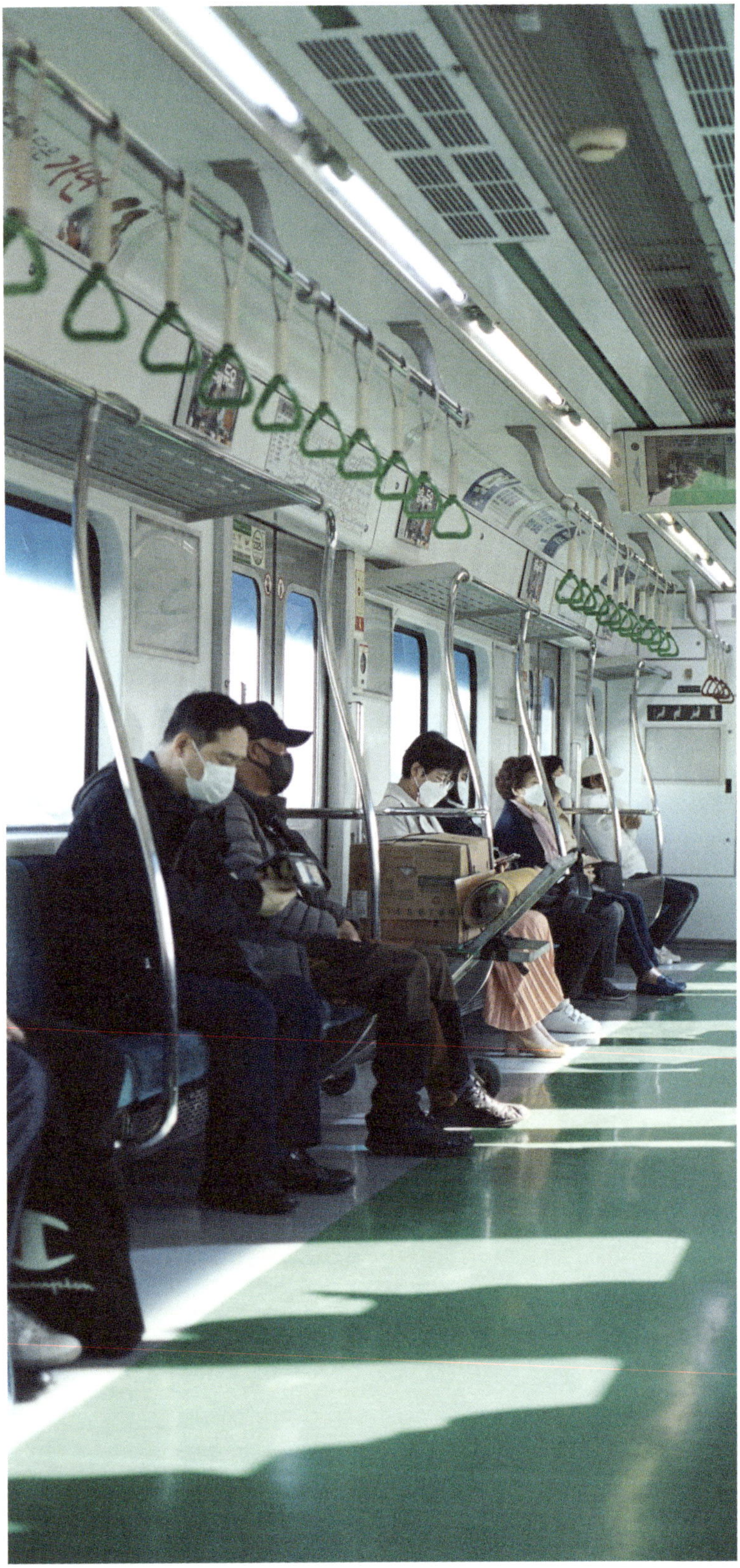

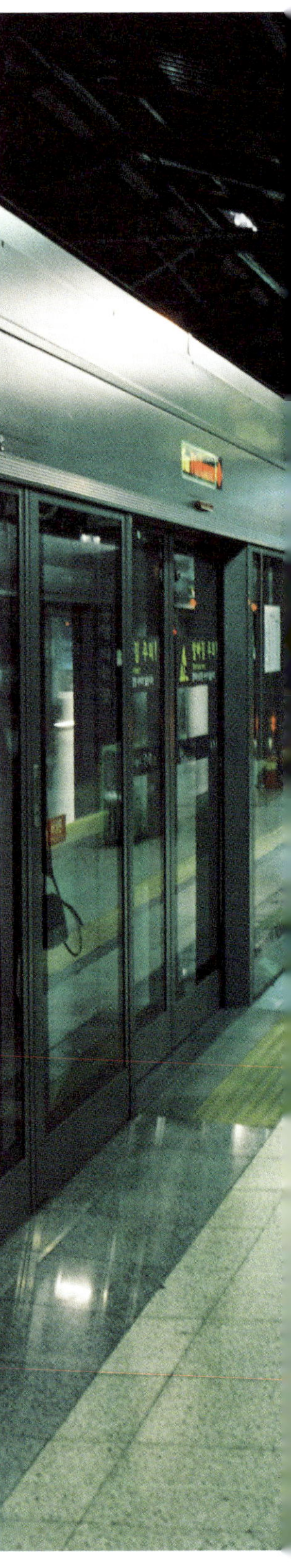

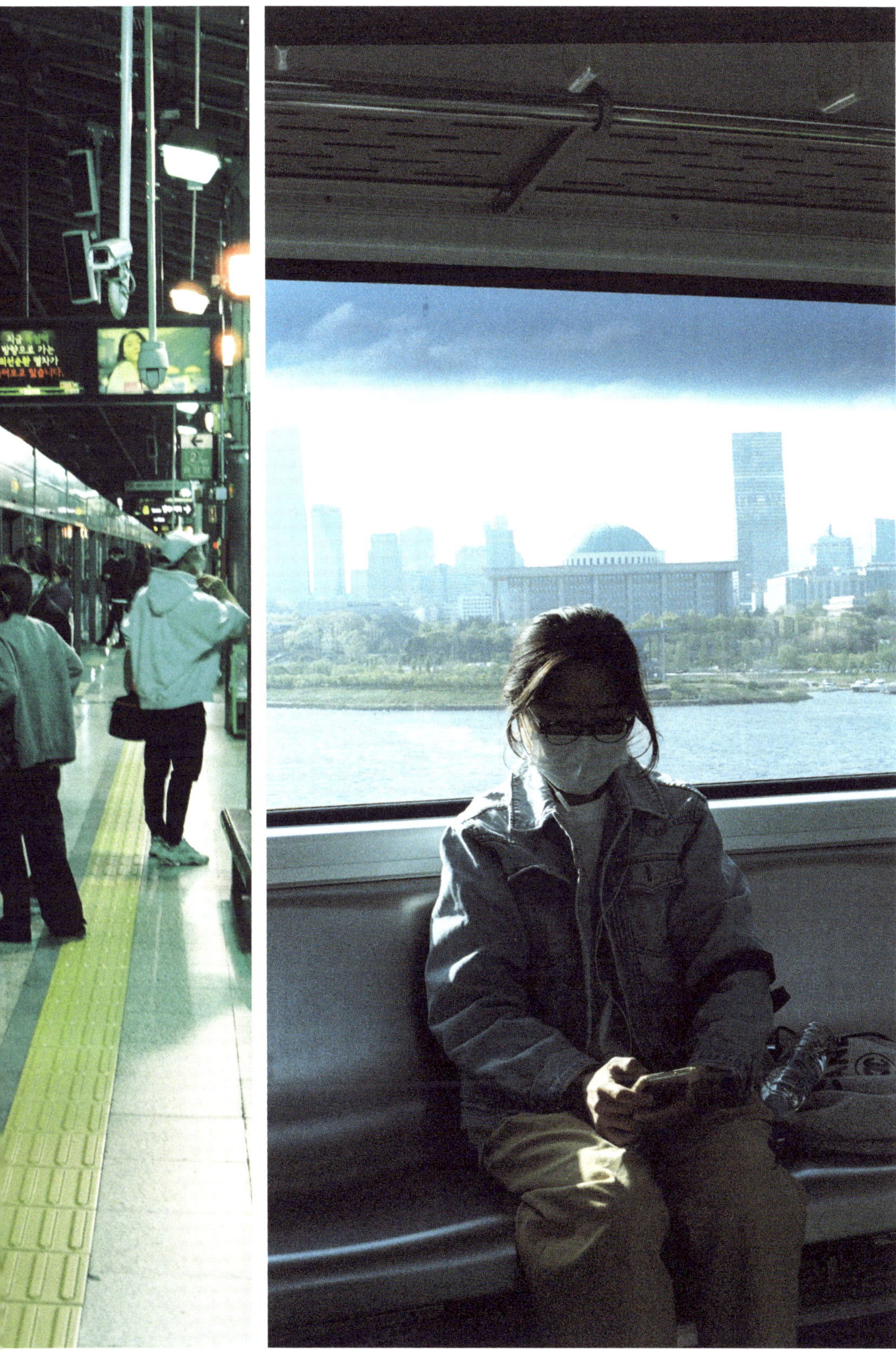

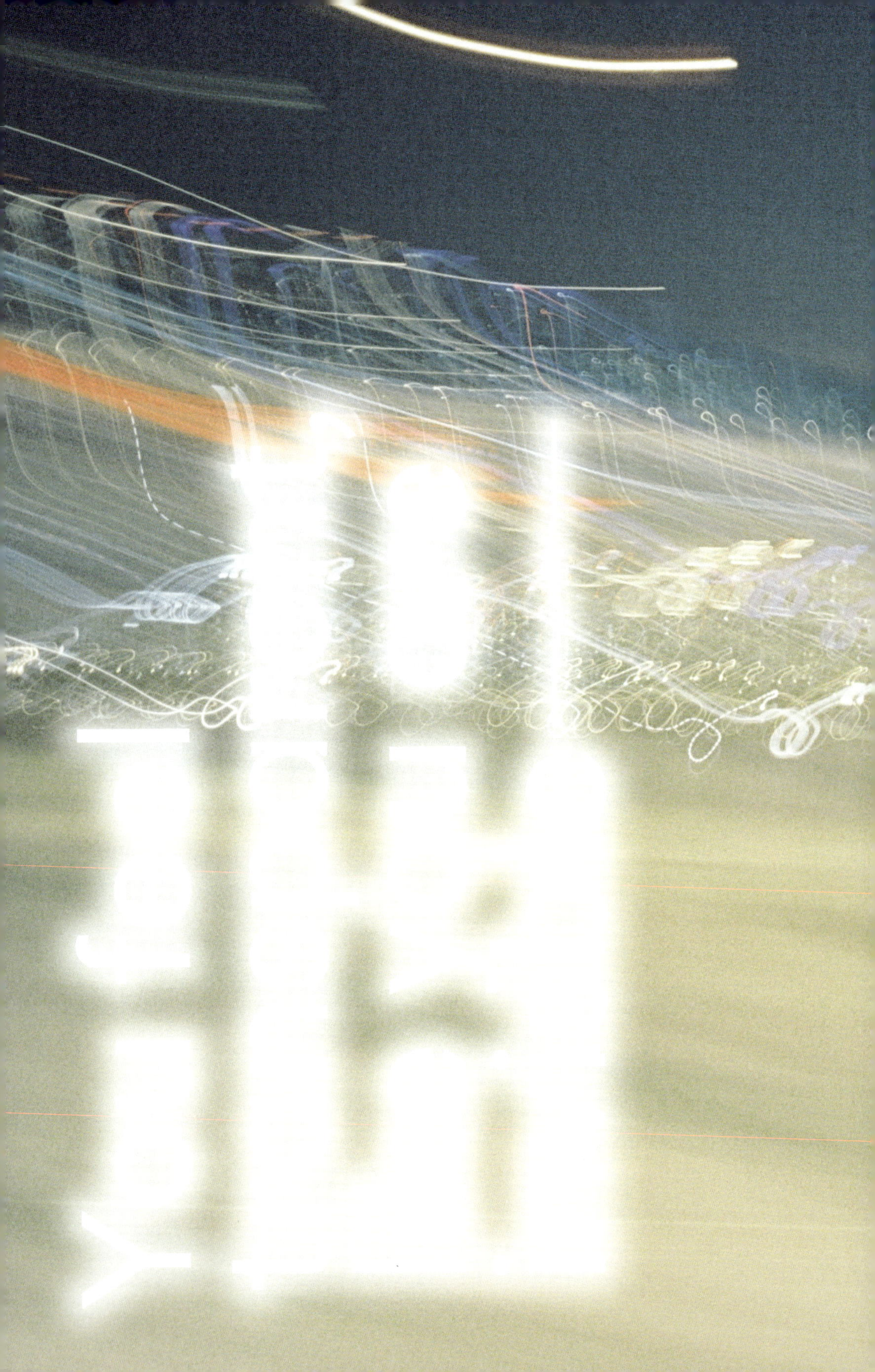

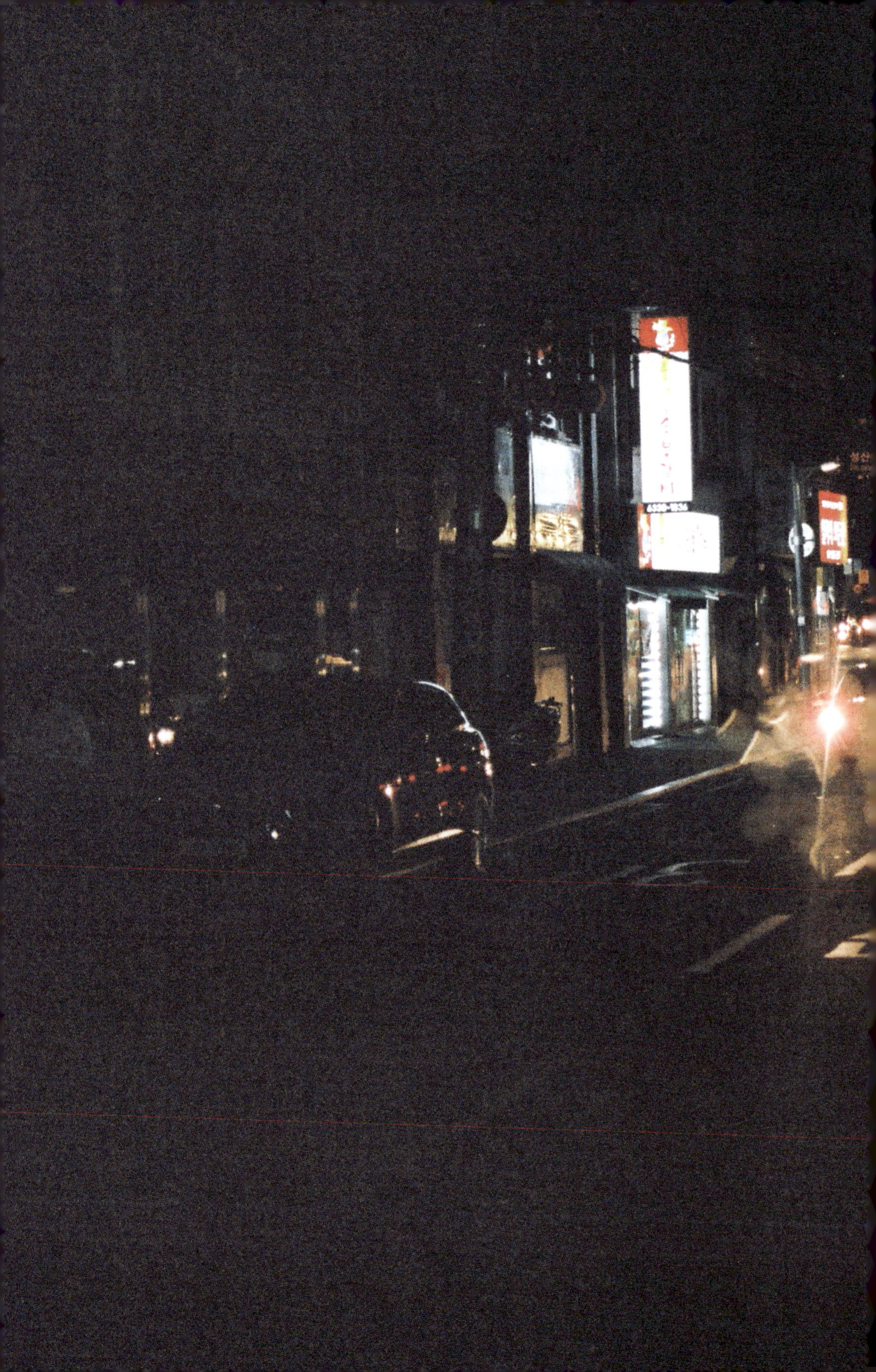

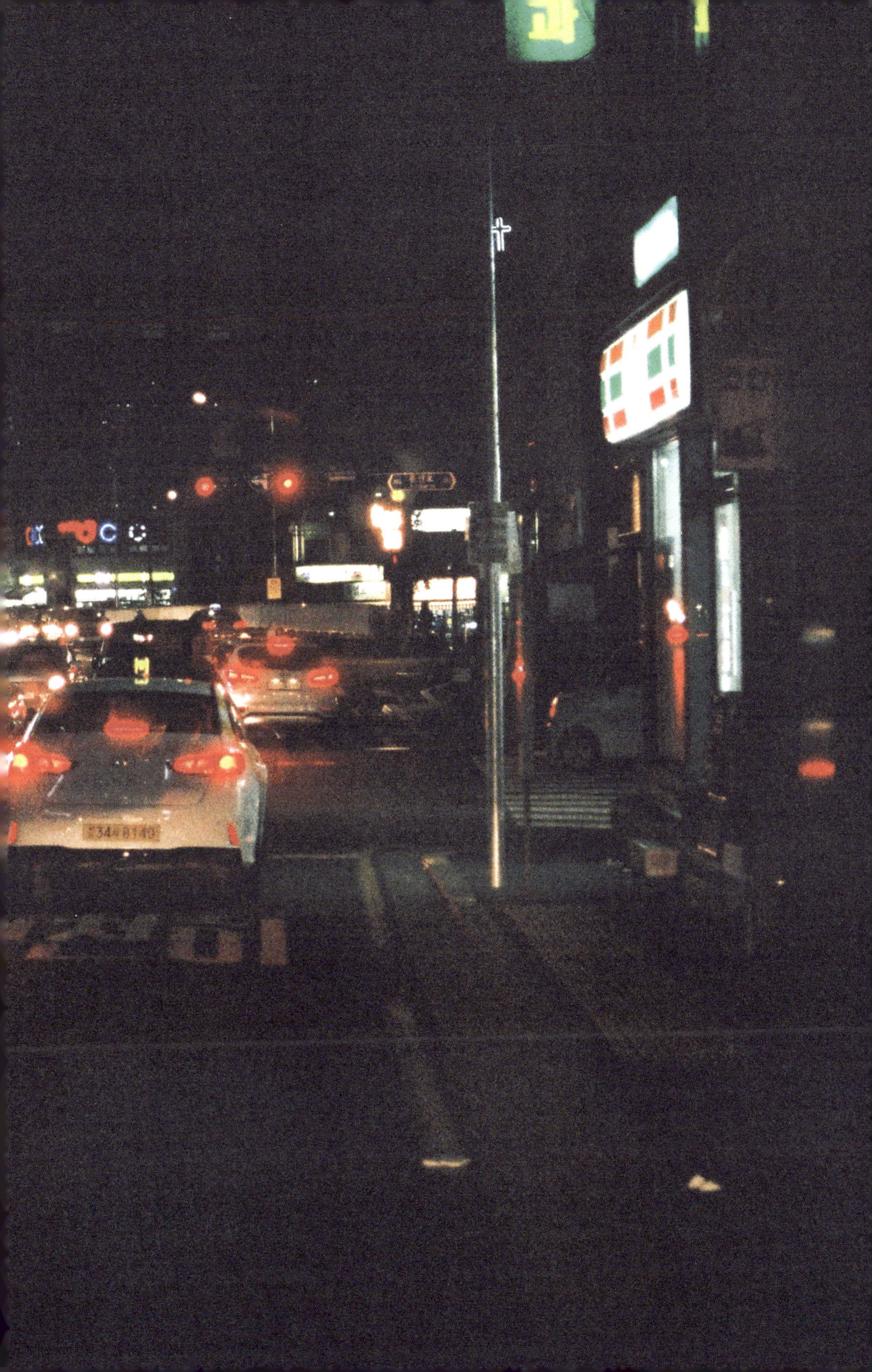

AGE·ING ATLAS

Words & Pictures: Kaon Kim | Maps: openstreetmap.org & map-stylizer by Absolute-Tinkerer

Talking about old age can be frightening. Getting old is often associated with weakness, loneliness, ugliness, and boredom. In most contemporary cultures, staying young both from the look and lifestyle is a big topic of interest. The truth is, no matter what anti-ageing procedures we take, we all eventually become old. In fact, our lifetime as an old person is getting longer. The statistics show that the number of people over 80 years is going to increase more than threefold in the next three decades (UN, 2017). Never before have people lived longer than today thanks to improved living conditions, hygiene, and preventive health care. The world's institutions of different levels are adapting to this demographic shift in their policies in terms of infrastructure, healthcare system, as well as community building. However, there is less attention paid to the consequences the longer lifespan brings to what it means to be old. How the media is projecting a person in his mid-sixties, for example, has not changed much from the time when we were expected to live only for few years further. Now that we expect to live another 20 years after retirement, we have to search for new models by which to grow old, and challenge stereotypes that there is only one way of doing so.

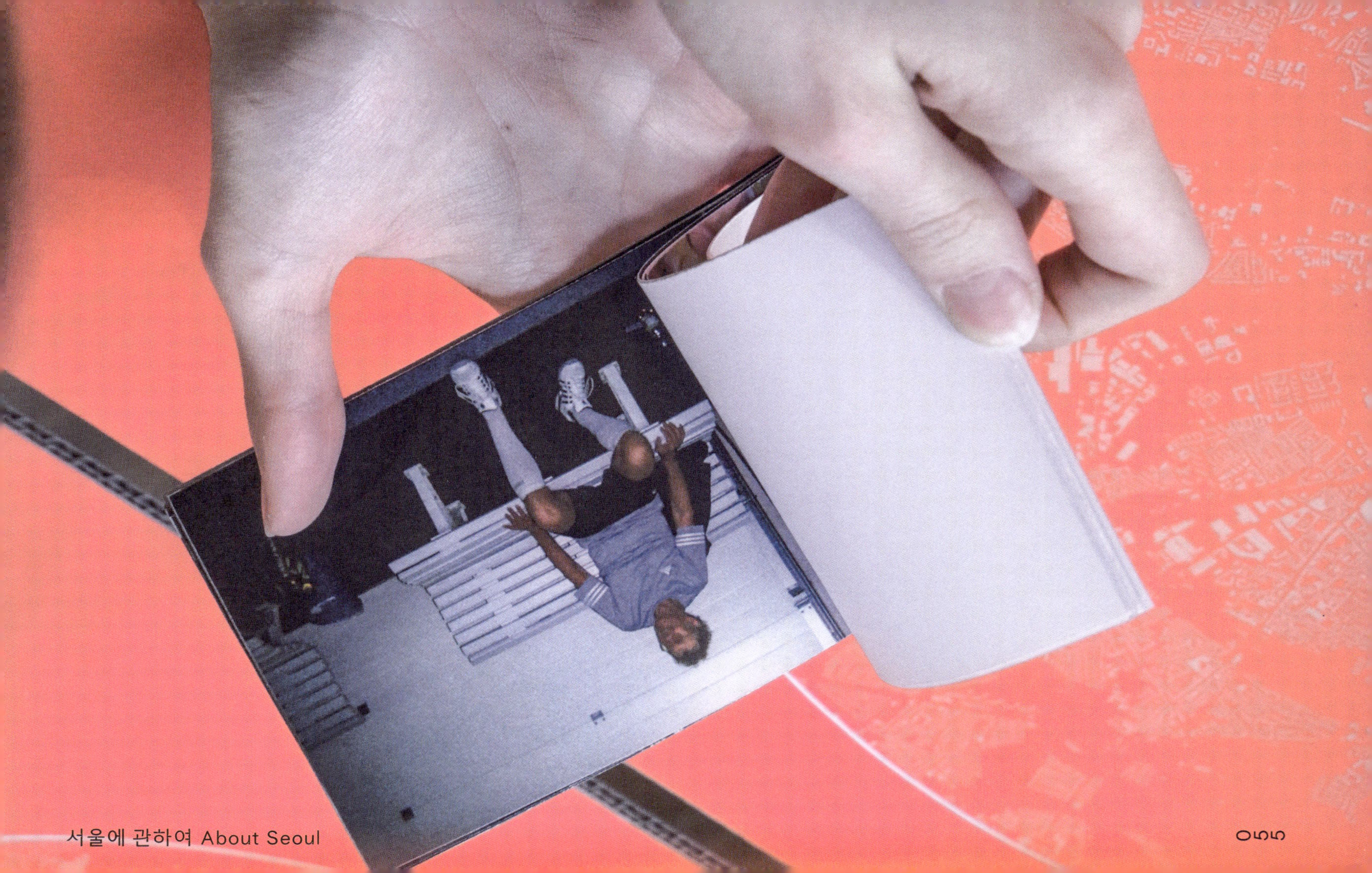

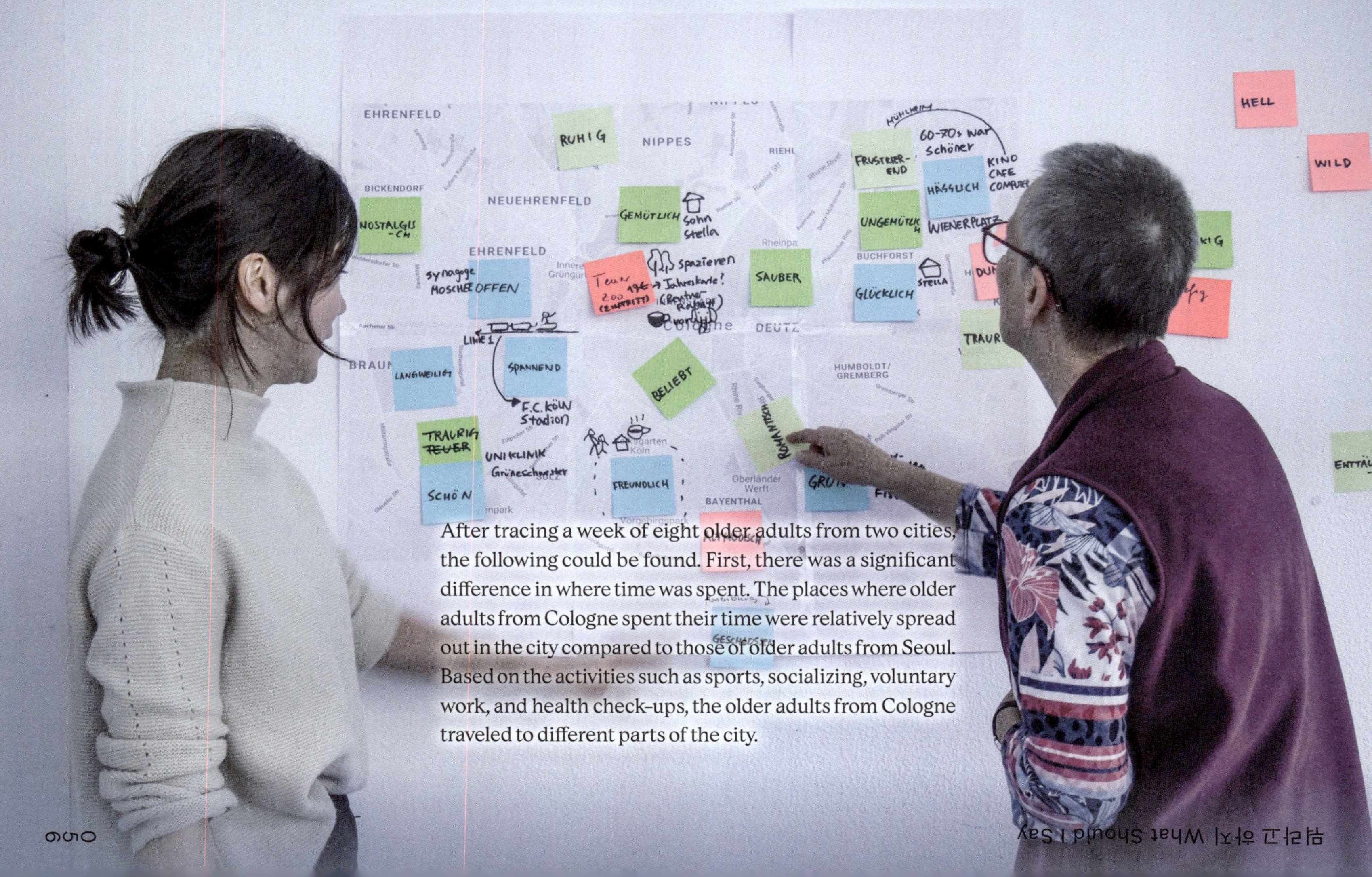

After tracing a week of eight older adults from two cities, the following could be found. First, there was a significant difference in where time was spent. The places where older adults from Cologne spent their time were relatively spread out in the city compared to those of older adults from Seoul. Based on the activities such as sports, socializing, voluntary work, and health check-ups, the older adults from Cologne traveled to different parts of the city.

COLOGNE (1,119,000)

→ Population over 65:
2020: 18 % | 2040: 20 %
→ 5.7 % of the population over 65
are receiving 'Grundsicherung
im Alter (Basic provision for
→ old age).' However, the report
notes that it can be assumed
that a considerable number of
unrecorded cases of older
people living in hidden poverty
because of shame or ignorance.
→ 30 % of 65–79-year-olds live alone.
→ 25 % of the population over 65
is involved in civic activities. The
older population is not evenly
distributed over the urban area.
The plan is to help the districts
gain a balanced age structure.

Source: 'Gesund altern in Köln,' 2012

On the other hand, there was overlap in the areas where three out of four older adults from Seoul liked to spend time: Tapgol Park and Jegidong neighborhood. These are neighborhoods whose main target population is people over 65. For example, the Seoul Metropolitan Government has implemented the principles of universal design in one of the streets near Tapgol park, which improved the physical access as well as the typography of signs. In Jegidong, there are dance clubs for the over-65s, cafes offering medicinal tea, traditional medicine markets, and doctors. One of the interviewees mentioned that it was not necessary to make an appointment with his friend because these places were already integrated into the daily routine of his circle of friends. Another interviewee mentioned that not every place in Seoul welcomes older people.

The differences can also be seen in the type of places. Older adults from Seoul visited public spaces more often compared to those from Cologne. An open lounge in a shopping mall and Incheon Airport were examples. In the interviews, the older adults indicated that they felt comfortable in such public spaces because they could stay there as long as they wanted without being noticed or having to pay anything. Free entertainment and free heating and cooling were attractive to them.

SEOUL (9,963,000)

→ Population over 65:
2020: 17 % | 2040: 32.4 %
→ 66.8 % of the population over 65 are
self-paying for their living expenses.
→ Research with 267 people over
65 showed that 33.9 % wished
for support in job seeking.
→ 40.7 % of the population over 65 are
living with their children. 34.5 %
of the respondents reasoned that
their children cannot afford to
move out and 31.3 % said that they
were incapable of living alone.
→ 62.2 % of the population over 65
are watching TV in their free time.
→ 37 % of the respondents
answered that they wished for
more leisure opportunities such
as traveling and camping.

Sources: Seoul Survey, 2014 /
'Prospective Changes and Policy
Agendas for Super-aged Society,' 2010

Atlas of Jinhan (67)—time spent in a week

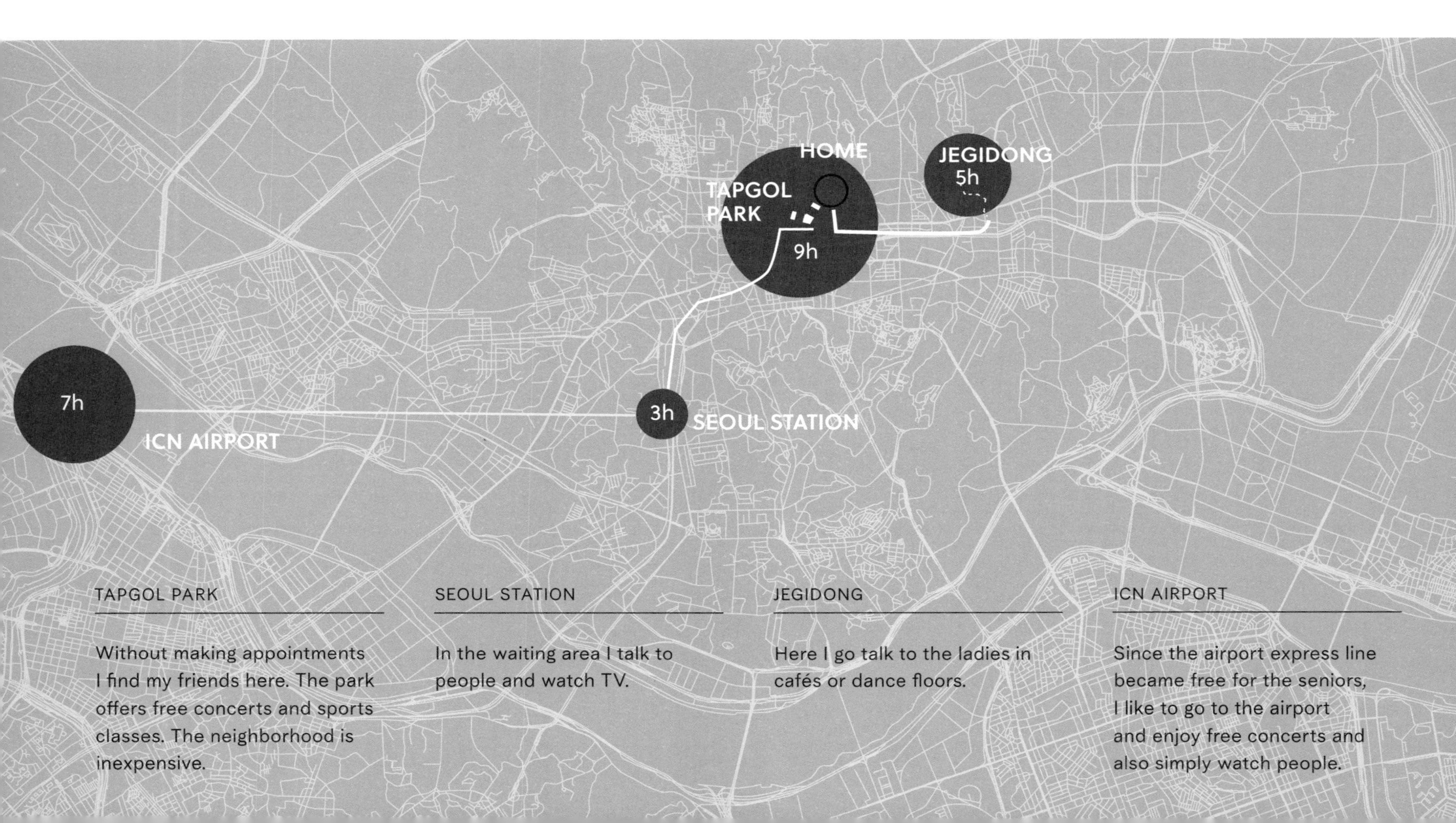

TAPGOL PARK

Without making appointments I find my friends here. The park offers free concerts and sports classes. The neighborhood is inexpensive.

SEOUL STATION

In the waiting area I talk to people and watch TV.

JEGIDONG

Here I go talk to the ladies in cafés or dance floors.

ICN AIRPORT

Since the airport express line became free for the seniors, I like to go to the airport and enjoy free concerts and also simply watch people.

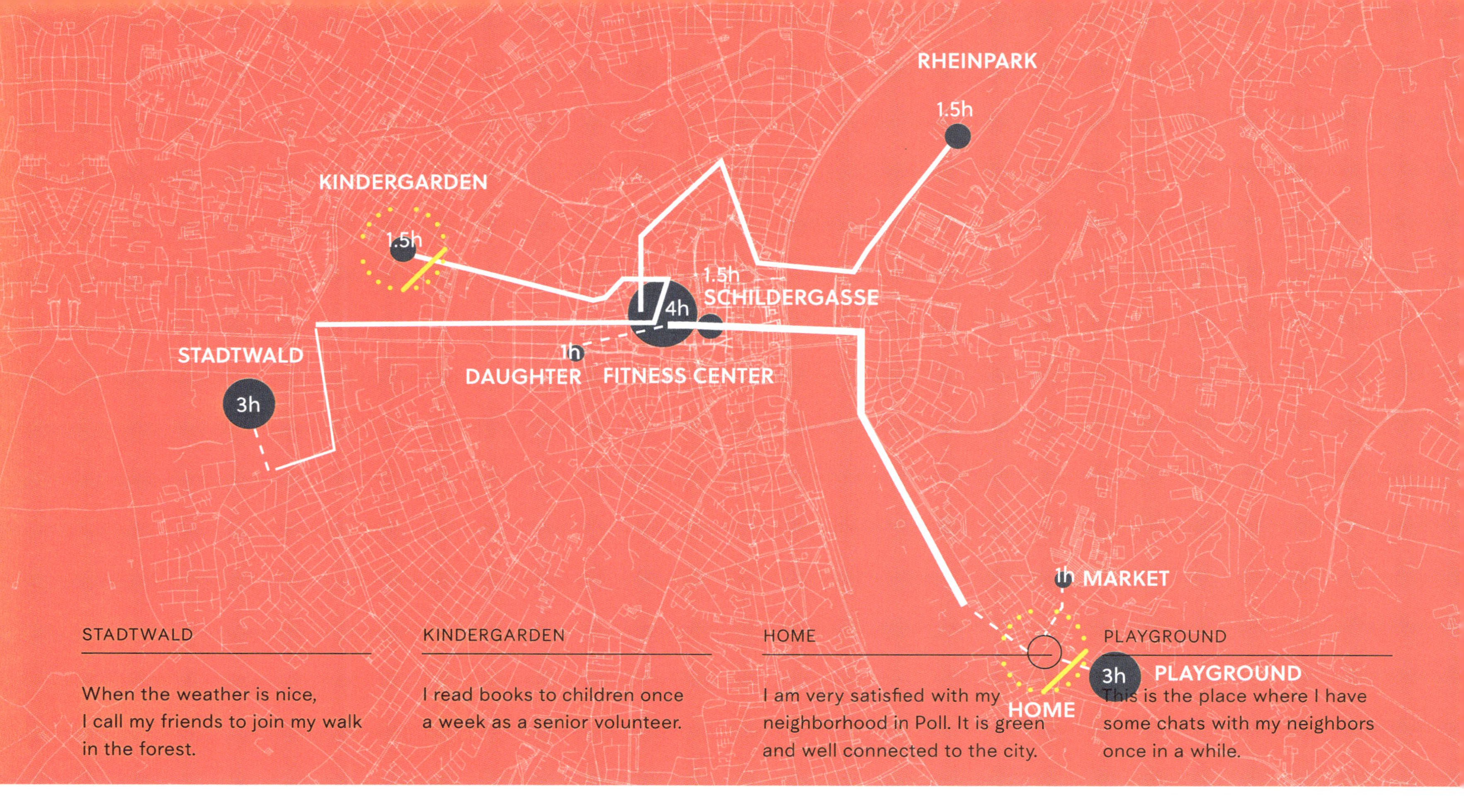

STADTWALD
When the weather is nice, I call my friends to join my walk in the forest.

KINDERGARDEN
I read books to children once a week as a senior volunteer.

HOME
I am very satisfied with my neighborhood in Poll. It is green and well connected to the city.

PLAYGROUND
This is the place where I have some chats with my neighbors once in a while.

Atlas of Hildegard (71)—time spent in a week

Atlas of Wondeok (75)—time spent in a week

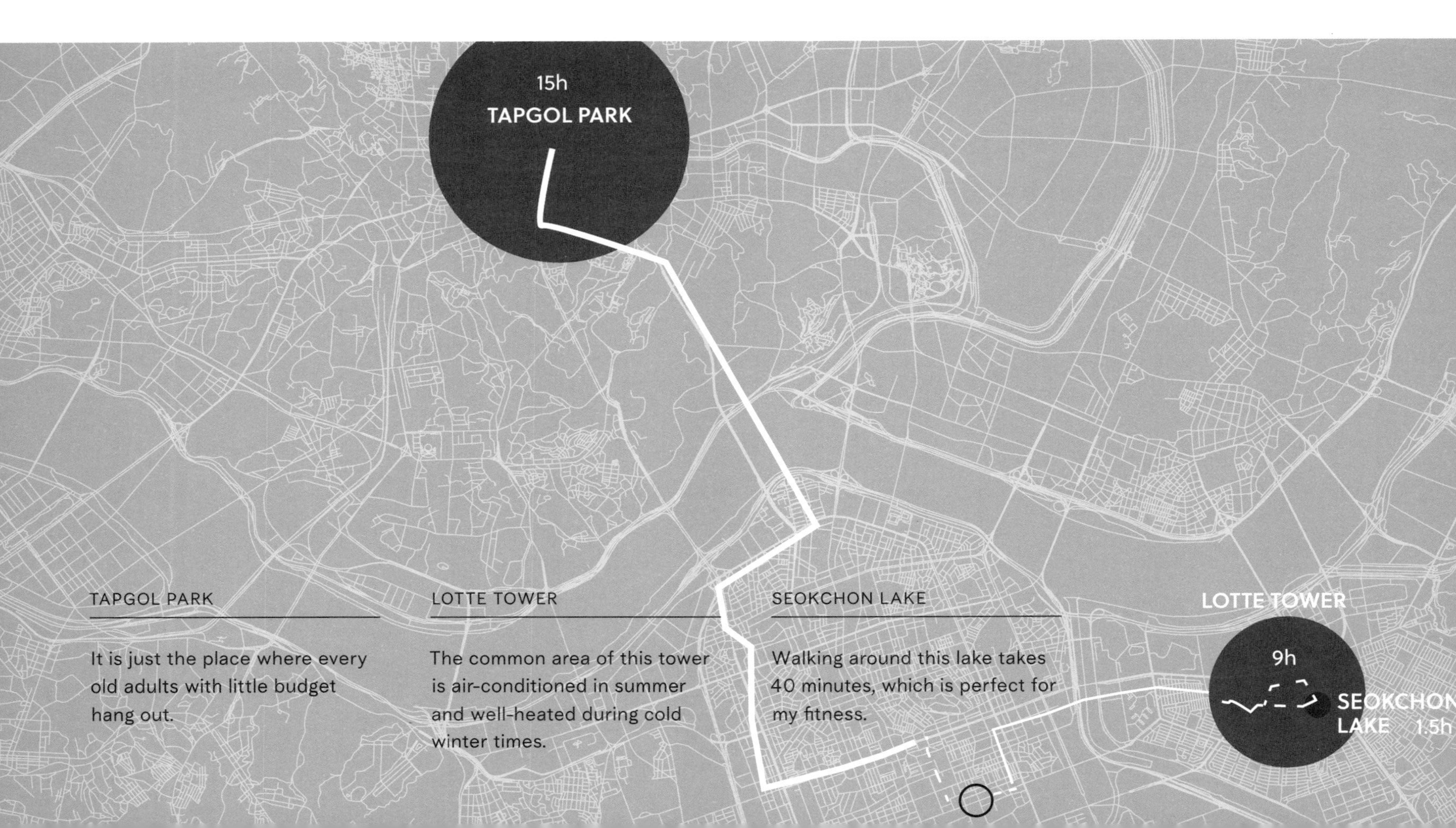

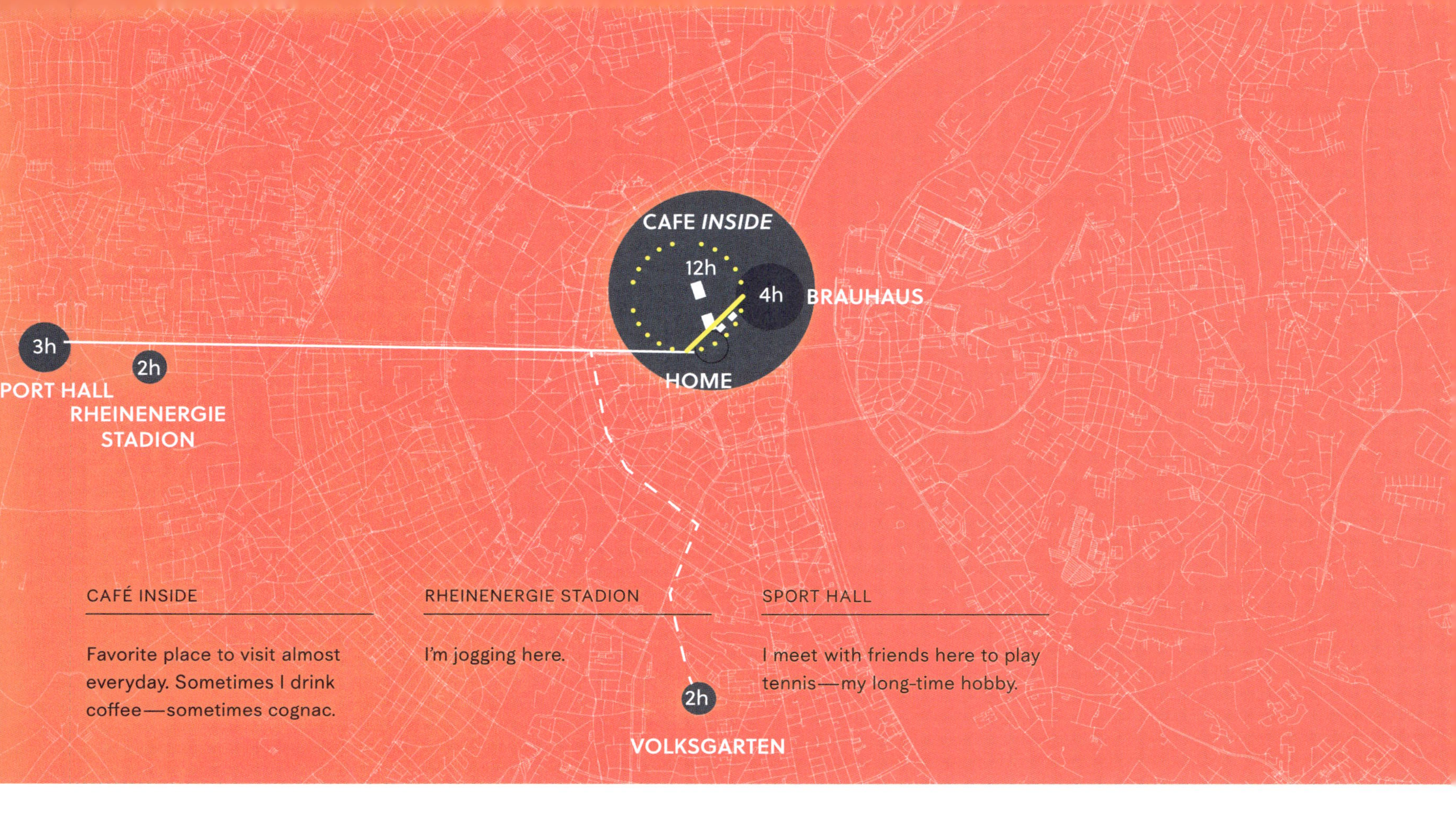

CAFÉ INSIDE

Favorite place to visit almost everyday. Sometimes I drink coffee—sometimes cognac.

RHEINENERGIE STADION

I'm jogging here.

SPORT HALL

I meet with friends here to play tennis—my long-time hobby.

Atlas of Toni (78)—time spent in a week

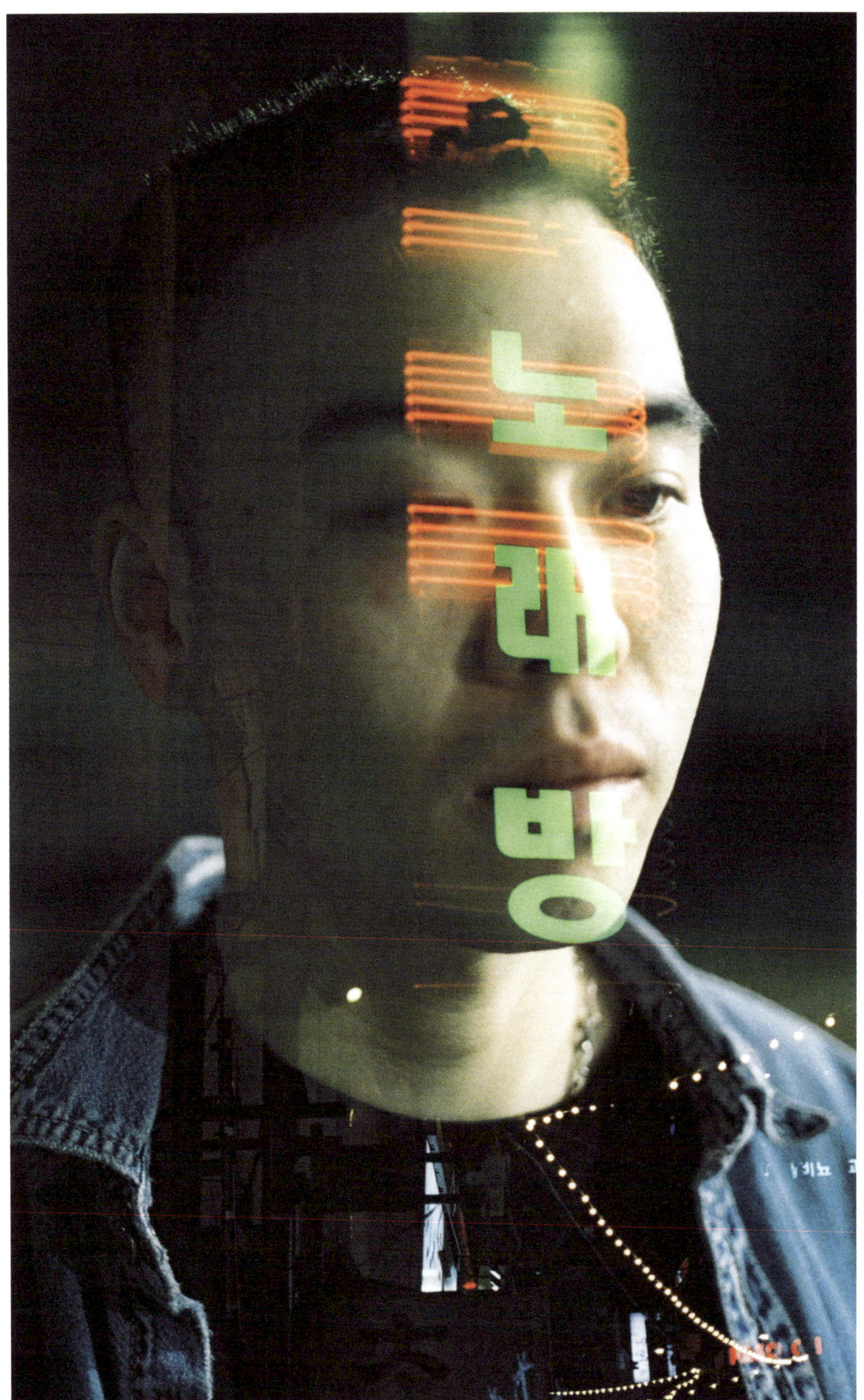
뭐라고 하냐

A God of fire

Interview with Seunghun Yoo

Interview | Pictures: Omid Fröhlich

HOW DID YOU GET INTO CERAMICS?

I didn't know about ceramics until the end of high-school. I decided to partake in a class assignment related to ceramics and that really got me hooked. I found the material and technique really exciting. From that point on I dedicated my creative energy towards that field—I even majored in ceramics.

WHAT INSPIRES YOU NOWADAYS?

Nowadays? My close friends. We can talk about our work and exchange our thoughts—they inspire me and I can inspire them back. When I started I was mostly inspired by ordinary things as well as traditional Korean patterns. I still find inspiration when I visit museums or look at books. I love to get inspiration by the old and mix it up with new things.

CAN YOU TELL ME WHAT MAKES YOUR WORK SPECIAL TO YOU?

I could show you some results, but maybe it'd be more interesting if I'd show you how to do pottery yourself. (He showed me how to throw clay and then we made some cups together. He fast dried them with a Bunsen burner.)

HOW DO YOU GO ABOUT WHEN STARTING A FRESH PIECE?

I work on the spur of the moment. I never really sketch my ideas out. It's adding an additional step between the inspiration and the actual work—which to me doesn't feel right. I prefer to translate my ideas straight into crafting. Another aspect that runs through my designs is storytelling. Each of my piece has its own story. Through all that usability remains important. In the end my pottery still is meant to serve a purpose.

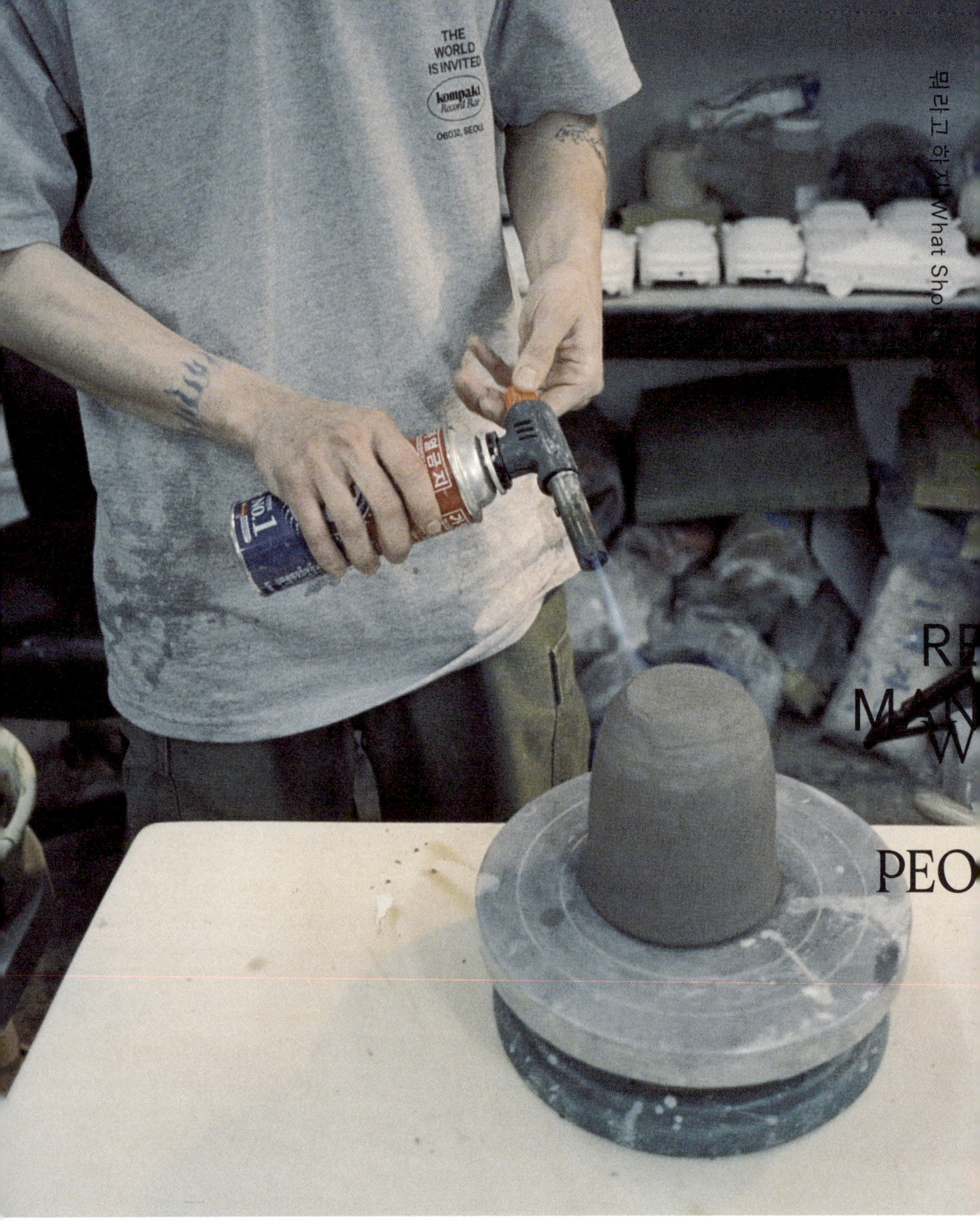

HOW DO YOU OVERCOME OBSTACLES WHILE DESIGNING?

A main obstacle are the ceramics themselves—they really are unpredictable. I'm often satisfied with my work before it goes into the kiln, but the burning process changes the shape a lot. In my opinion there is beauty in this uncontrollable change. That's why I'm not bothered that much by this—at least for my own work. With client work it's a different story. The kiln is really hard to control. It has a mind of its own—a god of fire, so to speak.

WHAT DOES YOUR EVERYDAY LIFE LOOK LIKE?

I love to work at night. So I adjusted my general schedule around it. I usually work at nighttime and go to bed at 4 or 5 in the morning. During the day I have meetings. Also I practice Jujitsu. I don't really have a fixed schedule. I am self-employed, which means I don't have a regular working week. I can work no matter what day it is: Weekend, weekdays—I don't care. But this also means my week never ends—which, I think is not good for my health.

SO, WHAT DO YOU DO FOR RELAXATION THEN?

For relaxing I practice Jujitsu. I also love drinking—alone or with friends. When I drink I feel comfortable. Music also is helping me to relax. I love DJing.

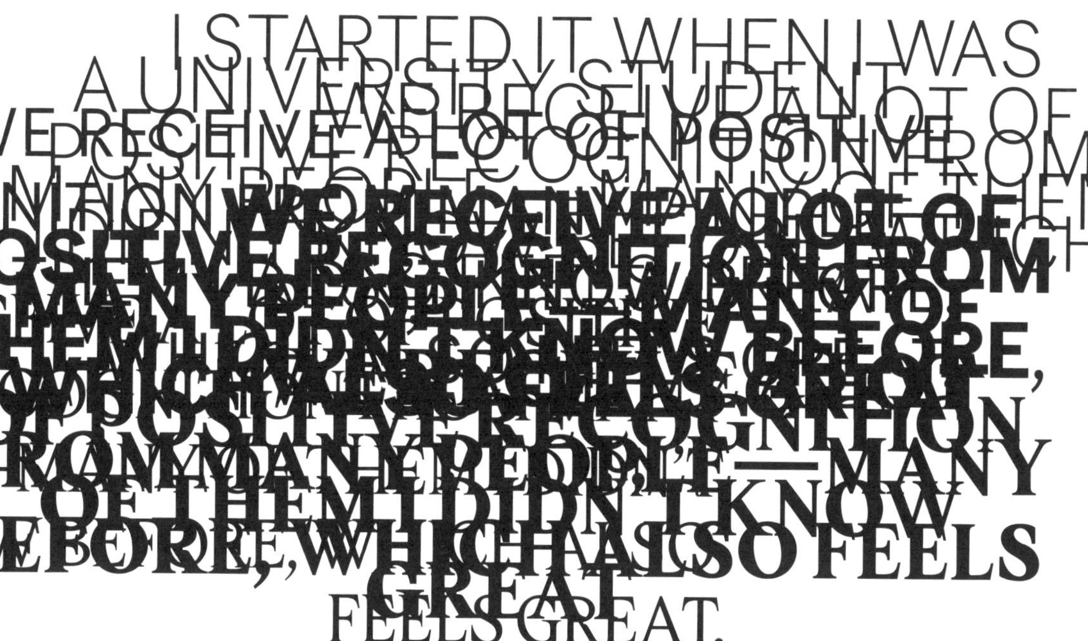

CAN YOU TELL ME OF A SITUATION OR THING THAT GAVE YOU JOY RECENTLY?

This studio 'QH'—my own brand. I started it when I was a university student. I was slowly building it up and nowadays many people like the brand. The income is not that high, but we receive a lot of positive recognition from many people—many of them I didn't know before, which also feels great. By now brands I love want to collaborate with me, so I am really happy.

WHAT DESIGNERS WOULD YOU RECOMMEND TO CHECK OUT?

I can whole-heartedly recommend Woojae's work.

WHAT DO YOU THINK IS THE STRENGTH OF YOUR CHOSEN
FIELD OF DESIGN?

I think as long my body supports me, I can make ceramics. These are
the merits of ceramics. It's not overly taxing and it is also not tied to a specific age. For example,
the time you can be active in a company as a graphic designer is much shorter. Same goes for
businessman, they will quit their work with 60. As ceramics is a craft, my craftsmanship will
grow over time—increasing the value of my work the longer I keep doing it. Ceramics always
played an important role in history. That's why I take a certain pride in making ceramics—I'm
standing in league with many important craftspeople and I myself am adding to this history.

WHAT IS YOUR BIGGEST CONCERN THESE DAYS?

'QH' is doing well these days. But I am thinking about how to make it
better. "You have to row when water is coming in," so they say. And I'm trying to figure out how
to best row this boat.

IS THERE ANYTHING YOU WANT TO DO OR TRY AS
A DESIGNER IN THE FUTURE?

My plan is to build a 'QH' factory. A huge multilayered workshop for
different crafts. The ground floor will be dedicated to car workshops, the second floor will
house a wood workshop, the third floor will accommodate for metal crafting, and on top of
the building: A penthouse, where I will do ceramics.

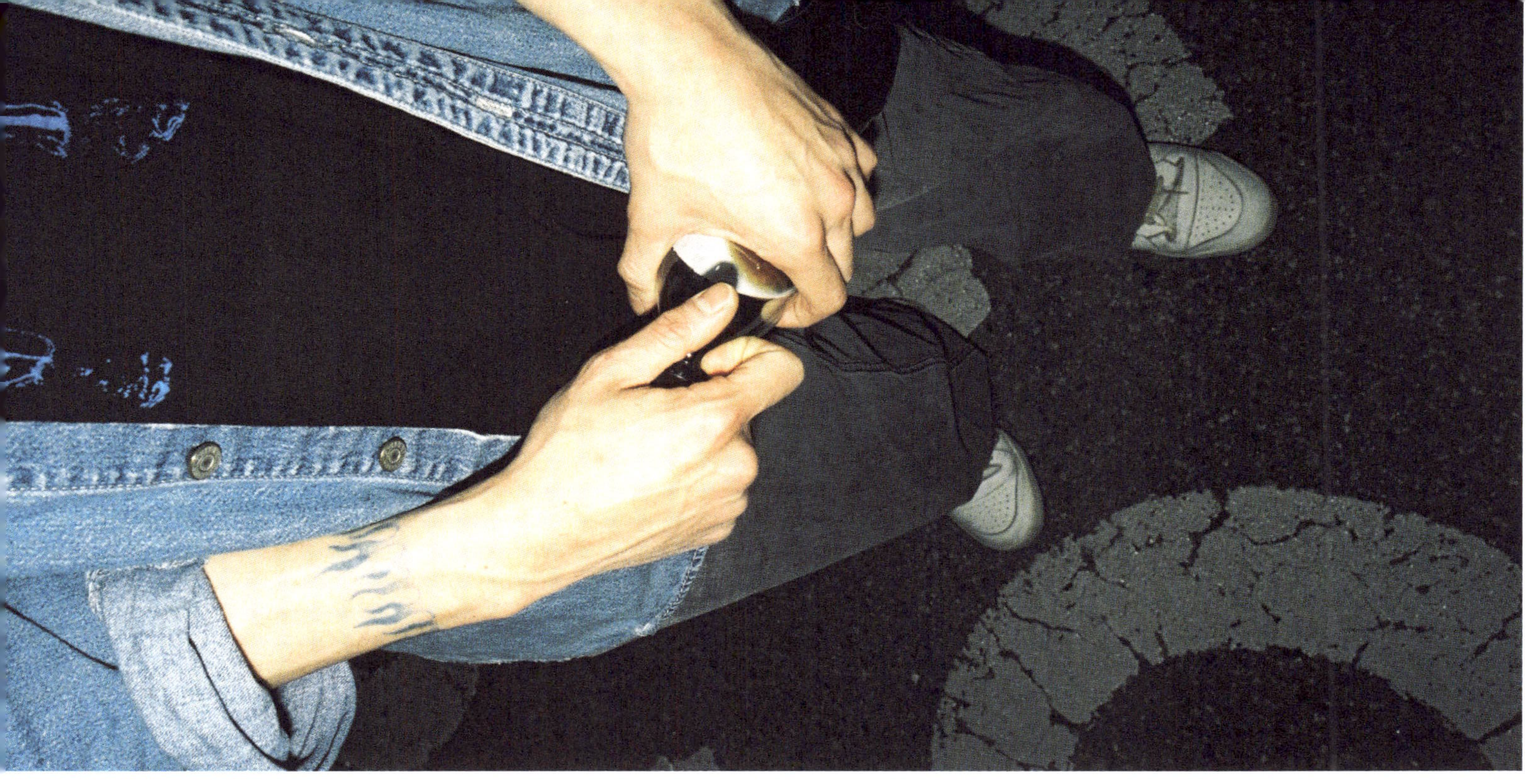

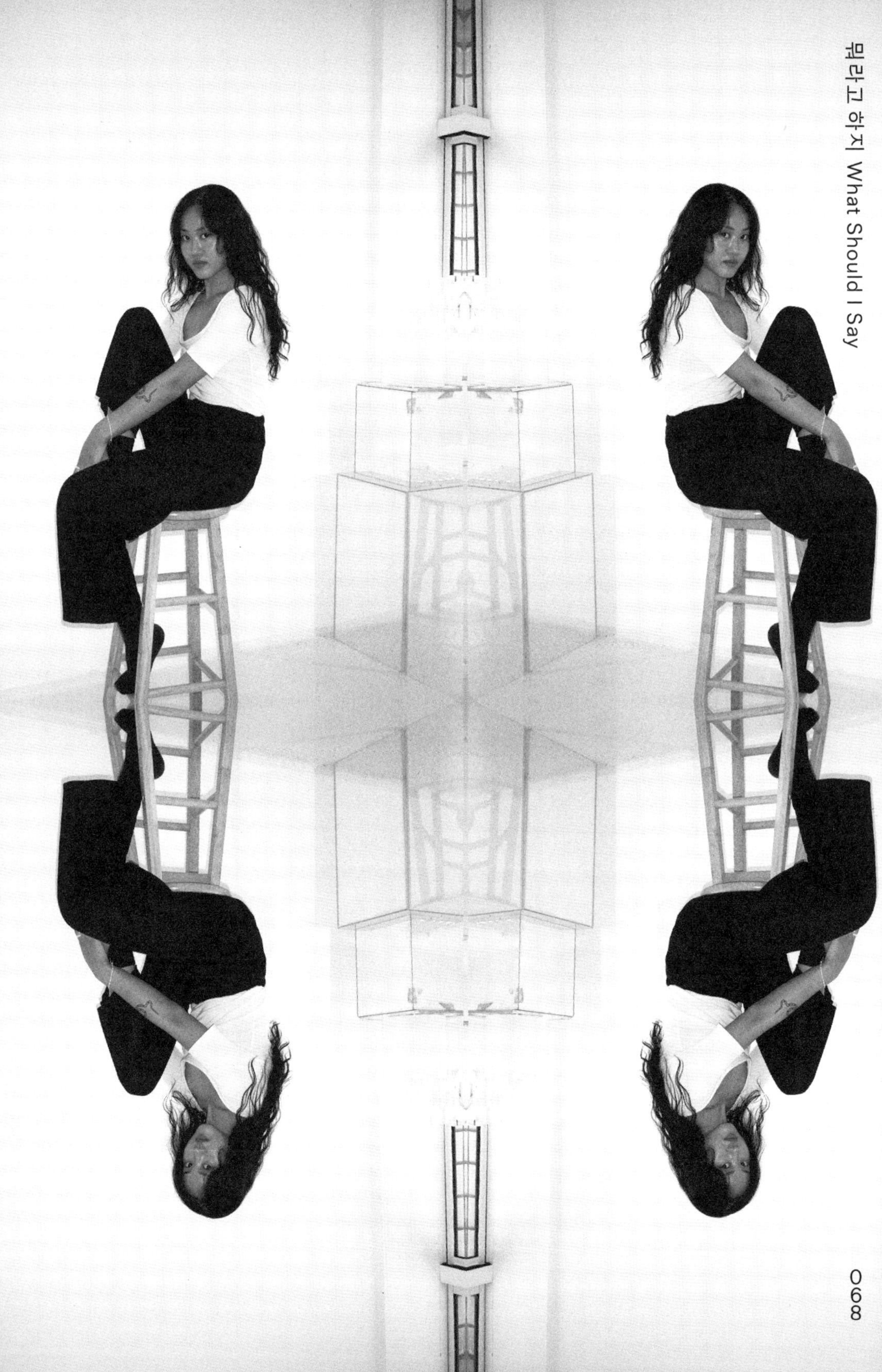

A way that works a lot better

Interview with Jieun Byun

Interview: Youjin Kim & David Wiesner | Pictures: Jieun Byun

YK: Please tell us a bit about you.

JB: Hello, I'm Jieun. I'm a UX-Designer in Seoul. I work for a digital design agency called 'Brex.' We specialized in digital design like websites, apps or branding.

YK: How did you end up doing what you do now?

JB: It wasn't my first job. I was working as a digital marketer before. But then I wanted to change my career to something with a better perspective for the future. I was really drawn to digital graphic design. So I looked up different kinds of areas where I could integrate my background in marketing. And I found that UX-design kind of combines all of that—graphic design as well as digital marketing. So I took a class and applied for a job.

DW: <u>Can you tell me a bit about the education process?</u>

JB: So, I studied business in university and then after school worked as a marketeer for about three years. Then I took a class at a private institution. It was a four month long course—it was a quick and fast course. And after that I had my own portfolio that I used to apply as a UX-designer.

DW: <u>In Germany it usually is quite hard to get a job outside of what you majored in. So your career path sounds exceptionally lucky from a German perspective. Is this a regular path for Koreans to take?</u>

JB: I know that in Germany everything hinges on the degree. I would say it is a little bit different in Korea. As long as you are willing to learn and passionate about something you can apply to something outside of your major. It is actually a quite common way in Korea. It will still be harder to get accepted, compared to someone who majored in that field, but there is a fair chance.

YK: <u>Especially UX-design is quite open for this kind of change in career paths, as it is more based on a certain way to think about problems—not so much on the crafting of an object. So I think the background in business can actually be quite helpful in this regard.</u>

JB: I think that is true too. In my company there are a lot of people that have a different kind of background. Even the manager that I'm working with—he has a music background.

YK: <u>Do you know how he started in UX-design?</u>

JB: I don't know exactly how he started in UX-design. I know he got burned out working as a composer working in the commercial industry. He always worked till late at night and so he wanted to switch jobs. He then studied again and now works as a UX-designer.

DW: <u>How do you keep on learning in your field?</u>

JB: I think I learn most by doing it. I work pretty much 14 hours per day. Every time I leave work I'm really exhausted and I kind of want to quit my job. But then I think of it in a different way. Everyday there is so much work to do and I'm stressed of dealing with the work. But at the same time I'm always researching, I appreciate my co-workers and learning a lot from them. So the work environment and staff always keep me inspired and continue to educate me.

YK: <u>How do you usually do your research?</u>

JB: There are a lot of different ways to do the research. Of course we do research Online. Then we do user-research where we meet with users and do one-on-one interviews to find the problem they have. Once we figure out what they need we build a prototype and do a second interview to check if the changes we made are actual improvements or not.

YK: <u>How do you start your design process?</u>

JB: Before we jump into a project we start with a research phase with the firm. For instance if we do a project for a bank (where we are tasked with doing a redesign) we download their banking app and go through every aspect of it. If we come across things we find noteworthy, we take screenshots and place them in a collaborative mood board—like 'miro' or 'sketchy.' And then we go through all these pictures and designs. So this is how we start into a new project.

YK: <u>If you encounter an obstacle in your process, how do you overcome it?</u>

JB: I think it is always better to communicate such problems with colleagues. Sometimes I don't know what kind of solution would be appropriate and I ask a colleague who is in charge of a different project. They then can take a look at this with a fresh pair of eyes. So depending on the problem I'm asking one of my fellow designers—could be UX- or UI-designers—who are not involved in my project for advice. I think that is my way to overcome obstacles in my projects.

YK: <u>During my time as a fashion designer I often had situations where I wanted to go into a direction that I thought to be fresh and good design in general, but whenever I showed them to our marketing guy he always said that customers won't like this and I should use more basic designs. So my question is, do you encounter problems implementing your ideas with your clients?</u>

JB: I haven't had any of these problems. That's is also why I really like UX-design. If you are doing graphic or brand design your designs will always be decided by the clients taste. But if you're doing UX-design you base your design on data. It could be Google Analytics or user feedback. So you always have data as a base for talking with your clients. You can validate your choices with numbers—60% liked design 'A' better than 'B,' that's why we choose 'A.' And most clients are okay with these numbers as arguments.

DW: <u>So it gives you a better base to stand on, in order to defend your design?</u>

JB: Yeah, sure. I think UX-design has to be this way.

YK: <u>Is there someone that inspired you lately?</u>

JB: I like the Netflix series 'Chef's table.' Each episode features a chef from a different country who introduces a different kind of dish. I love to watch these on Sunday mornings. Each of the chefs—especially the older ones that have been working in this field for several decades—

created their dishes that integrate the culture that they come from. I just find it inspiring to see how much they love this one thing—Cooking—and come up with new things because of their experience and love for it.

For example there was one baker in the show, and she said: Most bakers focus on the icing on the cake so that it becomes perfect. But it is not about the competition to make the perfect icing, it is about the creativity. So she started to create her own style by just smashing the icing on the cake. I found that liberating, as I think it is true: People often focus on things that don't matter. And the people that go their own way, they are the ones that become popular. I often think we are stuck in the theory while we are working. Because we think this is the only way to do things. But sometimes when you break these boundaries, you discover a way that works a lot better. And we couldn't think of this way before, as we were too stuck in our normal ways.

I don't think that UX-design is so much design-based it is more based on human thinking——it should make your life better in a way.

In my work practice I try to apply this from time to time. In UX-design we always think about the many theories that we can use to approach the problem, but then we often get stuck with the same approaches. But then we realize that there is not just one way to get through. So we go back to the start and come up with a better solution. So bringing this back to the 'The Chef's Table': There is not just one way to cook curry, to do the icing or cooking in general.

YK: <u>Can you talk a bit of some of your work that you're really fond of</u>?

JB: I want to show you the first mobile app that I designed. The app is called 'Flatmate' and is based on my experience living in Berlin. I found it very very hard to find an apartment or a flatmate in Berlin. I was always thinking: If only there'd be an app that could help you find a flatmate or room, that would be really helpful. So I took the idea from there and created a concept and prototype for an app that would help you to find like minded people and rooms. The mechanic in finding a fit would be similar to Tinder. You could swipe to right to find out more about the offer, find descriptions, ratings, and reviews. On the offer page it also shows the price for the room and you can locate the place on the map. I wanted the app to appear as friendly and reliable. I picked blue—as it is associated with reliability. I also picked the font 'Orkney' because it has these rounded corners which gives it a cute feeling. For the logo I wanted to integrate the idea of a new home, so I changed the upper stroke of the uppercase 'T' to the shape of a roof.

DW: Would you say that you are proud of it?

JB: I don't think I'm proud of it. It is the first project that I worked on by myself and the idea behind it came from my own experience looking for a flat in Berlin, where I thought: If there would be an app like this it would really help and my life would be so much better. I think UX-design should be this way. I don't think that UX-design is so much design-based it is more based on human thinking—it should make your life better in a way. And with this project I wasn't really focused on creating a pleasing design, but to solve a problem humans have.

DW: If you could change one thing about your work so that when you come home from work you are really happy, what would it be?

JB: Anything? I want to change the coffee machine at work—to a Nespresso machine.

YK: A small dream. (laughs)

JB: I'm pretty satisfied with the work environment and the people I work together with, but the only thing I don't like is the coffee machine.

YK: What is your daily routine?

JB: Before corona? I think it was pretty similar. The only difference is, that now I can't go to party after work. Otherwise it is pretty much the same. Because I work until late, so during the week I don't really have that much personal life. I go to work, and then I go home—that's my routine. On weekend I try to see friends and try to have a good time with them. Or I read a book. I think that's it. A very normal routine.

YK: What do you do with your friends usually?

JB: Before corona we tried out different new restaurants and went to parties, if there was a good gig. But at the moment we can't go to these public places. But here at my place I have access to the rooftop, so we go to the rooftop and drink together.

YK: From what I know you've got family in Australia. So I was wondering if you would prefer to stay in Korea or move to Australia at some point?

JB: I definitely don't want to work in Korea the whole time. Just because the working hours are long and they don't really value my time. For example: even today I have to work, even though it is Sunday. Just in general I have to work most of my waking life. I love doing my work, but I feel like they don't really value my time. This is what causes the most stress and frustration for me. Because you work really hard but you don't really get what you deserve. I definitely want to go back to Australia. I think the work culture in general is a lot better there. It is very hard to maintain a lifestyle outside of work in Korea.

DW:

JB: The weather here is starting to get warmer (we conducted the interview in April) so I started jogging again. I love jogging in the morning because it gives me excitement for the day. And just soaking in the sun does so much already to improve your mental health. I wasn't able to do that during the winter so I was really happy that the weather allows me to do that again. So now I'm back to jogging 30 minutes to an hour before work.

DW: Can you give us a few recommendations on designers that you like—preferably Korean designers?

JB: I don't know that many Korean designers to be honest. I like Dieter Rams. I think he is German. I came across his works during my UX-design studies and really liked their aesthetics. I think his aesthetics still hold up, so that people nowadays still like what he did 30 years ago. I think his designs are not trendy but have a longevity. Apart from that I don't know that many designers. Maybe one other UX-designer I came across, was featured in the Netflix series 'Abstract.' But I don't remember his name.

YK: What do you think is a benefit or something unique about the 'Korean Style?' Because, I think every country emphasizes certain traits which sets them apart from other countries.

JB: I think what makes Korean design special is that many designers here work abroad and then come back to Korea to start their own label or agency. So they got that mixture of something that is strongly rooted in Korean culture and aesthetics, but also very much influenced by western style. I think they strike a nice balance between those. But when it comes to UX-design, there are no real specialists in that field. Everyone is kind of in the beginning with UX-design. So in that regard I think Koreans have still a long way to go. But this is also a great opportunity to develop something unique.

DW: When you will retire someday in the future, what kind of 'legacy' or 'achievement' do you want to leave behind?

JB: I think most UX-designers or people that work in Korea in general have their own standards of what they want to achieve. Many want to climb the career ladder to end up in a high position. But I don't think that is my goal. I don't think of a job as a permanent thing. I think a job can always switch—especially these days. Because I already switched my job, I think that many jobs are really connected to each other. So a marketeer can be a designer, and a designer can be a developer. My goal is to become a person that can do everything—at least a bit of every position. I can't really imagine myself being just one thing.

Thinking of 'achievements' outside of the business world I want to have a family that I love. I will probably will have children, and retire in a house near the beach, so I can go to beach everyday.

YK: Is there anything that worries you these days?

JB: To be honest I work too much and this stresses me out. I can feel this affects my mental health—I'm actually somewhat depressed because of this amount of work. But then again, I'm also grateful that I can work and learn so much at my job. But there is only so much work I can stomach.

For me, this shows that people care about others. And that is a really good thing.

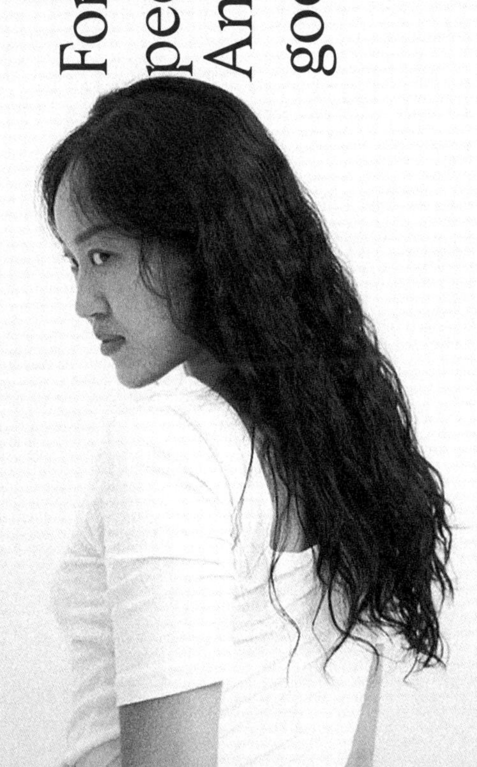

It is really a problem in Korea, that there are so few legal regulations that protect the workers. They need to work long hours or they get fired. Everybody knows it is too long but there are no other options.

YK: <u>Is there anything you want to try as a designer?</u>

JB: I want to make an interactive face filter for Instagram as a fun project. Just because I work with UI-designers a lot and I don't think you can separate UI and UX that much. But what my UI peers are better at, is the visual language. As a UX-designer I can also design visually, but I want to become better at this. If I have some extra time I would also like to learn developing, so I can do everything in the process by myself: sketch, prototype, and development. I think knowing all these parts would help me becoming a better overall designer.

DW: <u>You said you lived in Berlin for some time. What did you take with you from that experience?</u>

JB: There is a lot I took from being in Berlin. I can talk about one thing—because there is just too much if I would go into everything. I think the people in Berlin care about the environment. They don't usually use plastic bags, but carry their own bag when they go to a grocery store. Here in Korea people are still using plastic bags: When you go shopping or order food. Now it really hurts me to see this: People are using plastic without any awareness on the impact for the environment. But in Berlin people care about these things, and I respect that. Also they care about each other and look out for one another. I was surprised to see people handing out some of their used stuff for free (for example in Facebook groups). That was a big thing for me, when I moved there—that way I didn't need to buy furniture. People are not just throwing stuff away. Instead they leave it in front of their door, so you can take it away and use it.

For me this shows that people care about others. And that is a really good thing.

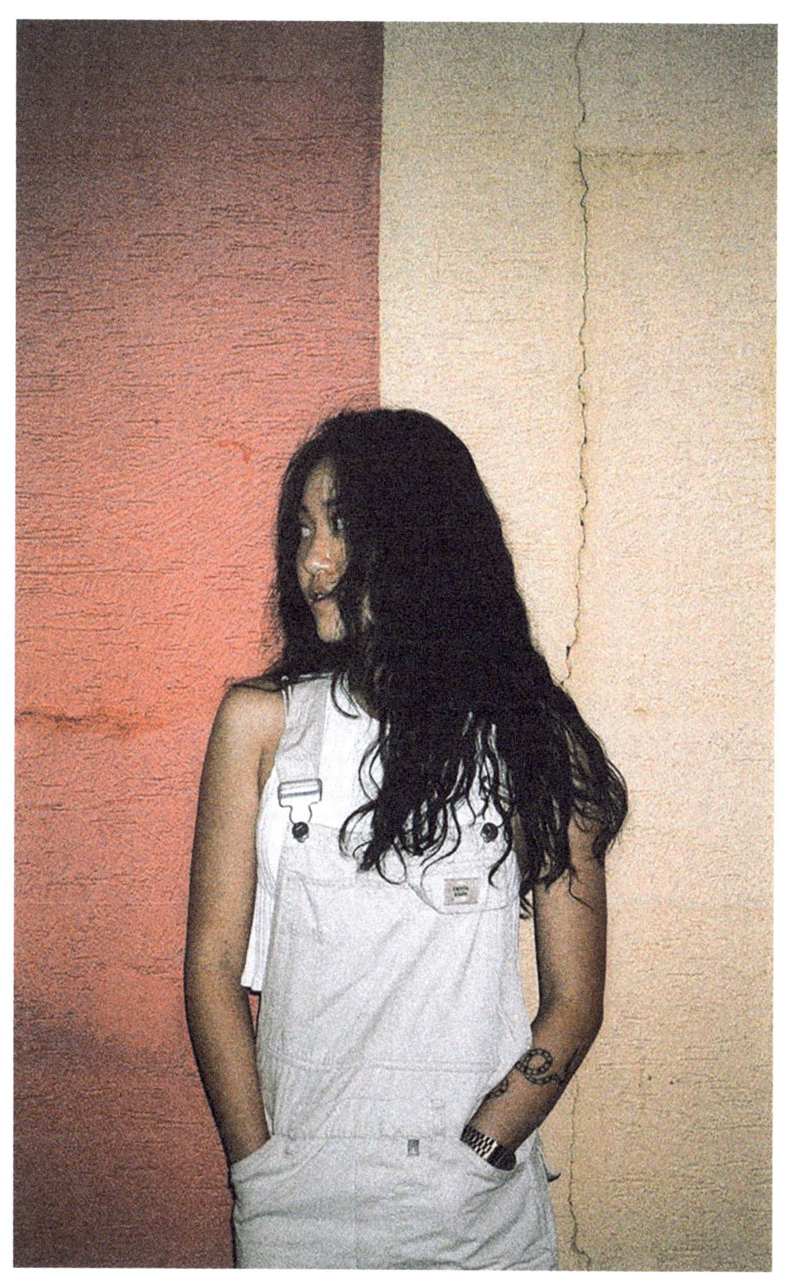

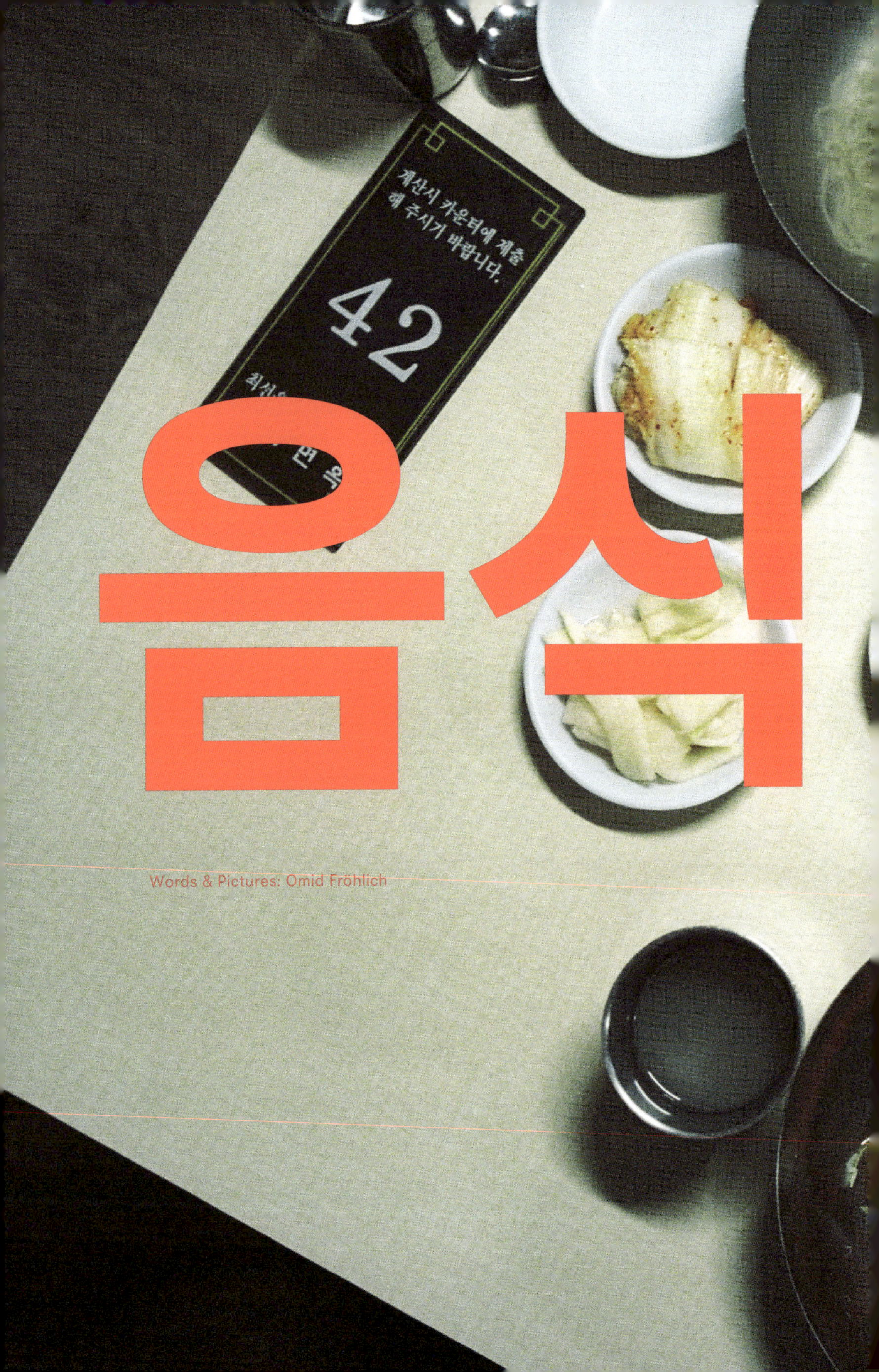
계산시 카운터에 제출
해 주시기 바랍니다.
42
음식
Words & Pictures: Omid Fröhlich

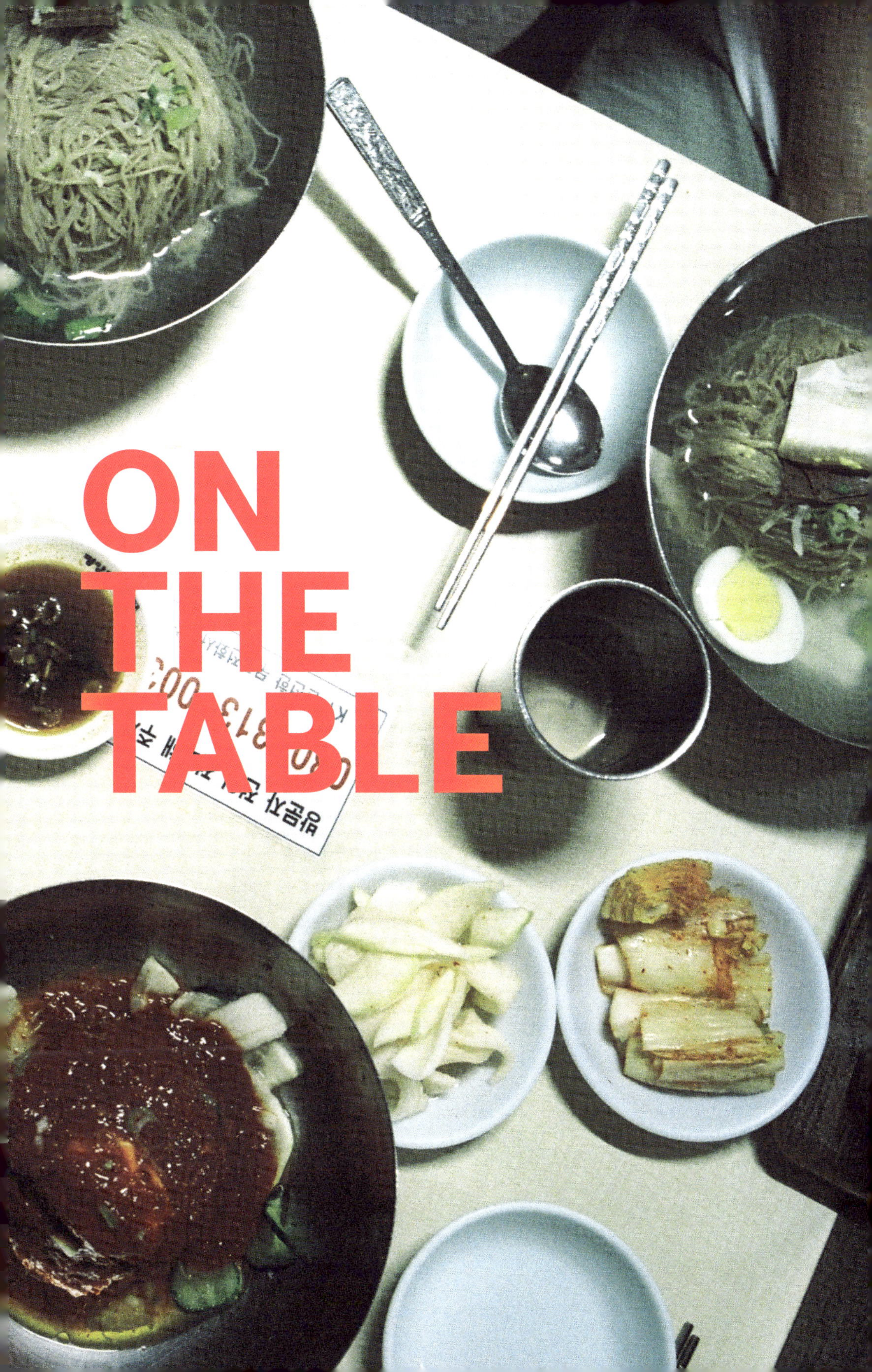
ON
THE
TABLE

One of the most important things during my time in Korea was food. As a trained chef I had to try every dish I got my hands on. From kalguksu (handcut noodles), bindae-tteok (mung bean pancake) over mandus (handmade dumplings) to bibimbap (mixed rice bowl) just to name a few.

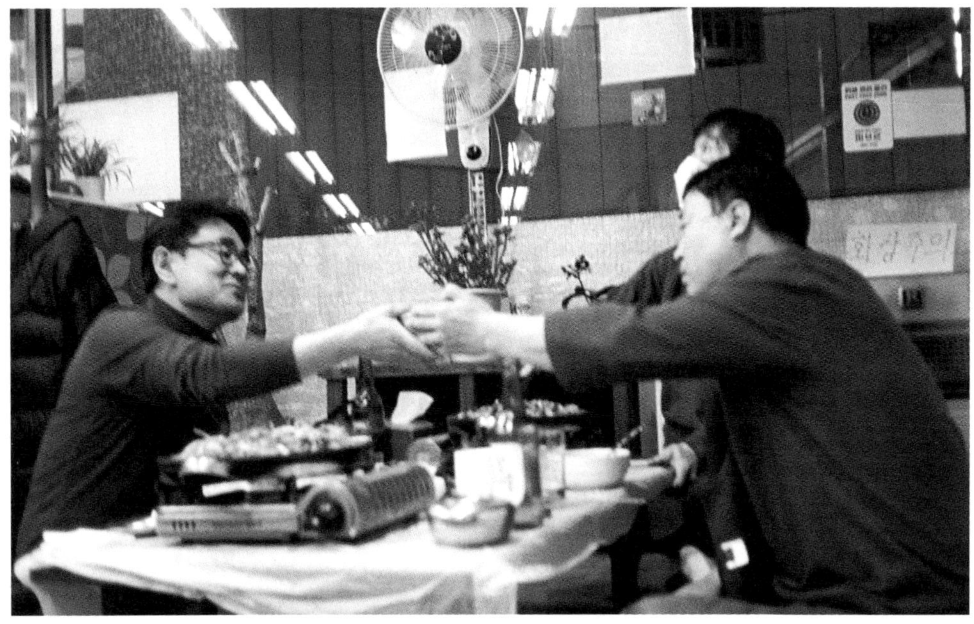

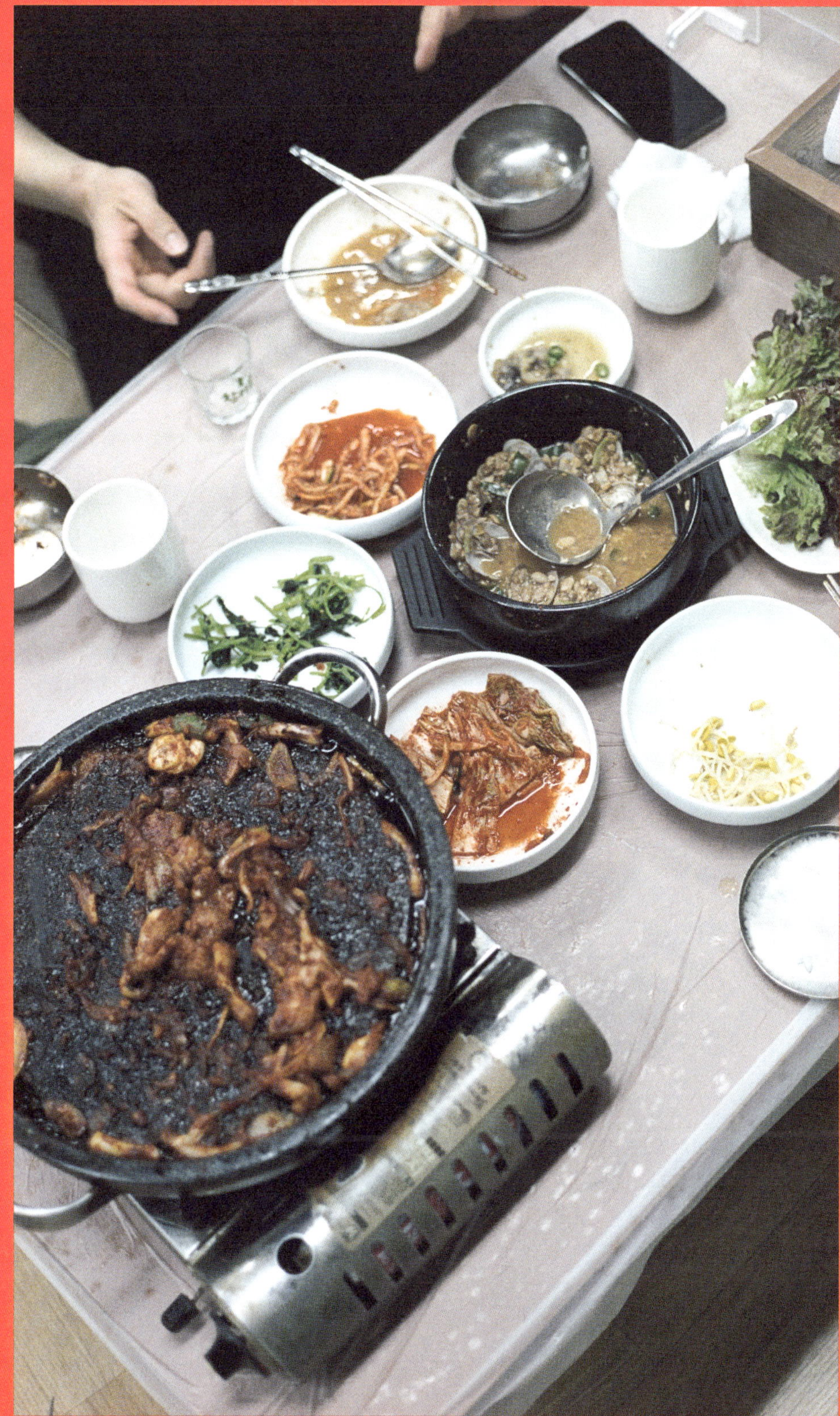

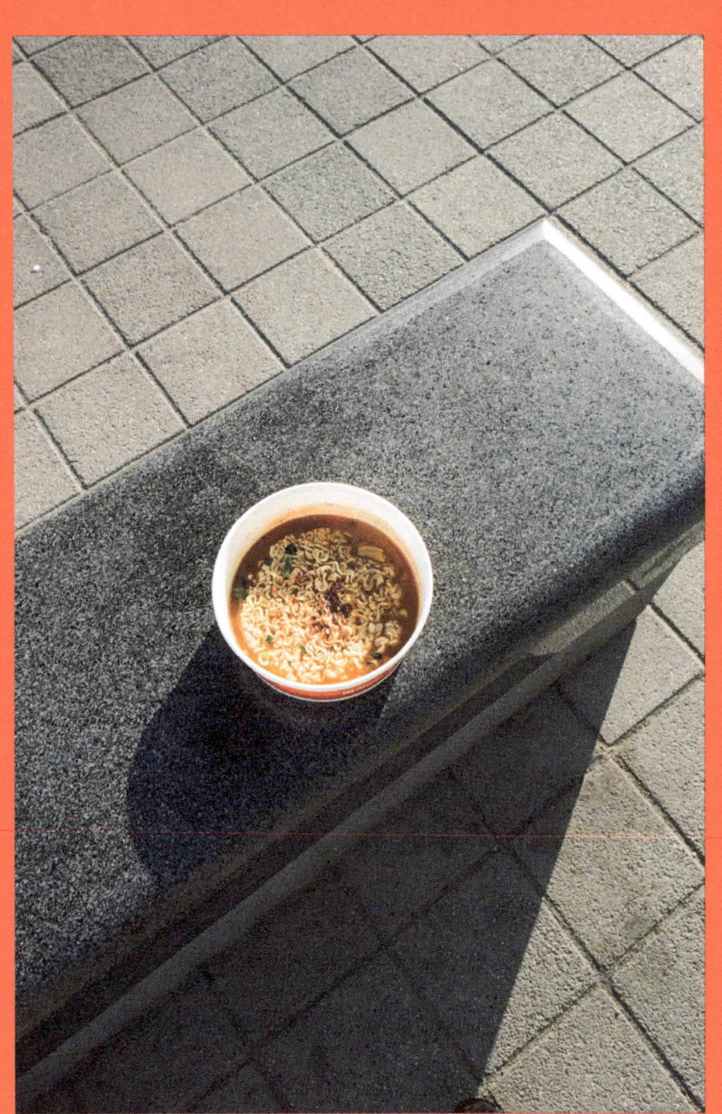

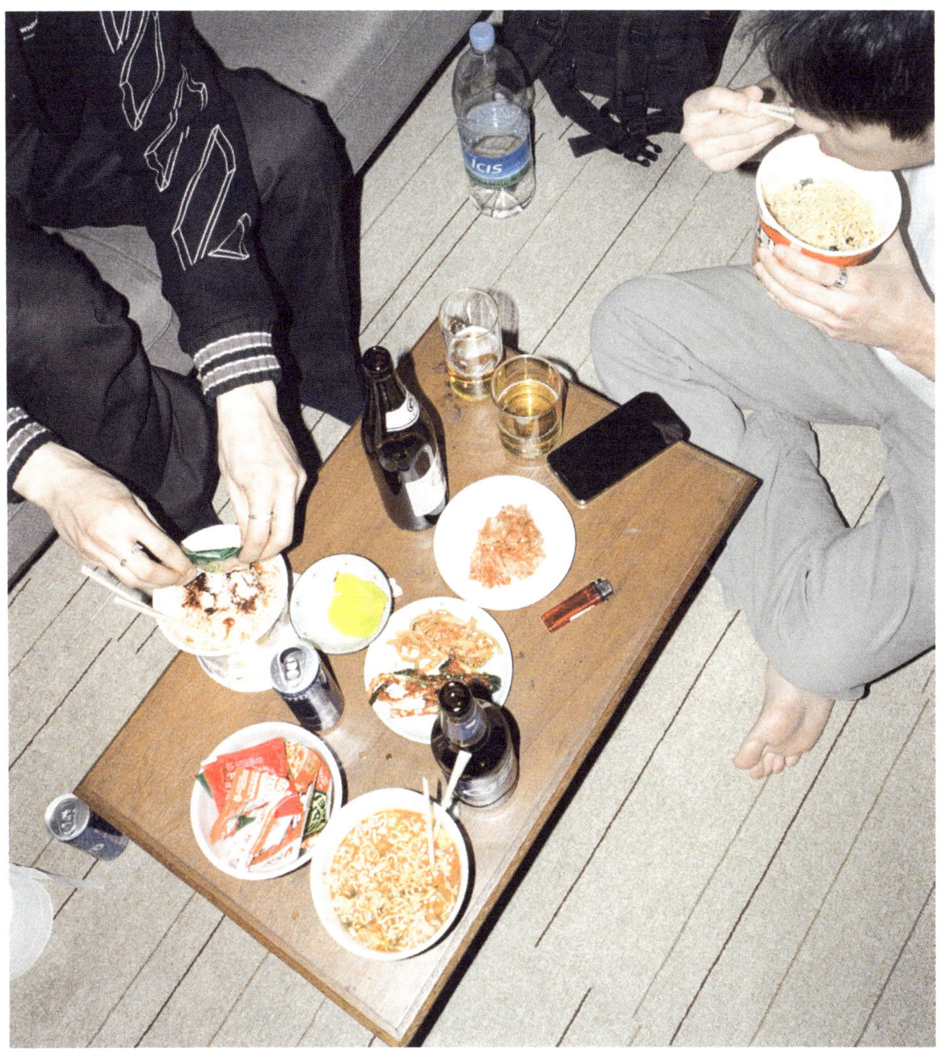

Another very common meal is ramyeon (라면)
which are instant noodles similar to ramen.
They come in handy during any time of the day
or night. Done in three minutes no wonder
South Korea is the country consuming the most
instant ramen per person. The famous brand
Nongshim exports their shin ramyeon success-
fully in the whole world.

Quite often I recognized scooters rushing by
when meandering through the hustling traffic
of Seoul. They belonged to delivery services
that are tied to ghost kitchens. Ghost kitchens
can be found all over Seoul. During Corona the
brick-and-mortar restaurants had to take big
losses. Many could only survive by offering food
delivery—as in-house dining was prohibited
for a long time.

      This benefited delivery kitchens in
two ways: They didn't lose money because
of 'dead' space in their restaurants—as they
never housed guests to begin with. While at
the same time the demand for food delivery
exploded. The covid-19 pandemic accelerated
the growth of the ghost kitchen industry by
approximately five years within only three
months. I personally loved their reusable plastic
dishes which they picked up right from your
doorstep after you finished.

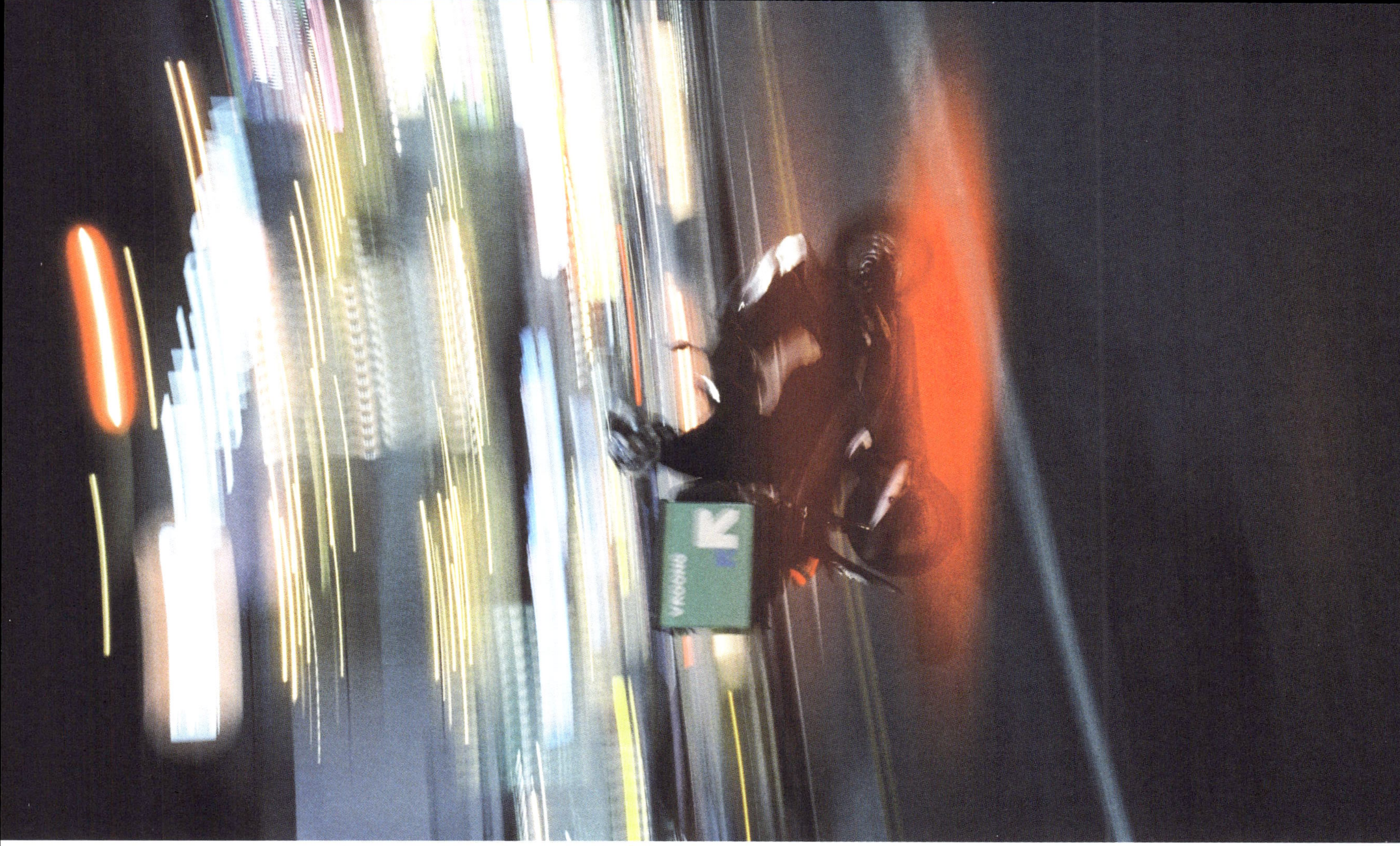

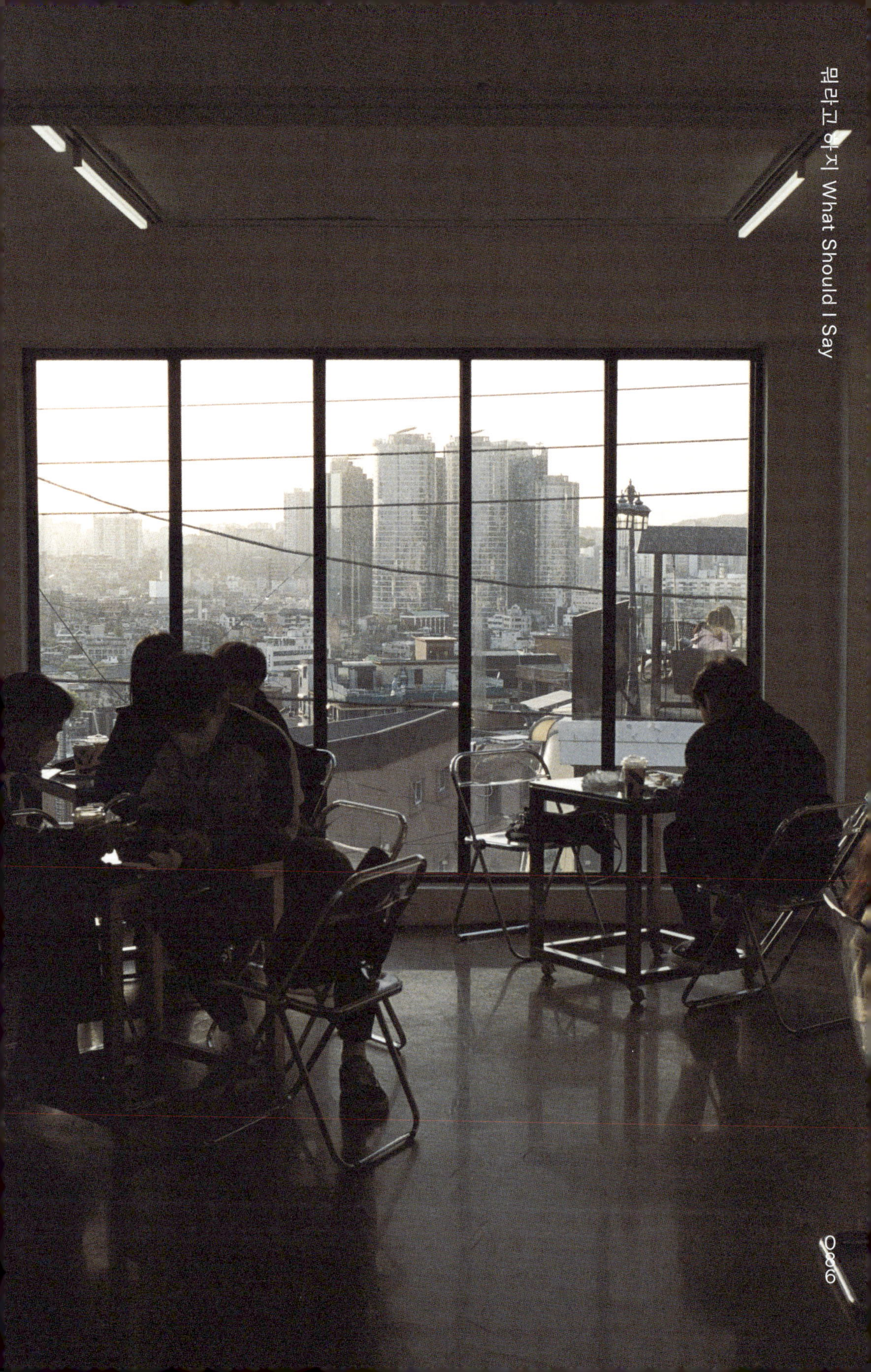

Going out to drink a coffee at a fancy café
is mandatory for a good weekend in Seoul.
The youth of South Korea has made it into
a tradition already. The cafés try to top each
other off with amazing locations or cool
food trends that are worth a picture.

'Instagram-worthy' is a word which
I was thinking a lot about when I was visiting
different cafes, one more fancy then the other,
seeing people taking a plethora of photos of
nicely arranged food and drinks.

The contrast is Gwangjang market which
is one of the oldest and largest markets in
South Korea where daily roughly 60,000
people go for lunch or dinner in one of the
endless choices of street food stalls.

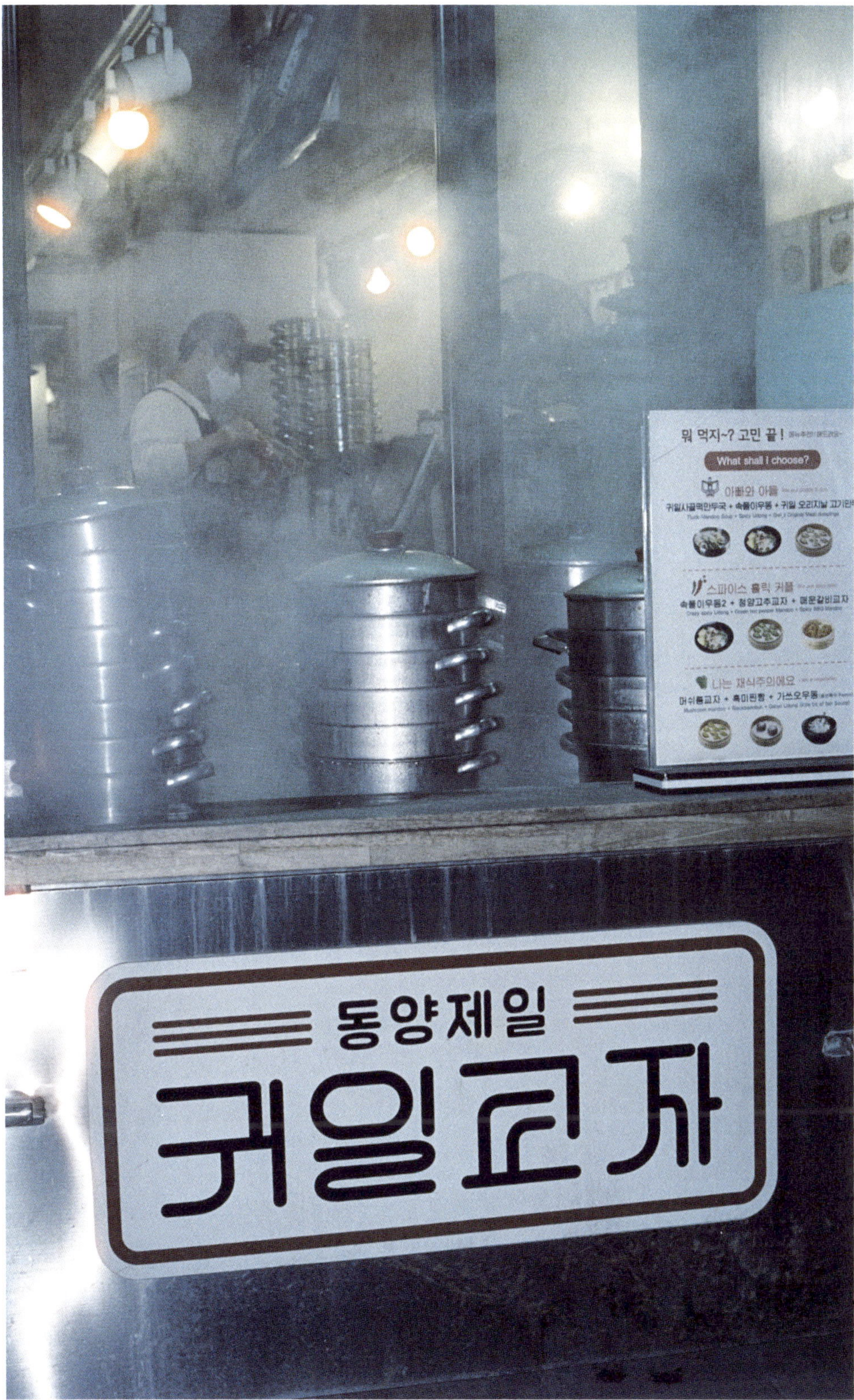
동양제일
커일교자
워 먹지~? 고민 끝!
What shall i choose?
아빠와 아들
스파이스 홀릭 커플
나는 채식주의에요

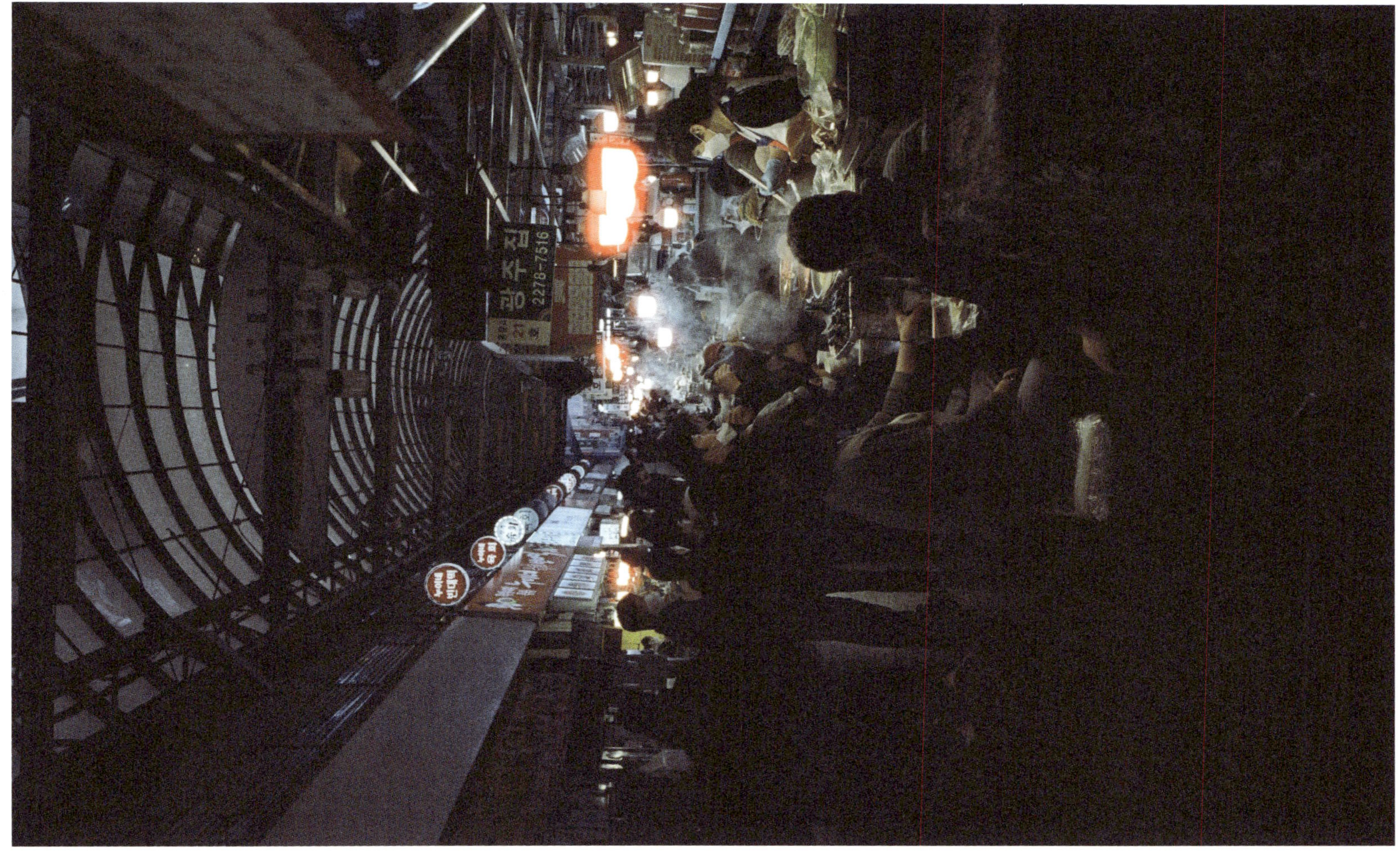
광주집
2278-7516

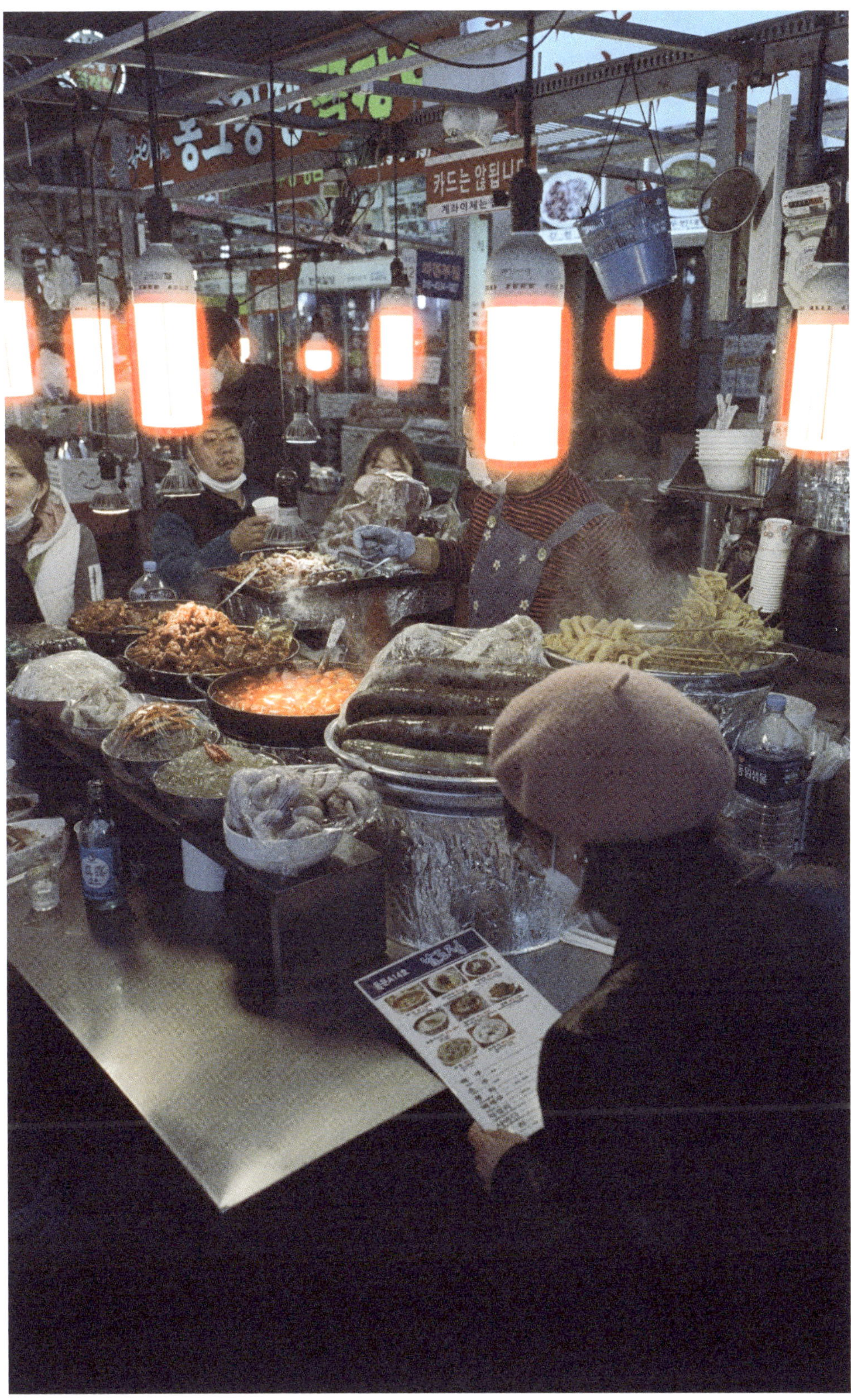

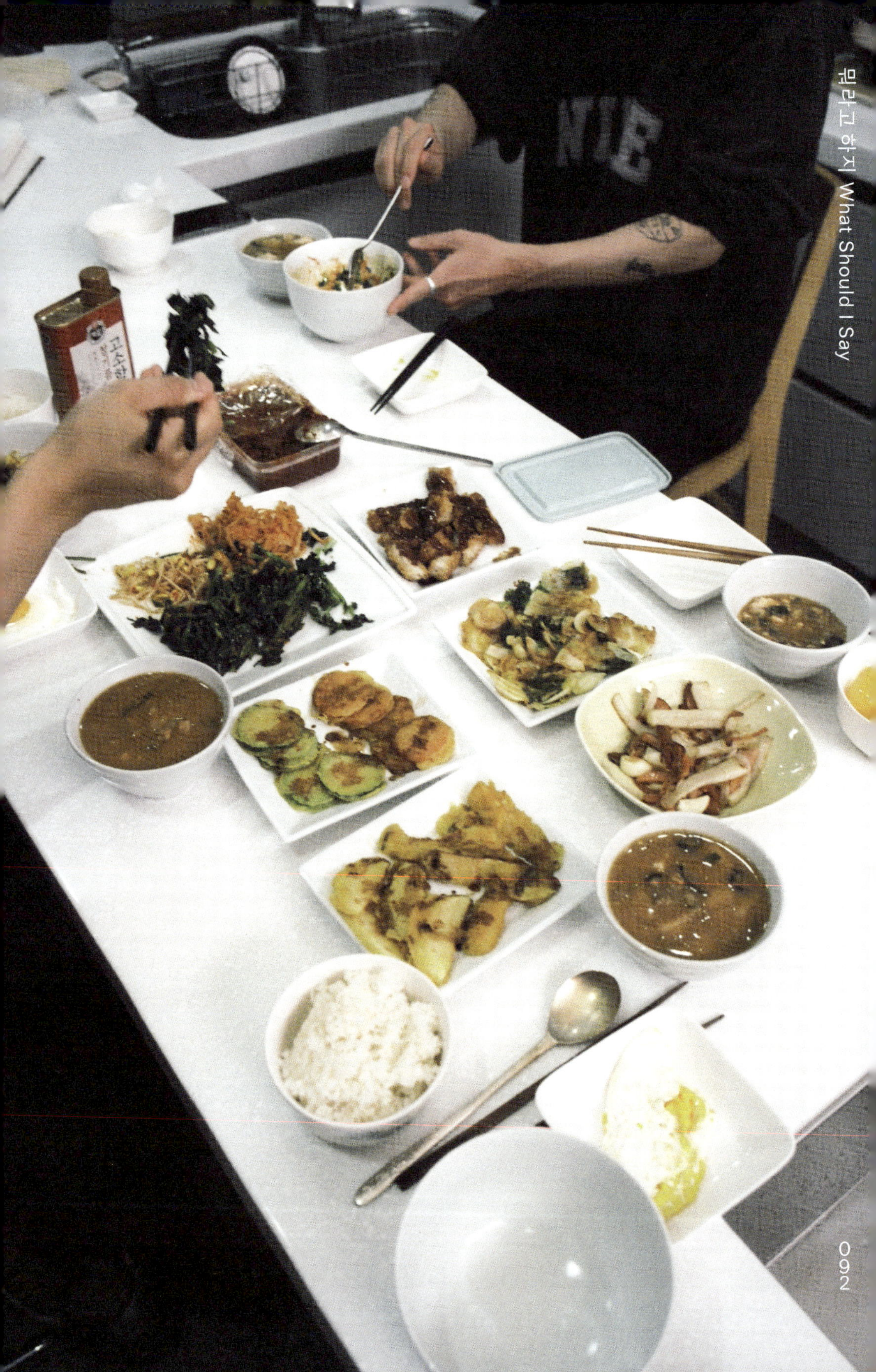
뭐라고 하지 What Should I Say
092

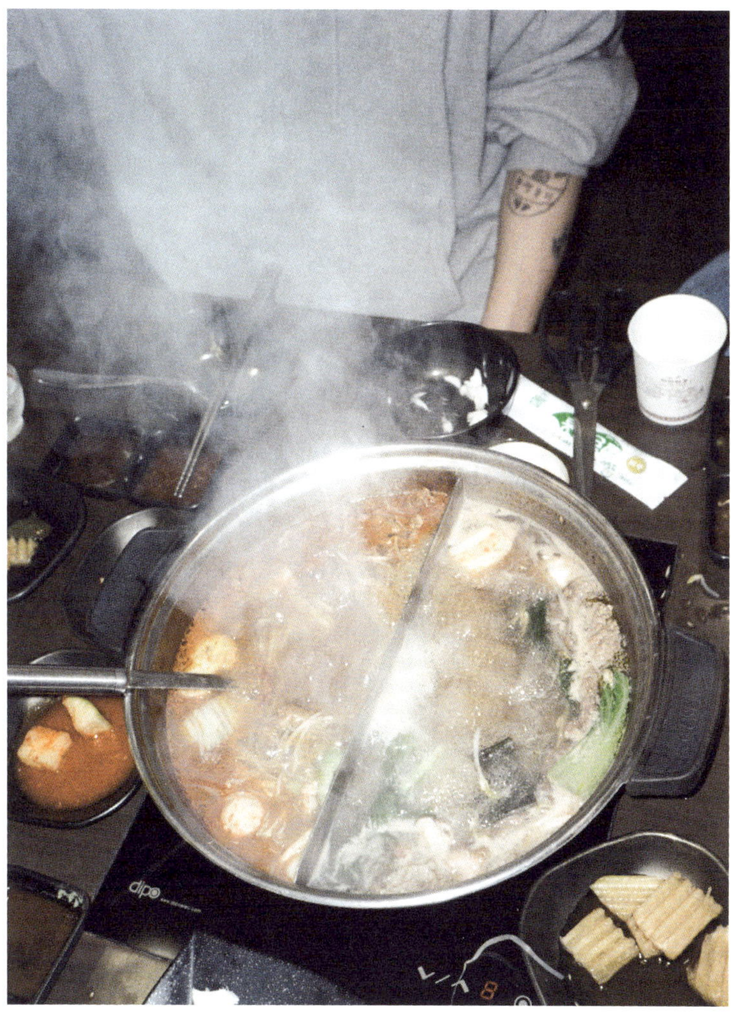

The Korean cuisine is special to me, as the
variety of dishes on the table are combined
with the company of people at the table.
Everything is shared which makes eating
a whole lot more social, then what I'm used
to from Germany.

Regarding the food I'm fascinated
by the balance between sweetness, acidity,
and spiciness—which is super unique.

IDENTITIES
& RECIPES

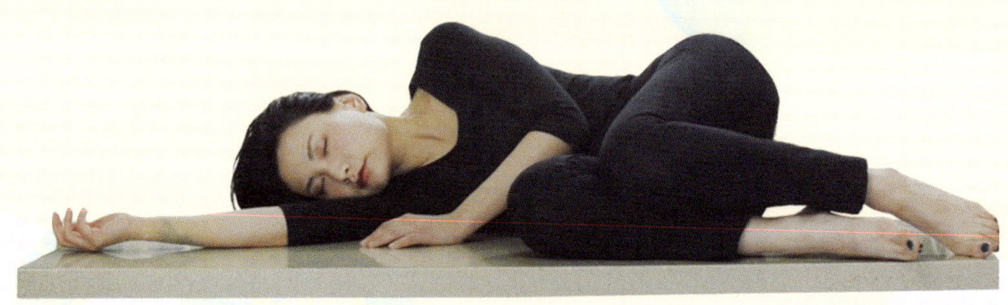

Words & Photos: Ji Su Kang-Gatto

Layout: Youjin Kim | David Wiesner

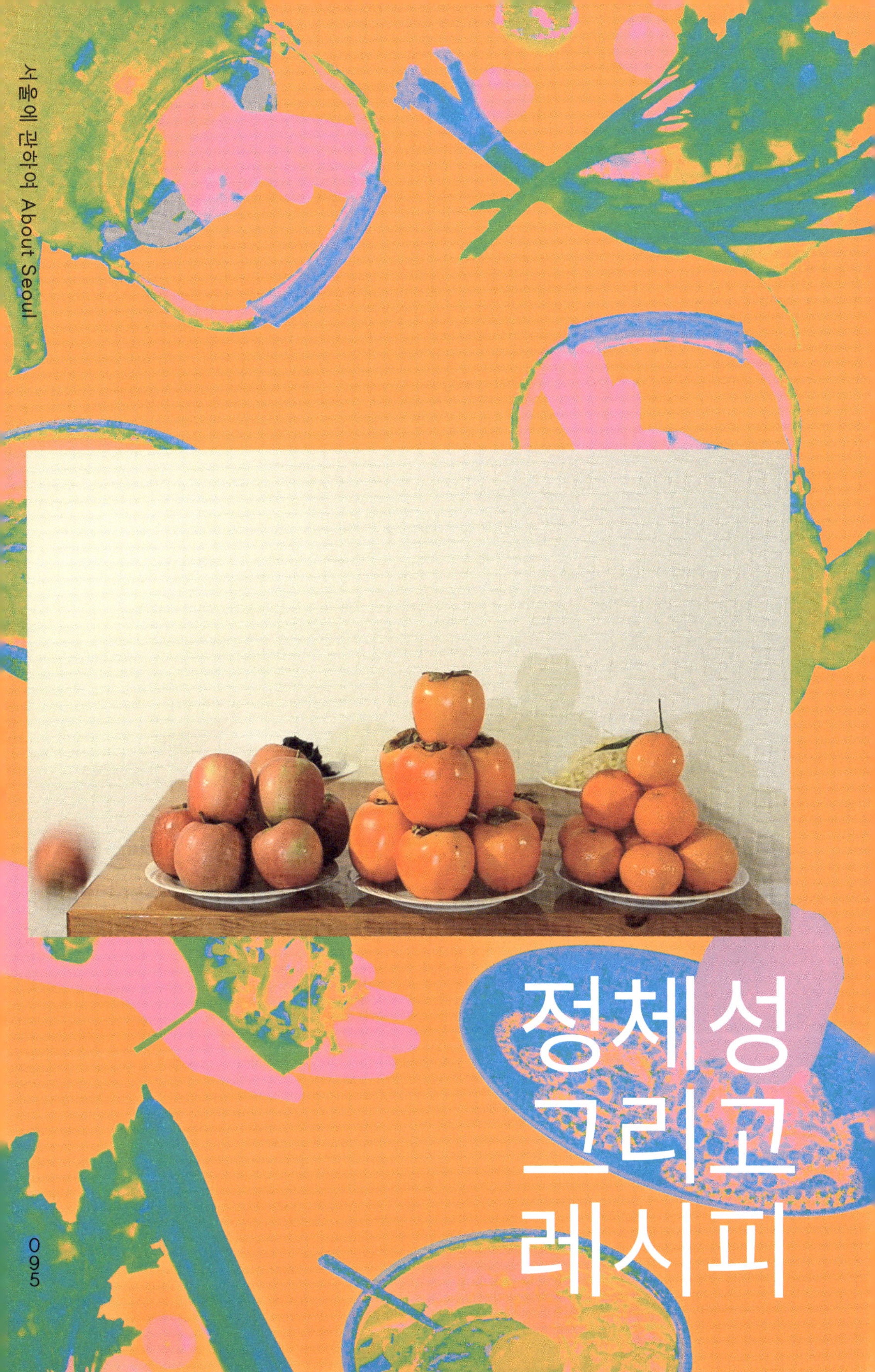
서울에 관하여 About Seoul
095
정체성
그리고
레시피

Ji Su Kang-Gatto is a video artist who was born in
Seoul, South Korea. But she grew up in Germany
since the age of two. She expressed herself through
her art project 'Identities and Recipes' which is not
only a cooking tutorial but also containing her identities being a German-Korean. Especially in her last
video called 'Vlog #8998 / Korean Karottenkuchen
& Our Makeup Routine,' she spoke about her personal story why she moved to Germany and how her
life was as an Asian living in Germany.

I began to plan my art project 'Identities and Recipes.' I also took it as an opportunity to
continue my postgraduate studies at the Academy of Media Arts Cologne. I have
started to focus on video art exclusively after graduating at the Kunstakademie Düsseldorf,
so it was a good support to be accompanied by a Media Arts School Cologne while
realizing 'Identities and Recipes.' My cultural background is the reason and breeding
ground for my work. Art needs to be authentic. So it is a logical conclusion that my
work is about myself. Besides that, I need to express myself through art. Doing art is a never-
ending search for identity.

The reason why I decided to express my identities with the cooking recipes was
because I think food is very much about identity. A dish can disclose a lot about
the culture and the environment of the people who invented it.

When I was already an adult I realized that my food has always been Korean.
I'm so used to German culture and language but I still do not know very well what type
of dish is typical for a German family on a Sunday evening for example. I have never experienced it. Even though my family had breakfast with bread, and my father used to
buy 'Brötchen' (small breads) every Saturday morning. But for lunch and dinner, we always
had a Korean meal. Rice and Kimchi were obligatory to have in our Kitchen. My
experience with German food mainly comes from the student canteen where my parents
used to take me sometimes.

My door to Korean culture has been food.

____

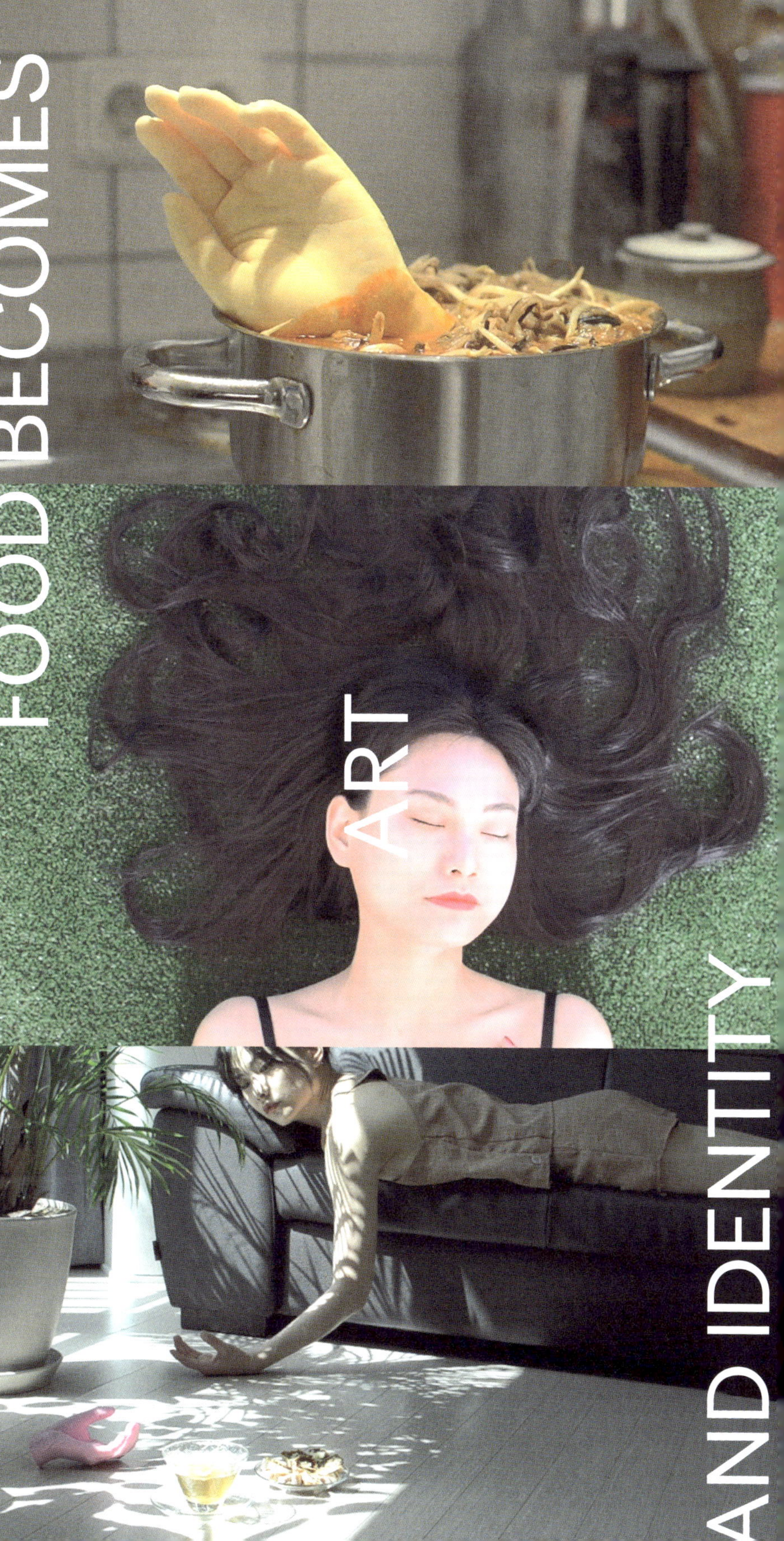
FOOD BECOMES
ART
AND IDENTITY

I was born in Seoul. Ji Hoe, who is my sister has not lived in Germany for a long time. She lived briefly in Seoul, but is back living with my mother in Masan. I moved away from this town after graduating high school and have been living in Düsseldorf ever since. But I will also leave Düsseldorf soon. Anyways, we have not been here for a long time. I told Ji Hoe that I wanted to make a film about us a bit like following the traces of the past. But honestly, I think I just needed an excuse to have a reason to come back here again. I have not been here for a long time and I've always wanted to come. As soon as I got here, memories came flooding back. Neither Mom or dad had a driver's license nor a car at the time. So, we mostly walked or used public transport. Once my dad and I were walking from the city center towards Johanniskirche. There were a group of girls that chased us. I don't know how old they were. I was about eight and the girls were probably teenagers. They shouted "Ching Chang Chong" at us and turned their eyes into 'slit eyes' and got in our way. They stopped us from continuing on our way. My dad tried to ignore them———just like he always did. And usually, it worked. But these girls back then were very persistent. I remember we quickly went into a drugstore, I think it used to be called 'Ihr Platz.' 'dm' (a German retail chain that sells household wares, beauty, and health supplies) did not exist back then. We went in and thought we got rid of them. But when we came back out, the group of girls were still standing out-side the entrance and kept insulting us. I don't remember how we got rid of them. Probably we quickly went into an alley or they lost interest or something. Anyway, my dad didn't respond to them or at least scold them, as I thought he would. He was strict with me at home in the past, so I remember very well that I was surprised as a child that he didn't fight back.

These things always happened to me when I was out alone or when I was with other people that look like Asians. Actually more when I was alone. But when I'm with white friends, this never happens. When we lived at Jahnplatz, I often went home alone after ballet class. At the intersection, my friends at the time always had to go in a different direction. So I walked the short distance alone. There is a large playground in front of Jahnplatz. It's still there and I liked playing there. But one time, there were older kids playing there. Maybe they were about 16, I was about eleven at that time. Maybe they were younger and they just seemed older to me. The playground is really big and I already had a bad feeling walking near the playground that day. They looked at me so strangely and I just didn't feel comfortable. But I had to go that way if I wanted to go home. I continued walking. But they shouted "Ching Chang Chong" repeatedly and made strange animal noises, which I can't even describe. I just wanted to ignore that, like I had done many times in other situations, and continue on without interruption. But that day, one of the bigger kids picked up a stone and started to throw it at me. It was not a small stone. At the time it seemed like a brick to me. I don't believe there were actual bricks just lying around. But the stone seemed incredibly large to me at the time. I immediately ran and heard stones flying at me. I didn't look back and ran home as fast as I could. Dad was at home that time. So I immediately told him what happened. I wanted him to come with me but I remember that I did not get the reaction I was expecting. Dad reacted as if I had said something kids usually do. Like a prank … but it was very scary for me. I wanted him to come with me to the boys and scold them. When we got there, the boys were no longer there. I think my dad was kind of relieved that they weren't there anymore. I was angry——or sad.

Maybe both.

———————

Ji Hoe and I used to speak German with each other. That is, when Ji Hoe was still living in Germany. She was seven when she moved to Korea with my mom. It's a bit complicated. So it was like this: Mom had finished her studies and had to go back to Korea and took Ji Hoe with her. Dad was not finished yet and stayed with me in Germany. A few months later he got sick. Stomach cancer. Last stage. So Mom then flew back to Germany with Ji Hoe. But because she had job interviews, Mom and Ji Hoe flew back and forth several times for 1.5 years. Ji Hoe was in first or second grade——she changed schools four times. Two in Korea, two in Germany. The first time she was enrolled in Rosenplatz School. Mom, Dad, and I. We were all there. Everything was still good then. No one had foreseen that she would change schools so often. Then she went to a school in Korea for the first time, in Jeonju. Then she went to another German school, but I can't remember the name. And then she went to elementary school in Masan and stayed there. Back when she was still at the Rosenplatz School. Ji Hoe and I spoke German with each other. But we spoke to our parents in Korean. We have a nine year age difference. It was much more noticeable back then, than it is now. When she was seven,

The reason why I named the title such an ordinary vlog and not even indicated any racist issues was because most of the racism I encountered, hit me completely unprepared——— it's kind of a form of sudden violence. It's always lurks in my normal daily life and might just surface without warning. So I wanted my audience to have kind of the same feeling as I did. unexpected offence.

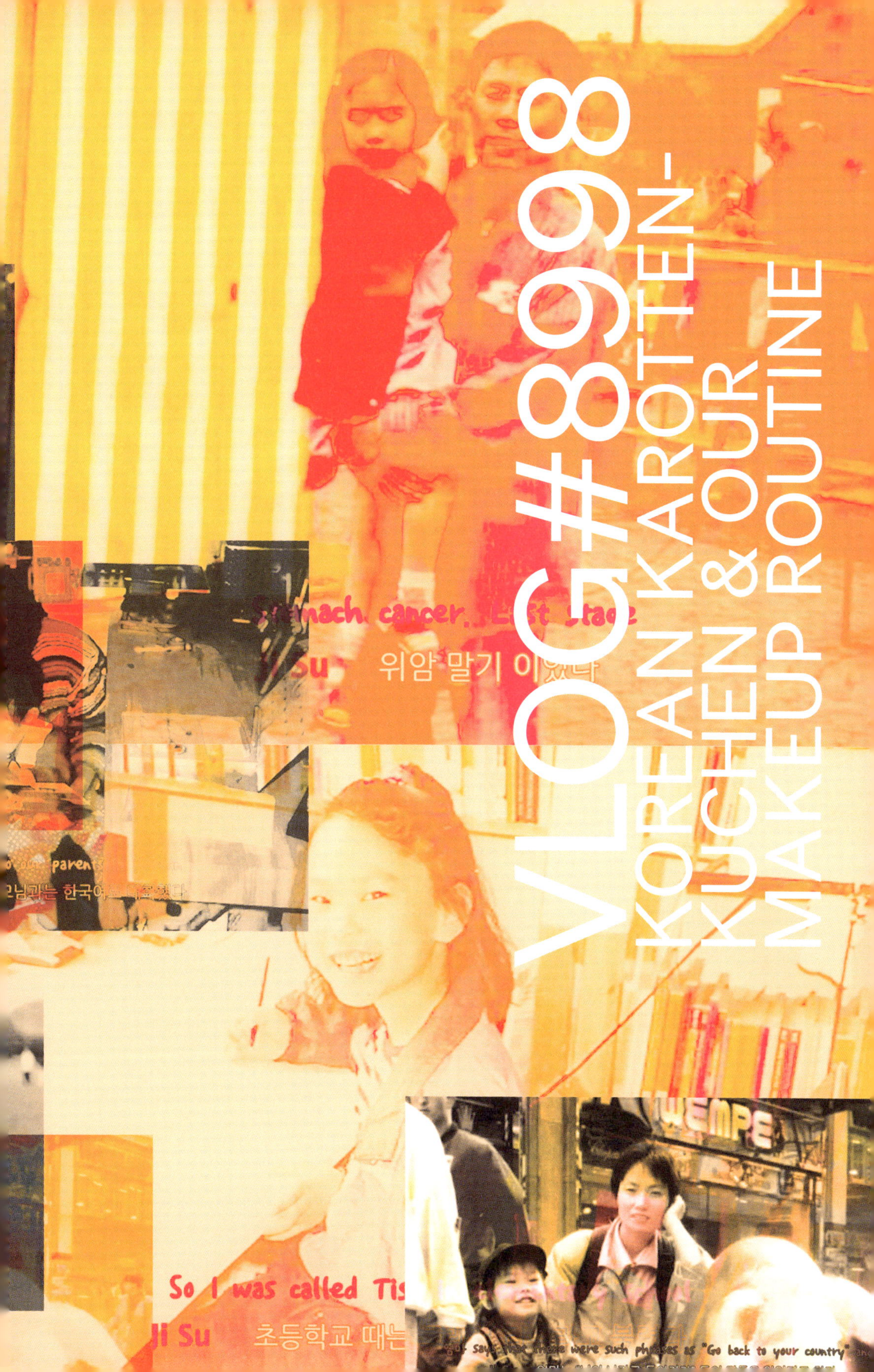
VLOG#8998
-KAROTTEN-
KUCHEN & OUR
MAKEUP ROUTINE
KOREAN
Stomach cancer, Last stage
위암 말기 이었다
Ji Su
parents
한국여
So I was called Tis
Ji Su
초등학교 때는

I was 16. I often took her to afternoon sports on my bike. But she often annoyed me and I just wanted to have my peace. I didn't feel like playing with her because I was much older. I didn't know that soon we would no longer live together.

After Dad's diagnosis——when he knew he was sick——pretty badly sick, he wished to be in Korea. My parents were long-term students. He went to Korea only once during the 14 years he was in Germany. There was not enough money to visit Korea more often. When Dad wanted to go to Korea, the four of us stayed in Korea only briefly. Mom found a job there and Ji Hoe was taken to where she went. I was an exchange student at a catholic girls' school at the time. I think it was after half a year of chemotherapy that Dad passed away. It was a shitty time. A few weeks after the funeral, I flew back to Germany. My parents wanted me to go back, so that I could get a better school degree.

Ji Hoe doesn't speak German anymore. We speak Korean with each other. I can still remember that I was so surprised because she had already forgotten German after only a few months in Korea. But she remembered again within two weeks when she was back in Germany. When Dad was sick and we were all in Germany, Ji Hoe spoke German again. Then she went back to Korea and forgot German. Ji Hoe says that she can't remember the memories I am telling here. She was around seven. I have memories when I was around seven years old. Ji Hoe says she doesn't remember these stories——or Dad. When she thinks she is remembering something of that time, she's unsure about the realness of these memories. Because we have told her so much about it or shown her so many family photos, to her it feels like these memories are not her own.

Mom says that there were such phrases as "Go back to your country" and so on. But she says that uneducated people usually say that. She says "There was no such thing in the academic environment". But she also says that her former professor told her that she "should go back to her country and look for a job there." I can also remember times at the central train station and on the bus where we were called "Japsen," "Ching Chang Chong," eyes pulled into 'slits,' etc. That all happened quite often. I think it also happened to Mom and Dad more often when they were walking alone. This is how it was for me. We always ignored such comments. I ignored it, but it still bothers me. I hate the word "Schlitzaugen." "Schlitzi" is what I was called next to "Sushi" when I was in school. I was totally hurt by it, but I don't think I said anything. I kept quiet so often. I also didn't tell my parents about such experiences every time. I didn't want them to be sad. But I also thought that they can't change anything anyway. Dad's no longer alive and Ji Hoe has been living in Korea for years. I continued to be in Germany. Racism has increased not only since the pandemic. The AfD is in the state parliament (The AfD is a German far-right political party). This says it all. But since the pandemic, I'm starting to think that with the right trigger anyone can suddenly turn on you because of e. g. one's appearance———even people who I would never have expected to do so. I have seen it many times in my school days that Asians were labeled as the 'good foreigners.' But the labeling or the stereotype as the 'good foreigner' can be traded for hate in an instant. At least from what I experienced. Even though I have experienced racism so often myself, rarely have I expected it. I lived my everyday life and then it just happened. However, in the early 2020s during the early days of the pandemic I was actually afraid to go out alone. I only went out with Federico and still I was constantly afraid of being attacked. When the virus was declared as a pandemic, my fear had calmed down. I don't want to experience being so scared ever again.

    I really don't.

————————————

I asked my parents very often: "Why Germany?" Dad was a German teacher at a high school in Seoul. My parents both studied German. What interested them so much in Germany and the German language that they moved here with their child? My parents always tried to integrate well but their mother tongue remained Korean and over the years, especially Dad's longing for Korea grew. German is the language in which I can express myself best. Just as Ji Hoe sometimes imagines what her life would have been like if she had grown up in Germany. I have also imagined what my life would have been like, if I had grown up in Korea instead of Germany. Especially as an Asian-looking woman, I am categorized into certain groups in Germany. Especially as a young adult it happened to me very often that people would judge my personality. It was mostly men who would judge my behavior without getting to know me. They said: "Oh, you ARE such a girl." or " But you are not like THEM." I instantly knew what they were talking about but for a long time I didn't know what to make of these statements. Only when I heard more explicit sentences like "I'd like to fuck you. Asian women are supposed to have such tight vaginas" from my bosses. I realize that many men in particular perceive me in a very stereotypical image. Submissive, well-behaved, sweet and, or in an over-sexualized context. I know I am wrong to think that growing up in Korea would have been less problematic. Korea with its patriarchal society is anything but an utopian haven. Although it doesn't really exist anyway. I don't think my parents saw Germany as an utopia when they came here. But maybe a little bit as a haven? I can imagine that they came to Germany, full of hope with their passion for German literature. I also don't think they suspected at the time that their two daughters would grow up so differently. I believe that Germany WAS a place of longing for Ji Hoe. But now I am no longer sure since the racist attack … I'll ask her again though.

Both Germany and Korea are anything but sanctuaries or places of longing for me. By now I'm pretty tired. Totally exhausted from continuously fighting to belong somewhere, but I always remain an outsider.

———————

Picture: Johann Husser

exemplary

KUNHA

works

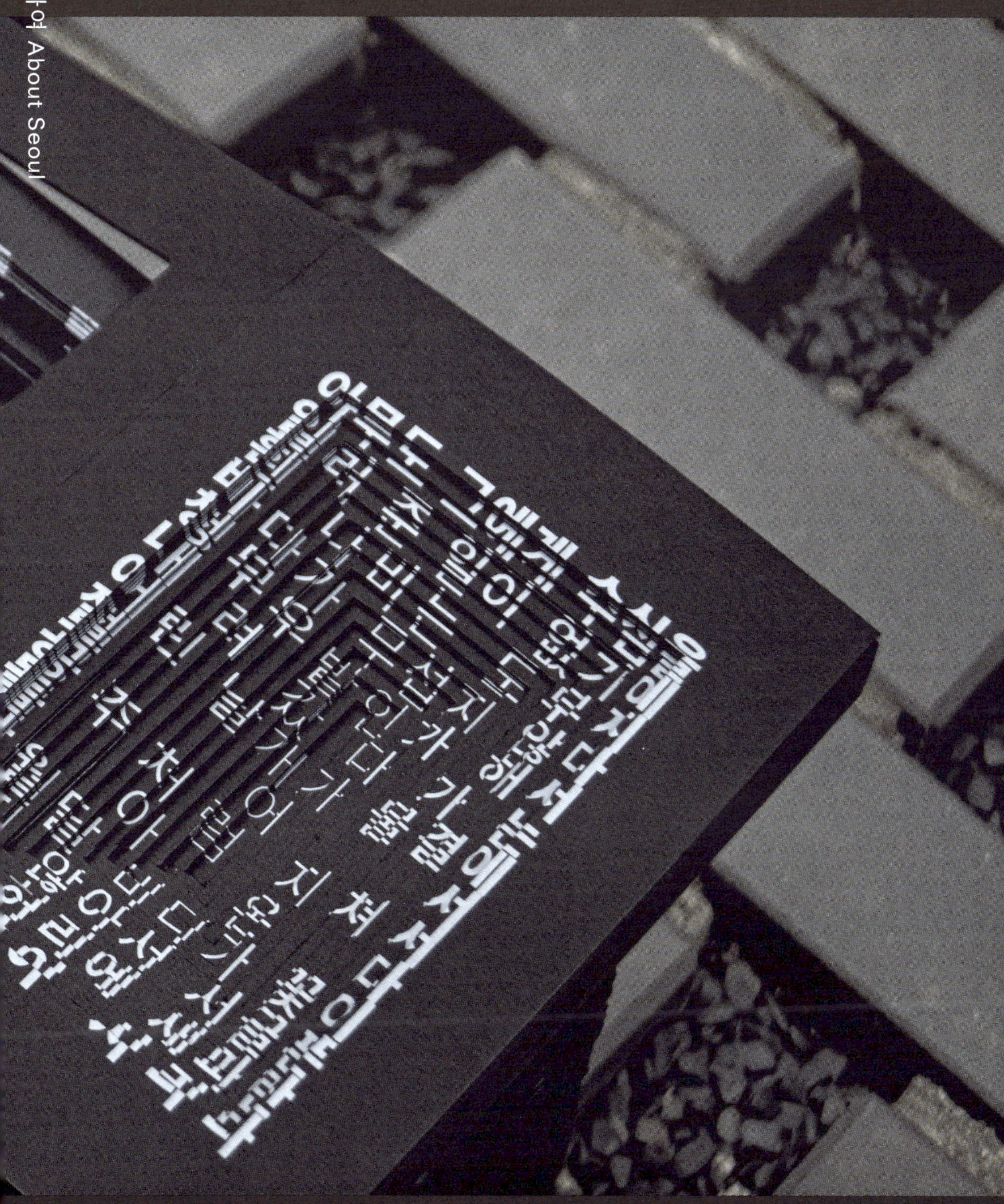

↖Concrete Poetry
Book design based on the poem 'The Sea and Butterfly'
by Kirim Kim.

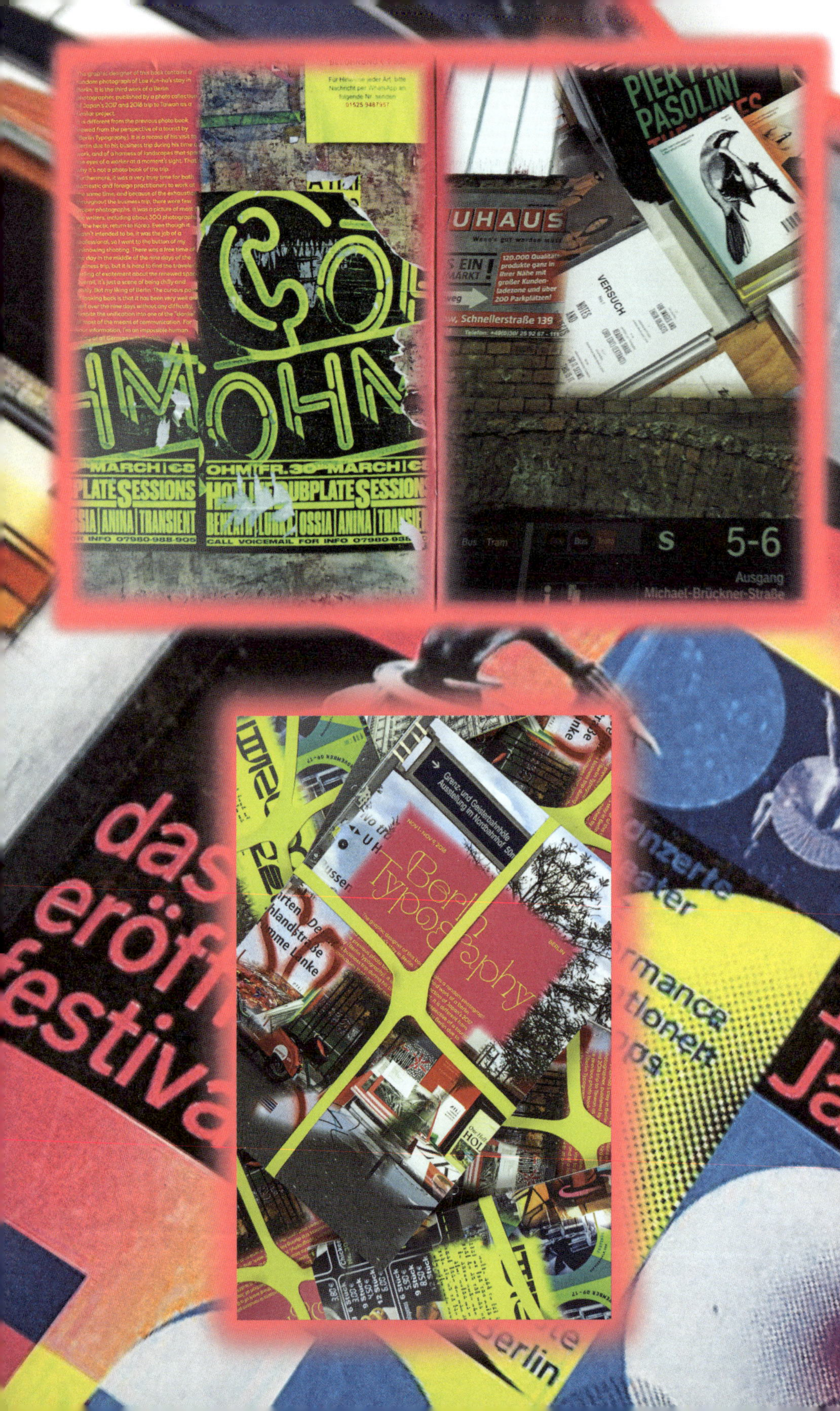

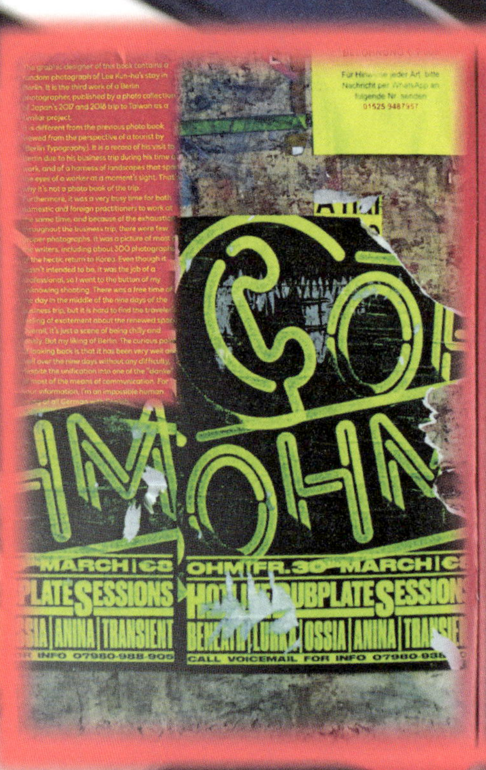

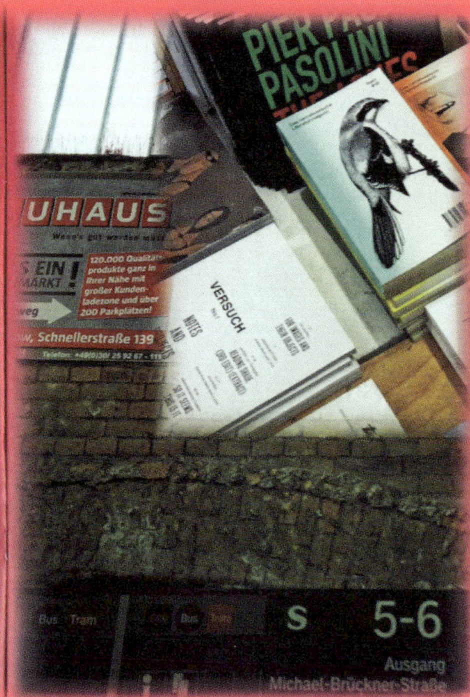

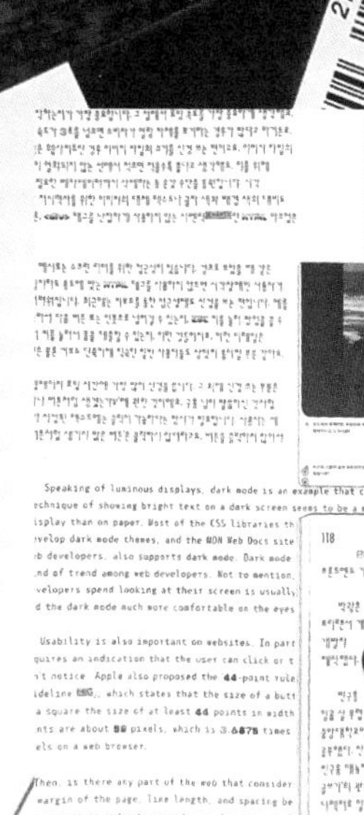
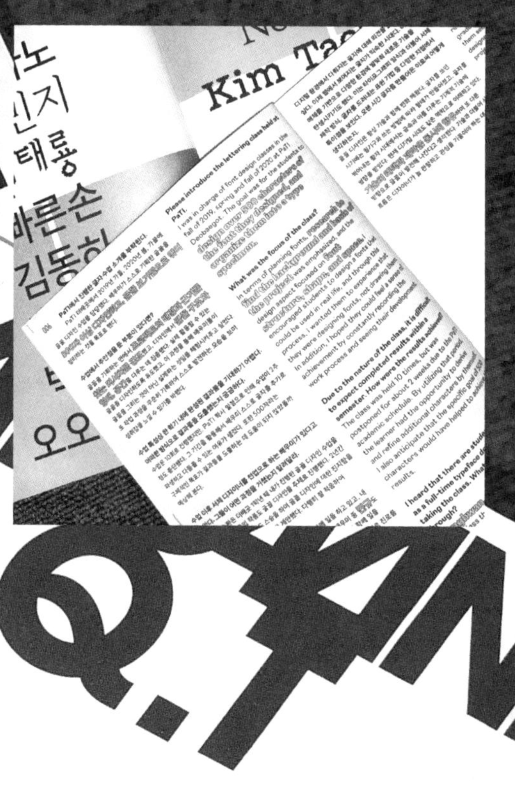

→ Magazine Q.T
Layout for the summer issue, 2022.
← Berlin Typography
Layout for the November issue, 2018.

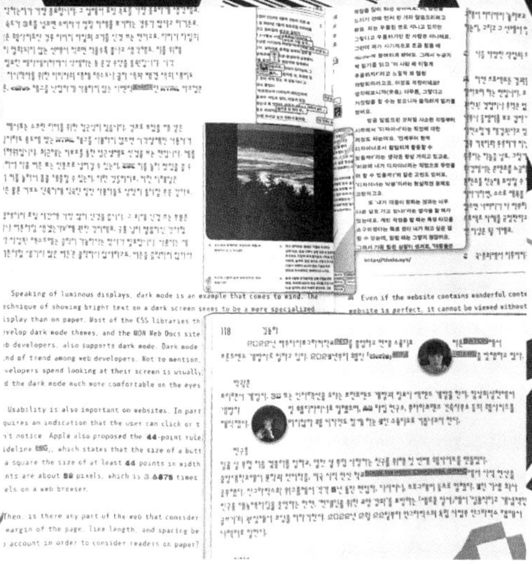

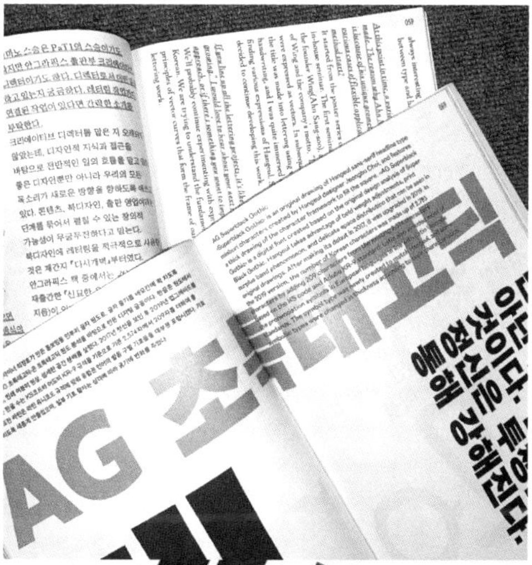

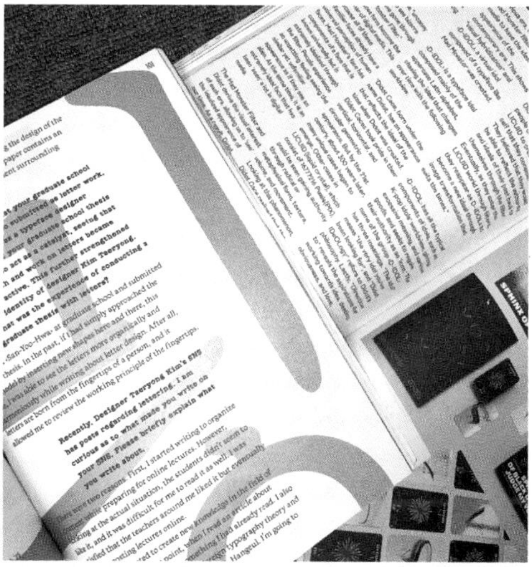

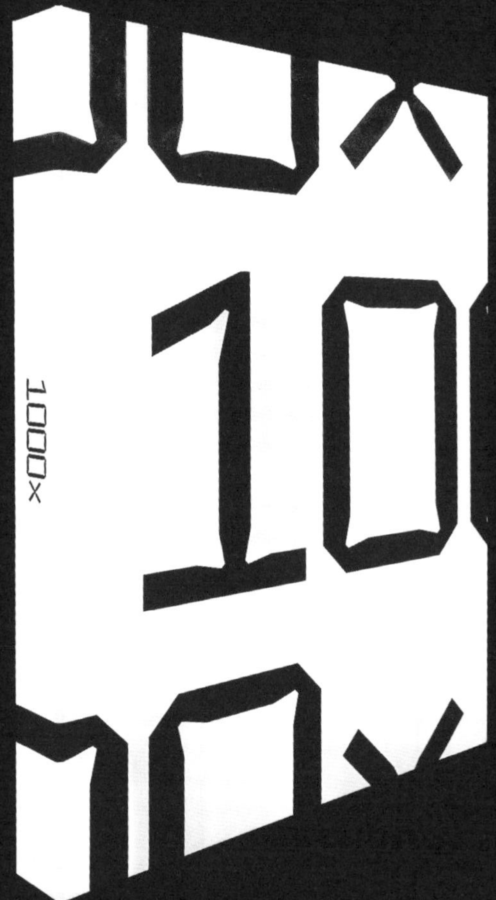

↑↗1000×

A collection of photos taken at 1,000 times magnification to find
the hidden properties of books.

1000×

이 책은 육안으로 확인할 수 없는 책 속의 숨겨진 물성을 찾아 드러내고 있다. 작업자는 책의 구매 시기, 제본, 인쇄, 후가공을 기준으로 50권을 먼저 선정하고, 현미경을 통해 1,000배 확대 촬영했다. 관찰 범위는 책을 상·중·하 세 구조로 나누어 진행되었다. 이 세 가지 구조는 책 머리부터 책 등과 책배, 인쇄된 책 표지 천연, 책 꼬리를 포함하고 있다. 그리고 현미경으로 들여다보았을 때 일반적으로 생각하지 못했던 흥미로운 지점을 찾아 탐색했다.

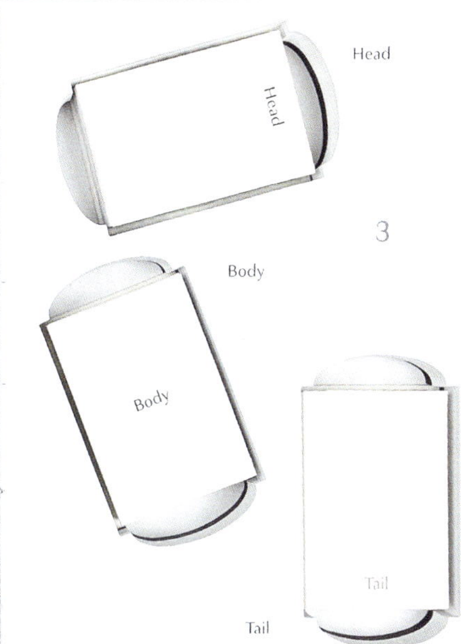

1000×

이 책은 육안으로 확인할 수 없는 책 속의 숨겨진 물성을 찾아 드러내고 있다. 작업자는 책의 구매 시기, 제본, 인쇄, 후가공을 기준으로 50권을 먼저 선정하고, 현미경을 통해 1,000배 확대 촬영했다. 관찰 범위는 책을 상·중·하 세 구조로 나누어 진행되었다. 이 세 가지 구조는 책 머리부터 책 등과 책배, 인쇄된 책 표지 천연, 책 꼬리를 포함하고 있다. 그리고 현미경으로 들여다보았을 때 일반적으로 생각하지 못했던 흥미로운 지점을 찾아 탐색했다.

1 Until Death Do Us Part
2 글을 뒤지다 Command F
3 Irma Boom: The Architecture of the book
4 VOSTOK No.5
5 책 번역 달력 (2017)
6 스위스를 훔치다
7 Arjan de Nooy
8 첫서답과 O
9 Sheila Hicks, Weaving as Metaphor
10 TIME IS MONEY
11 Ms. HERESIES
12 record of the day
13 BOEKEN / THE BEST DUCH
14 DESIGNHGERS
15 Ordinary Pictures
16 섬
17 타이포잔치 2015 프리비엔날레 포스트
18 미수갱이 쪽주
19 문능의 양식
20 JASON DODGE WITH ISHION HUTCHINSON ON ALL FOURS I AM A SEAT FOR THE WIND
21 PLATFORML L
22 BAKER SALON
23 타이포잔치 2017
24 KIAF 2018 ART SEOUL
25 올림픽 디자인:그래픽 프랙티스와 프로세스

26 셰익스피어 전집
27 펠티 포켓도 포스터 및 관광 포스터 채종별
28 초력(효고녀 글씨모기집
29 타이포그래피의 원리
30 프린트 사공카 꿈
31 타이포잔치 2017 서울 아티스테이션 협업 전시: 연결하고 봄, 구체적 공간
32 한국어 어낼 라-러-정스트
33 김기림-바다와 나비 구체시집
34 시간옵
35 Alternative Moons
36 패키지 디자인 레시티
37 GRAPHIC DESIGN IN JAPAN 2018
38 1990년대 한 라미술
39 TEXT: GRAPHIC 2007-2011 (No.1-20)
40 PUBLIC HOME
41 일반적 구성
42 거울여겨
43 김기림-우리들의 8평소 종이가지 구체시집
44 미술책 2018 글꼴멋가침
45 네어로 문자 기행
46 The Heart of Berlin
47 N&Q: Notes and ques
48 RECHTS / AVERECHTS
49 과제 1. 타이포그래피 포스터
50 계동 2018

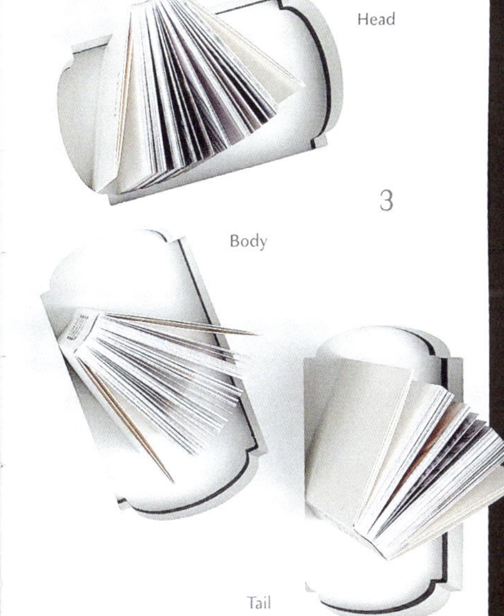

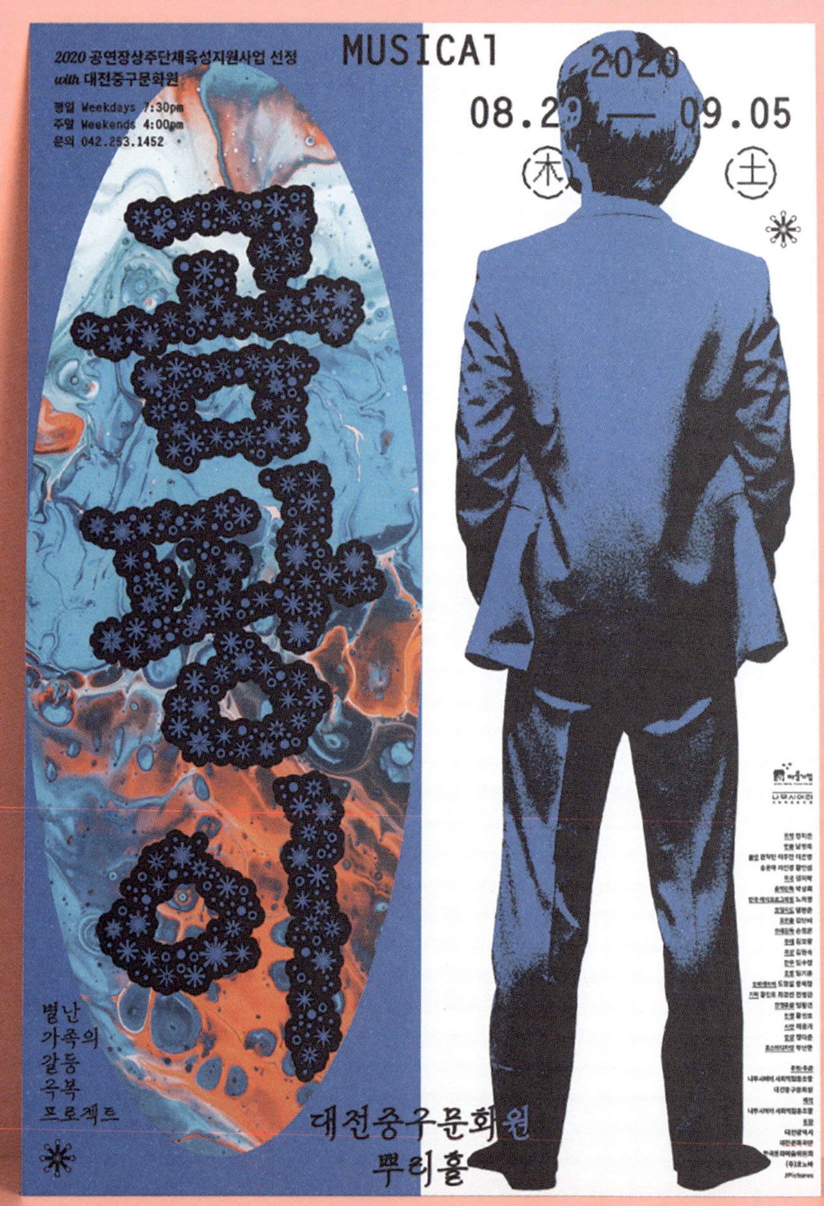
2020 공연장상주단체육성지원사업 선정
with 대전중구문화원
평일 Weekdays 7:30pm
주말 Weekends 4:00pm
문의 042.253.1452
MUSICA1
2020
08.2 — 09.05
(木) (土)
공짜밥이
별난
가족의
갈등
극복
프로젝트
대전중구문화원
뿌리홀

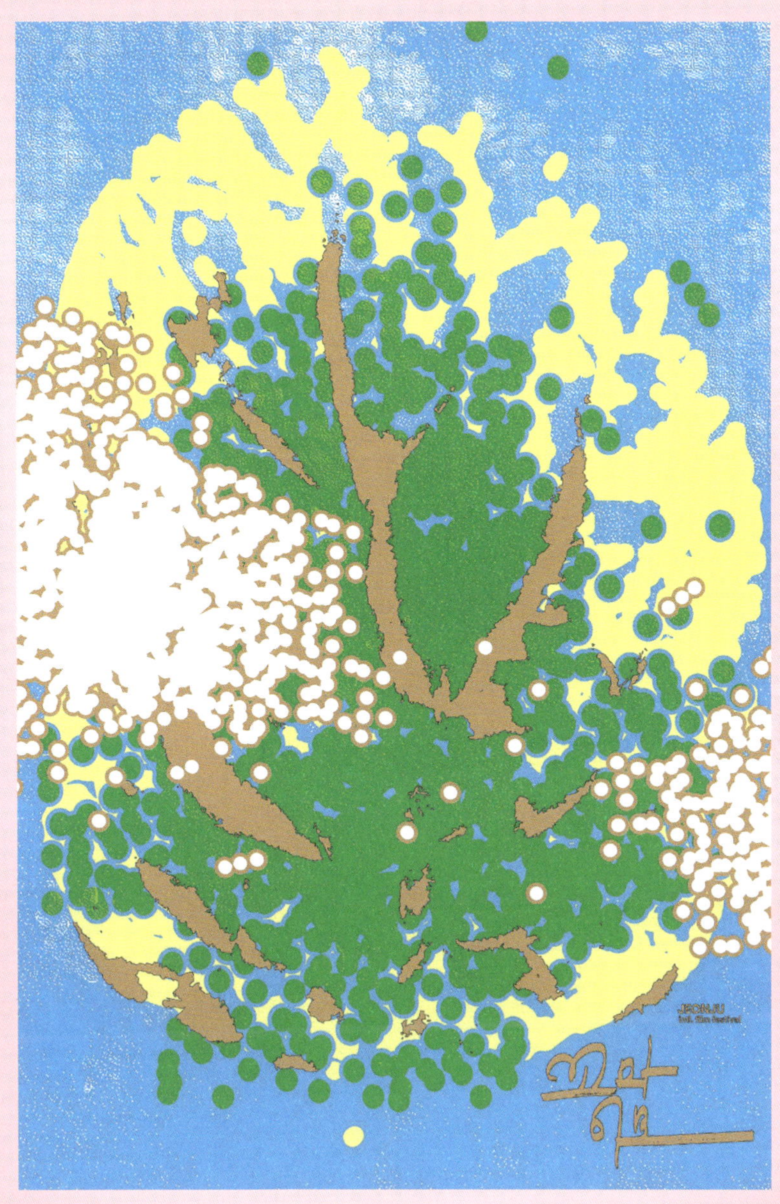

← Mold
Poster for a musical, 2020.
→ My little aunt
Poster for an independent movie, 2022.

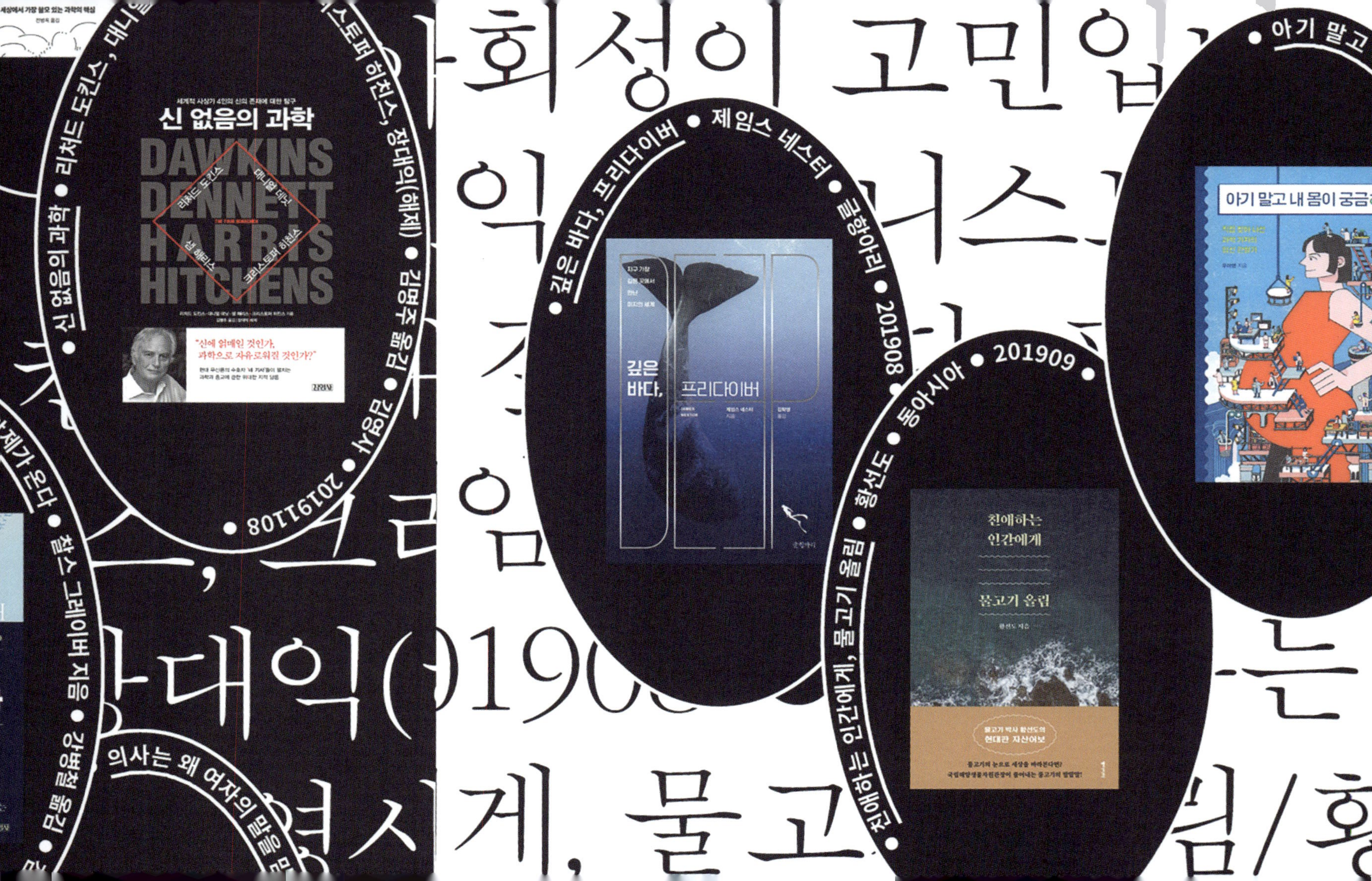
회성이 고민입
익 스
임

신 없음의 과학
세계적 사상가 4인의 신의 존재에 대한 탐구
DAWKINS 리처드 도킨스
DENNETT 대니얼 데닛
HARRIS 샘 해리스
HITCHENS 크리스토퍼 히친스
리처드 도킨스·대니얼 데닛·샘 해리스·크리스토퍼 히친스 지음
김명주 옮김 / 장대익(해제)
"신에 얽매일 것인가, 과학으로 자유로워질 것인가?"

깊은 바다, 프리다이버
지구 가장 깊은 곳에서 만난 미지의 세계
제임스 네스터 지음 / 김학영 옮김

친애하는 인간에게
물고기 올림
황선도 지음
물고기 박사 황선도의 현대판 자산어보

아기 말고 내 몸이 궁금해

리처드 도킨스, 대니얼 데닛, 샘 해리스, 크리스토퍼 히친스 ● 장대익(해제) ● 김명주 옮김 ● 김영사 ● 20191108
찰스 그레이버 지음 ● 강병철 옮김 ● 제가 온다
깊은 바다, 프리다이버 ● 제임스 네스터 ● 글항아리 ● 201908
동아시아 ● 201909
친애하는 인간에게, 물고기 올림 ● 황선도
의사는 왜 여자의 말을

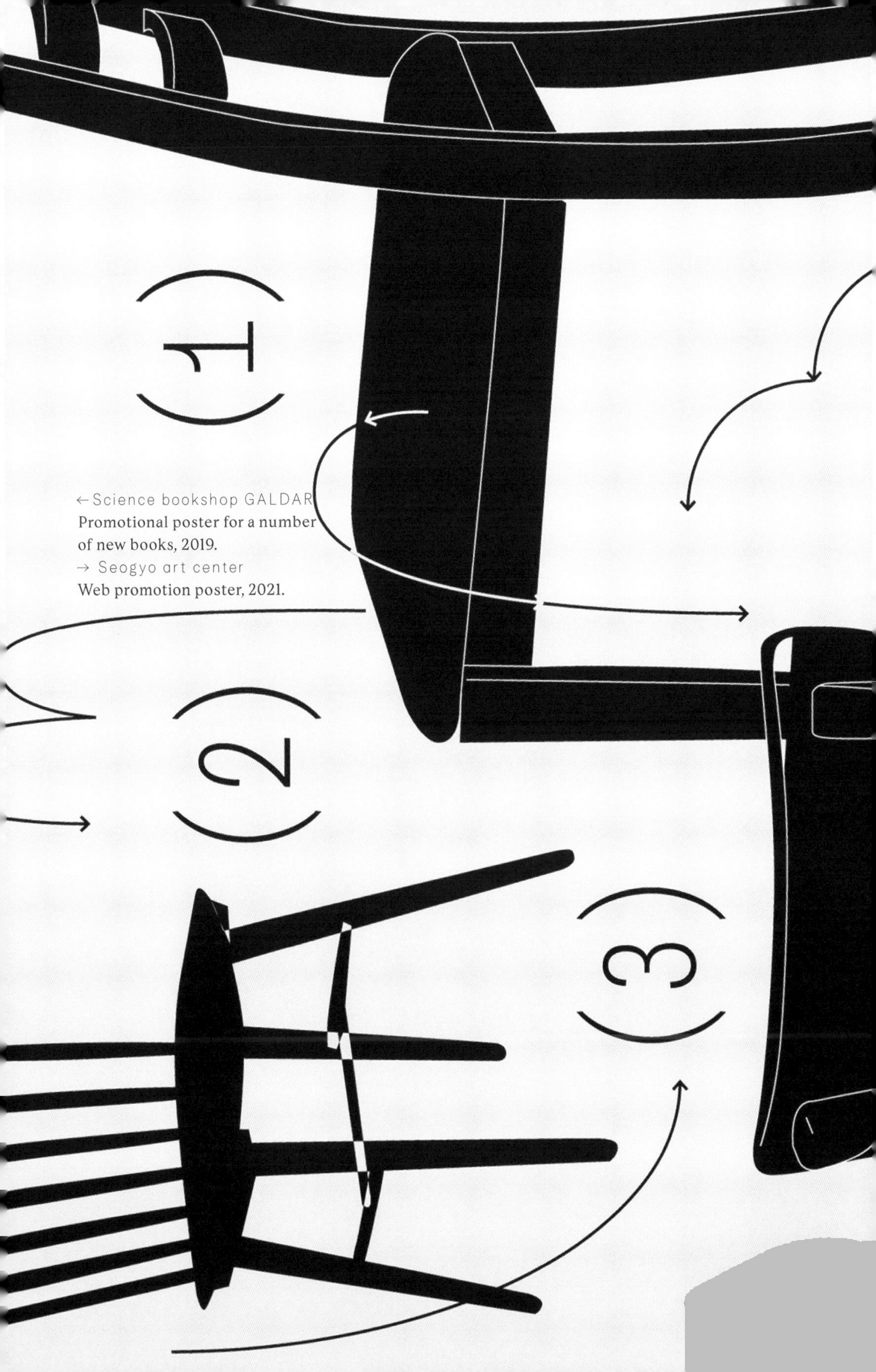
← Science bookshop GALDAR
Promotional poster for a number
of new books, 2019.
→ Seogyo art center
Web promotion poster, 2021.

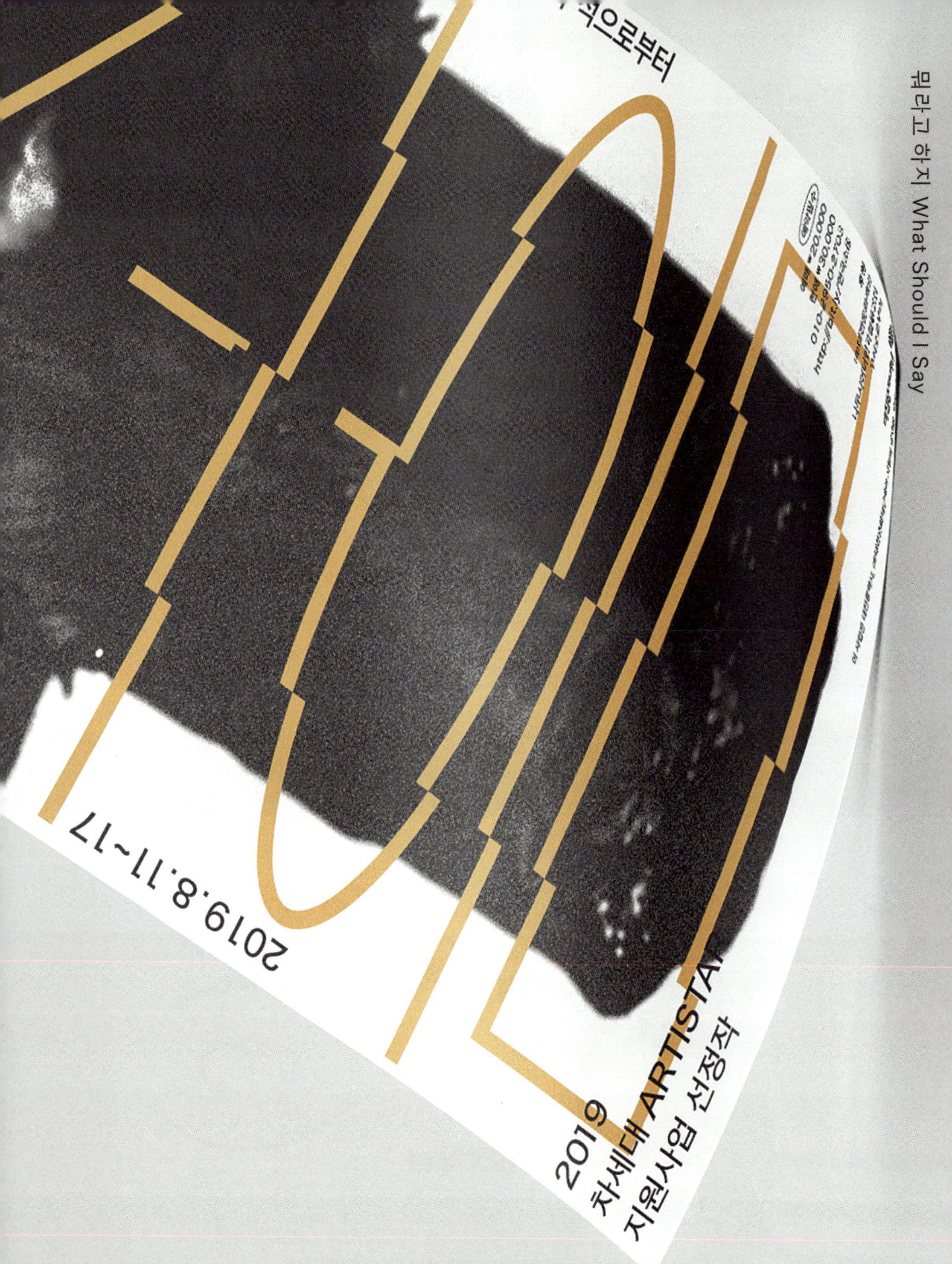

↑Noise
Promotional poster for a play, 420 × 594 mm, 2019.
→ Soje, remember the city
Poster for an urban archive project in Soje, 2020.

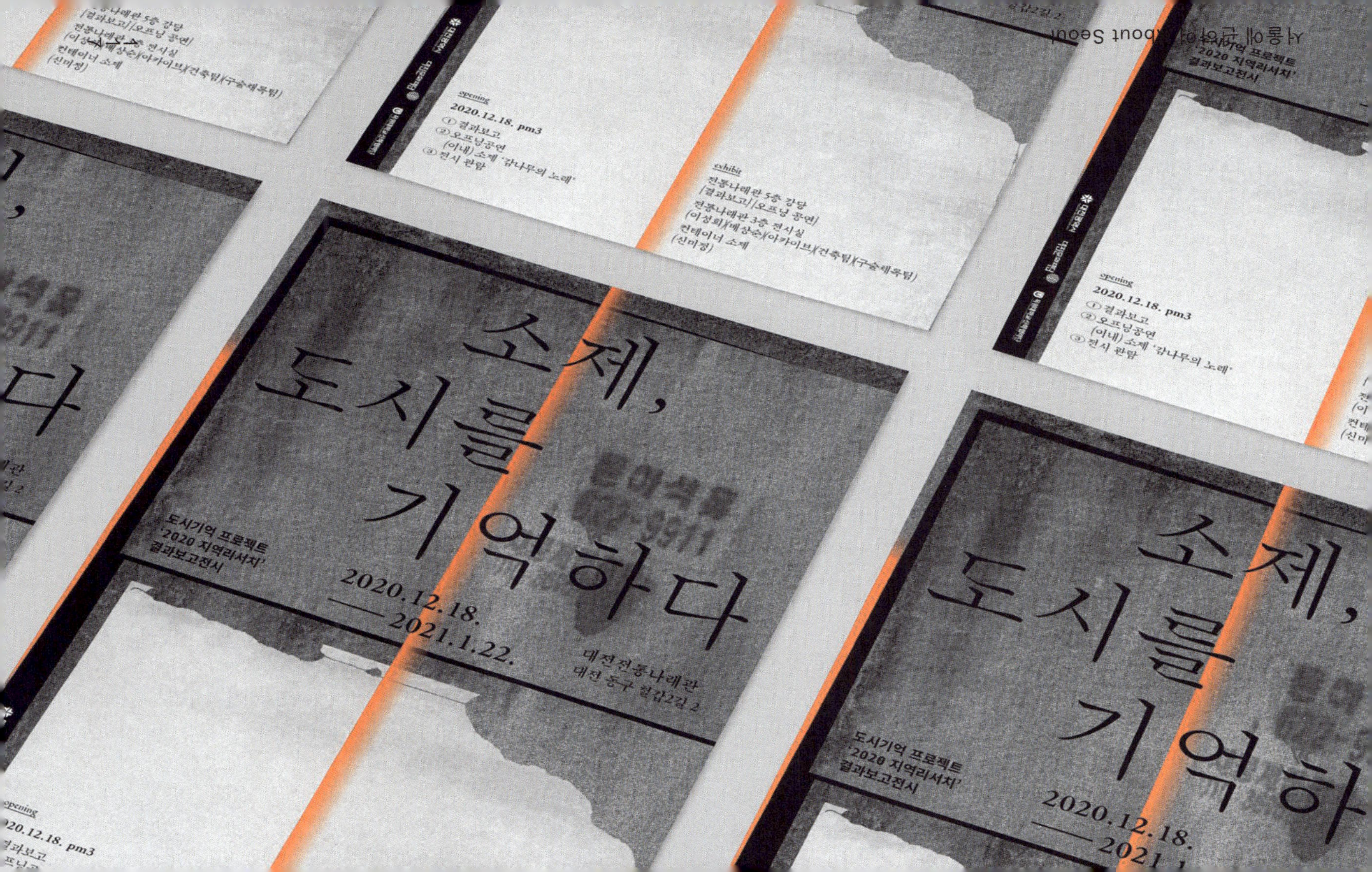
서울에 관하여 About Seoul
도시기억 프로젝트
'2020 지역리서치'
결과보고전시
opening
2020.12.18. pm3
① 결과보고
② 오프닝공연
(이내) 소제 '감나무의 노래'
③ 전시 관람
exhibit
전통나래관 5층 강당
[결과보고]/[오프닝 공연]
전통나래관 3층 전시실
(이성희)/(배창숙)(아카이브)/(건축팀)/(구술채록팀)
컨테이너 소제
(신미정)
소제,
도시를
기억하다
도시기억 프로젝트
'2020 지역리서치'
결과보고전시
2020.12.18.
2021.1.22.
대전전통나래관
대전 동구 향갑2길 2

WOOJAE

ПЕПСИ
U.S.S.R.
SHELL
Lubricants
SHELL
SKODA
MICHELIN
FOMAPAN
FPAN-36-10/10°
DX 135-36
от 100/36
JEONJU
intl. film festival
THE CARS
WE DROVE
INTO
CAPITALISM
BORIS MISSIRKOV
and
GEORGI BOGDANOV
AGITPROP presents

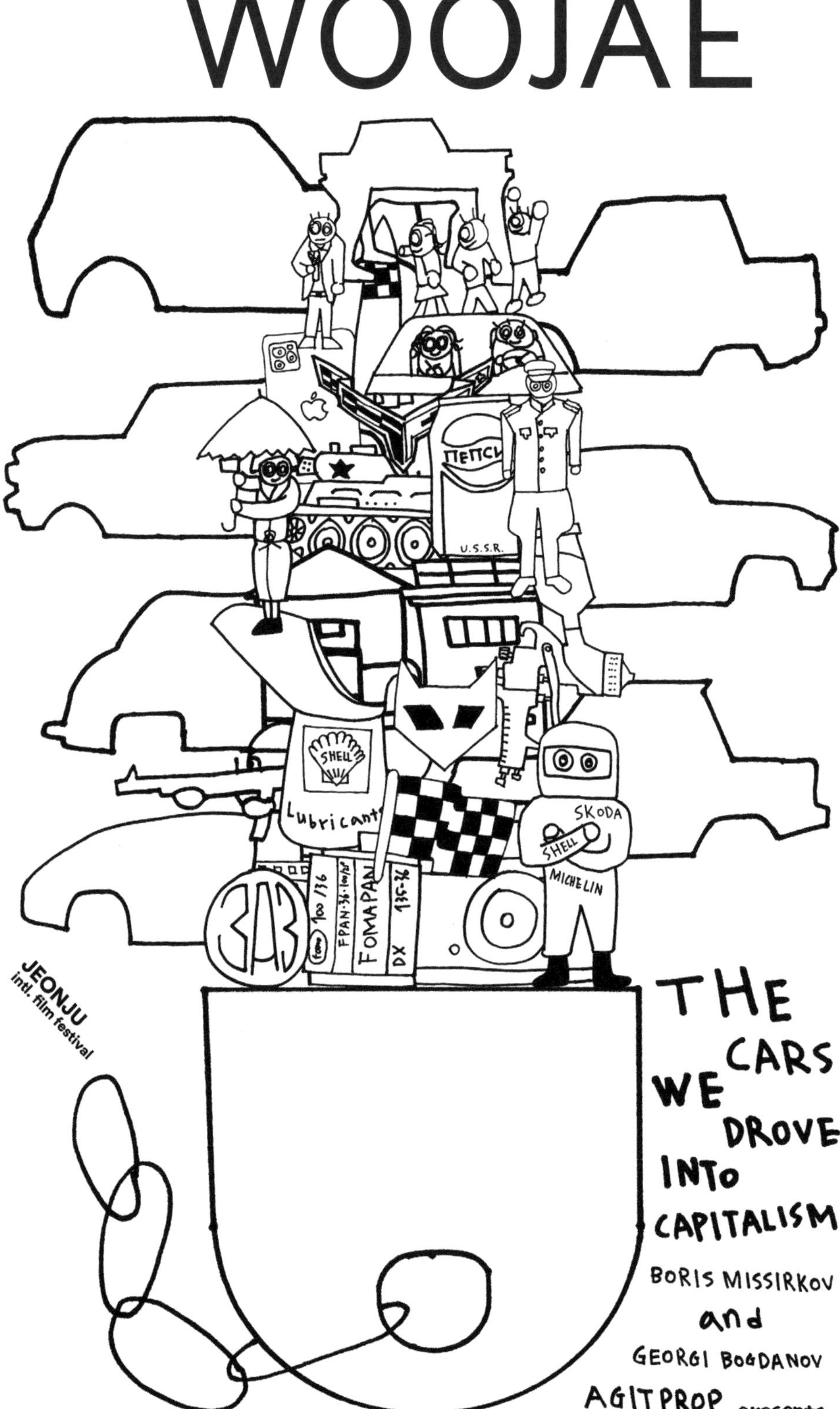

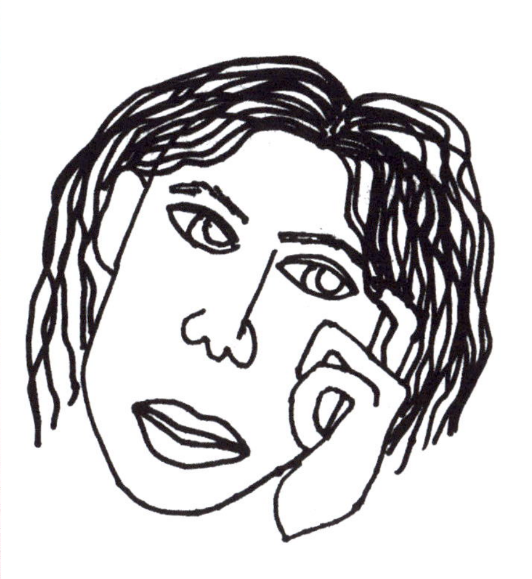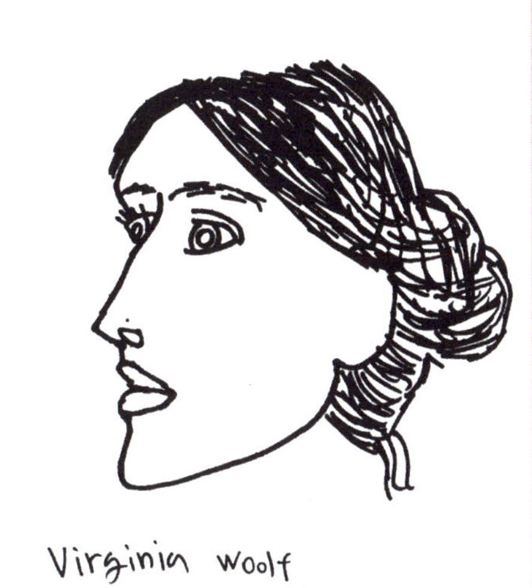

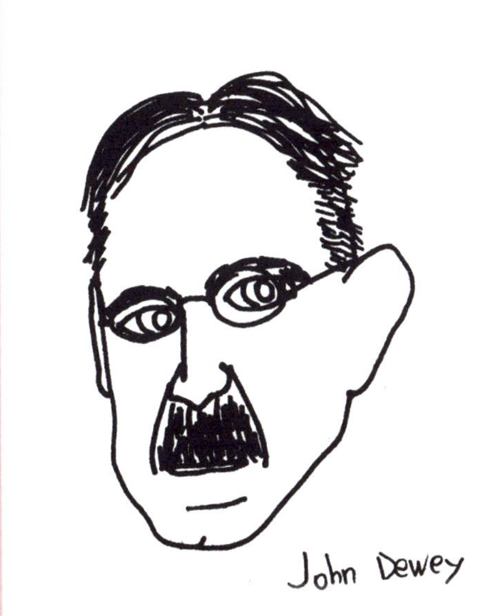

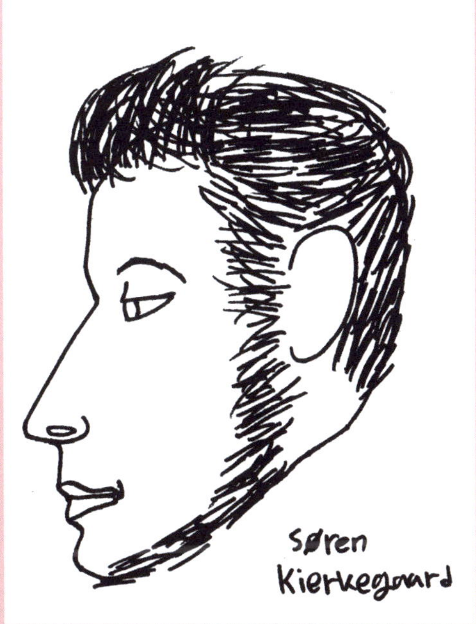

↑Portrait Series
Illustrations of historical figures.
↖Jeonju Intl. Film Festival
Poster for the Jeonju Intl. Film Festival.

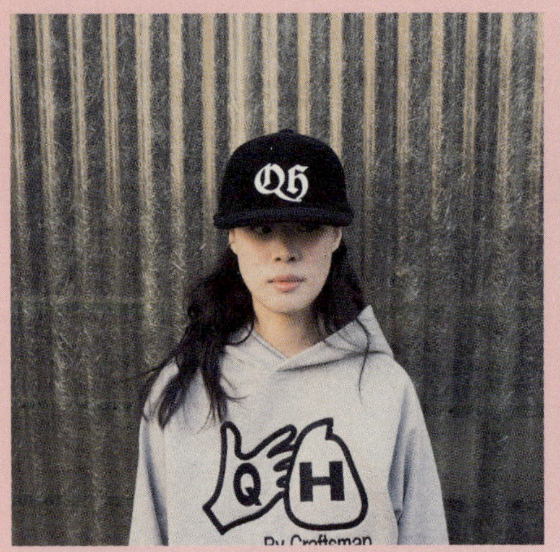
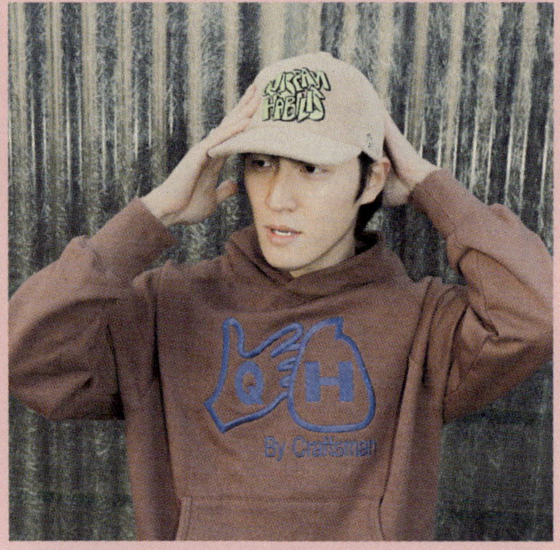

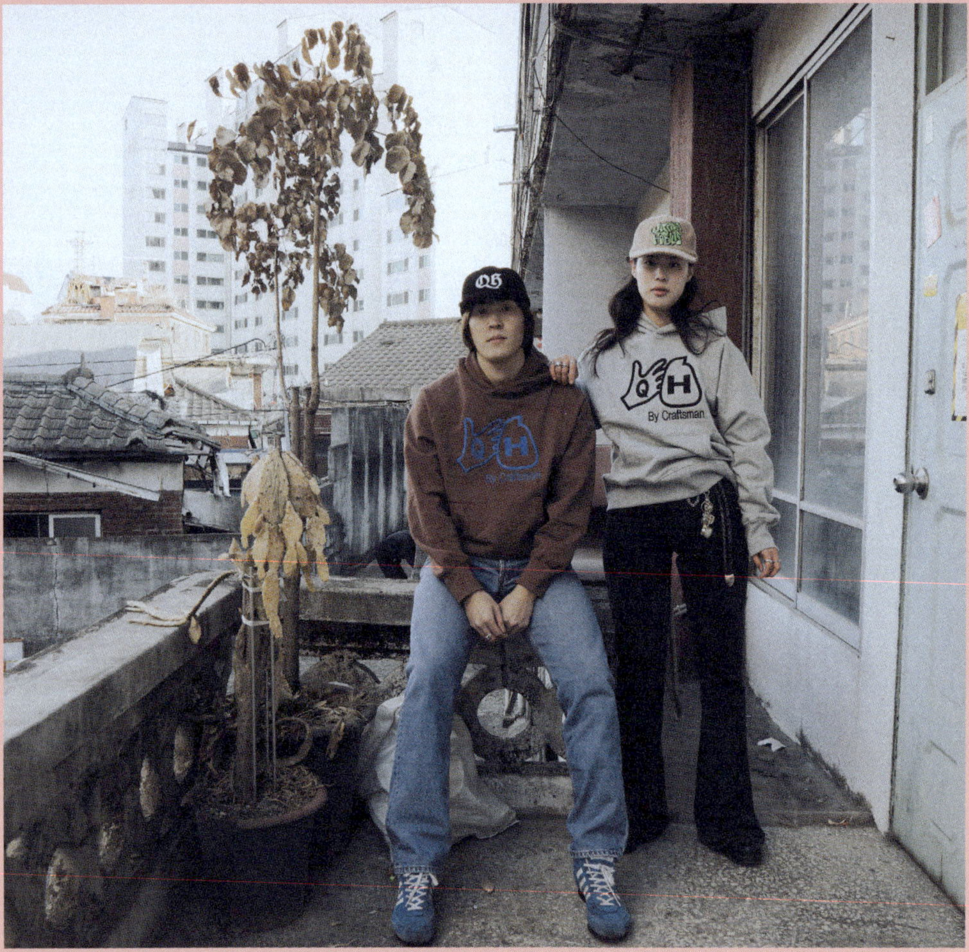

↑↗Quispiamhabils Clothing
**Editorial shot for Woojae's clothing and
accessory lable Quispiamhabils 'QH.'**

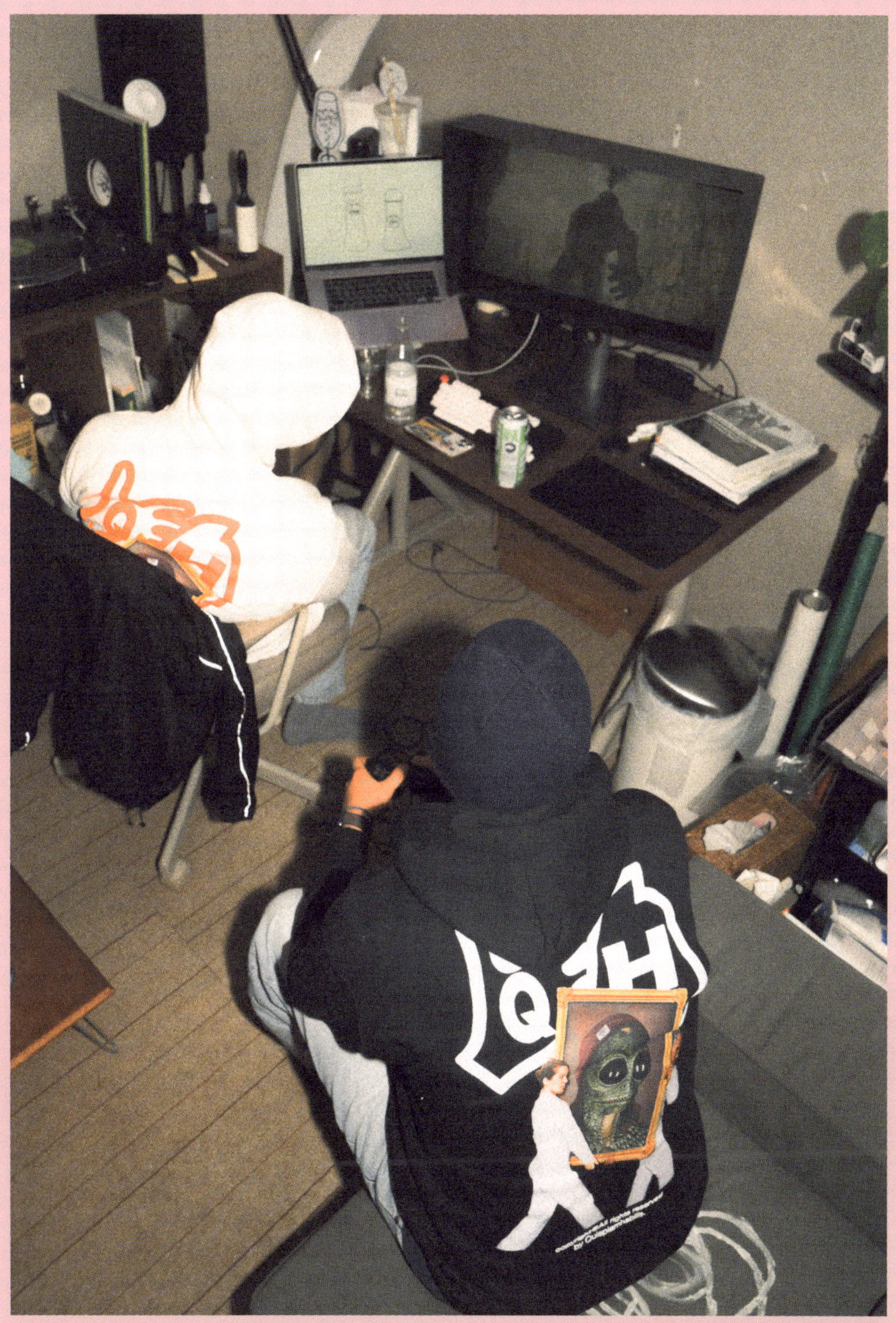

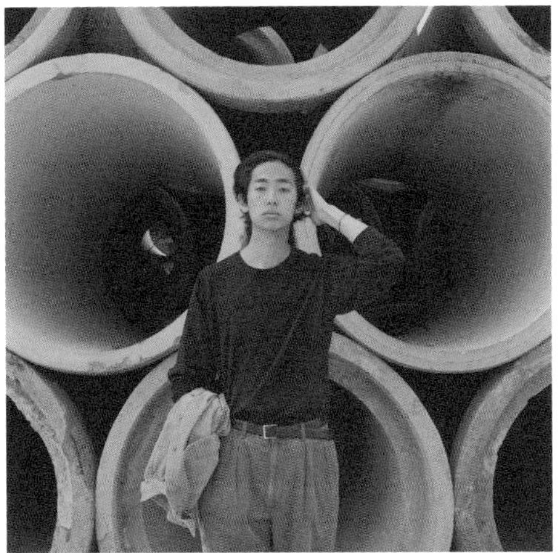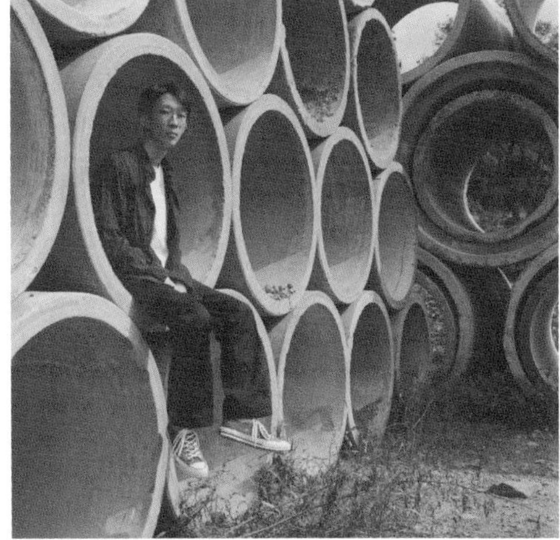

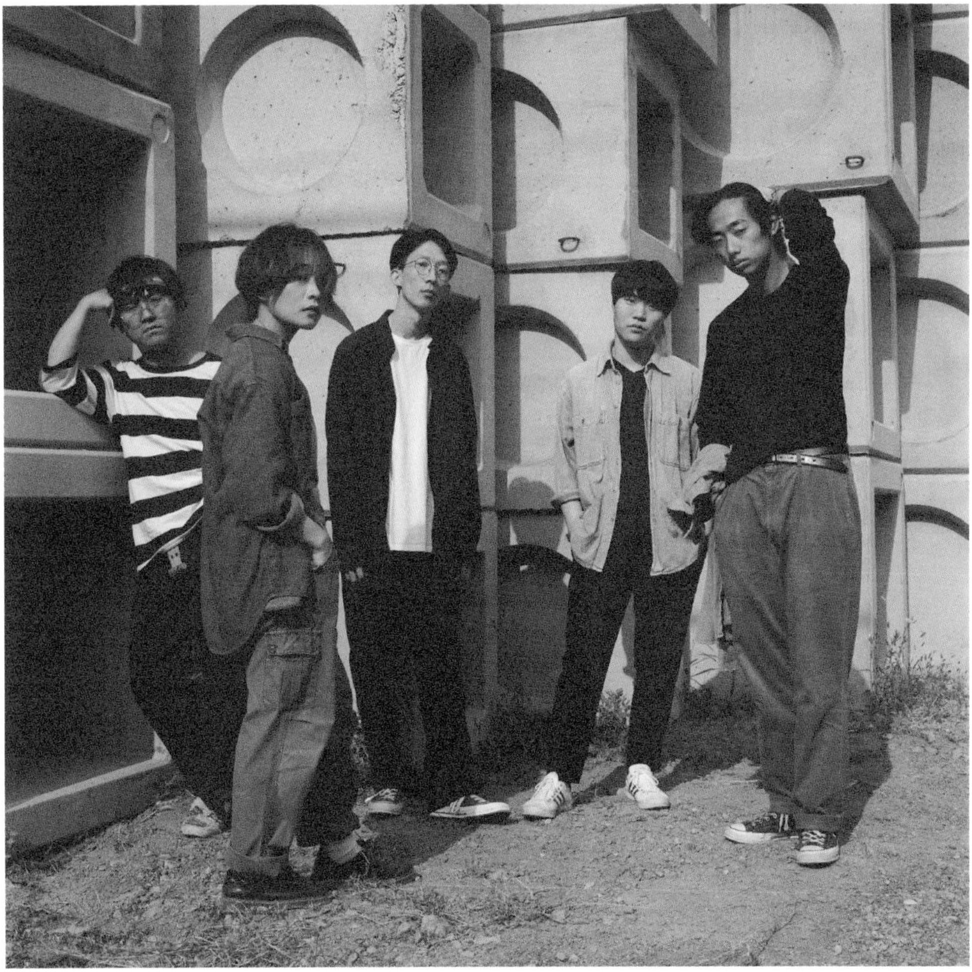

↑↗In the Endless Zanhyang We Are
photo shooting for the post-rock band
'In the Endless Zanhyang We Are.'

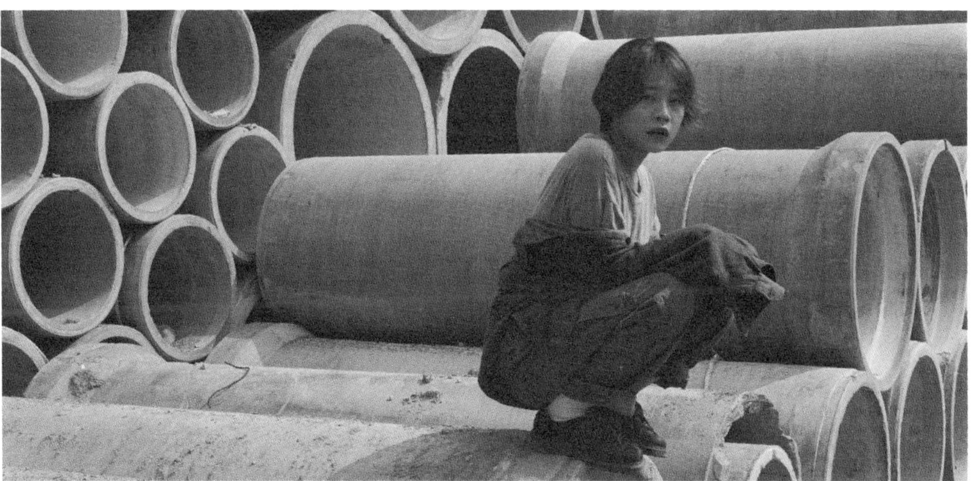

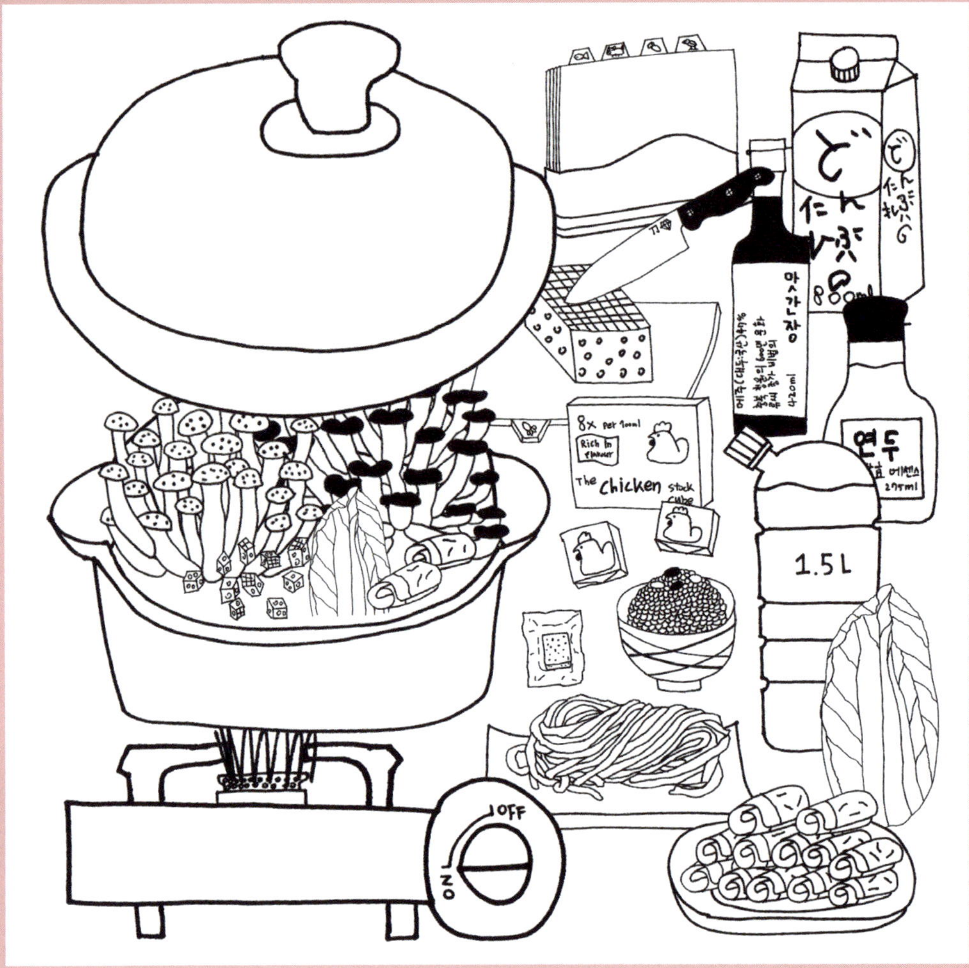

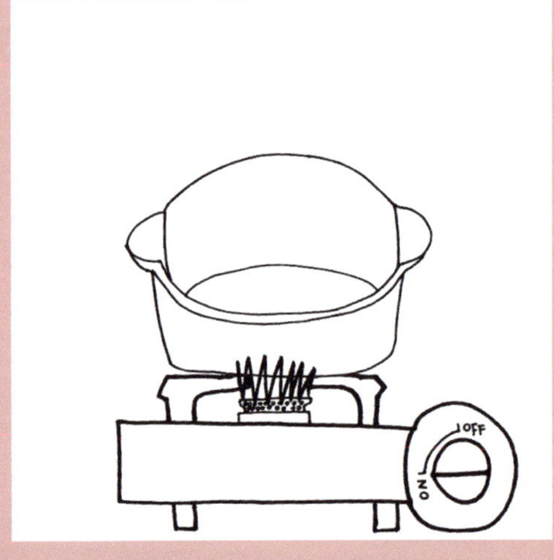

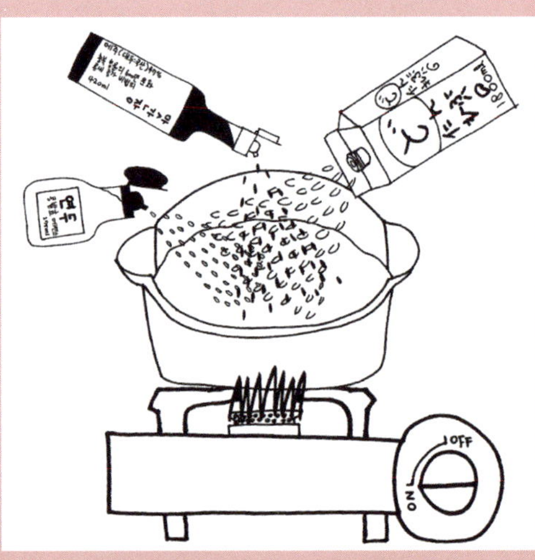

↑ ↗ Making Sukiyaki
Illustrations on how to cook Sukiyaki.

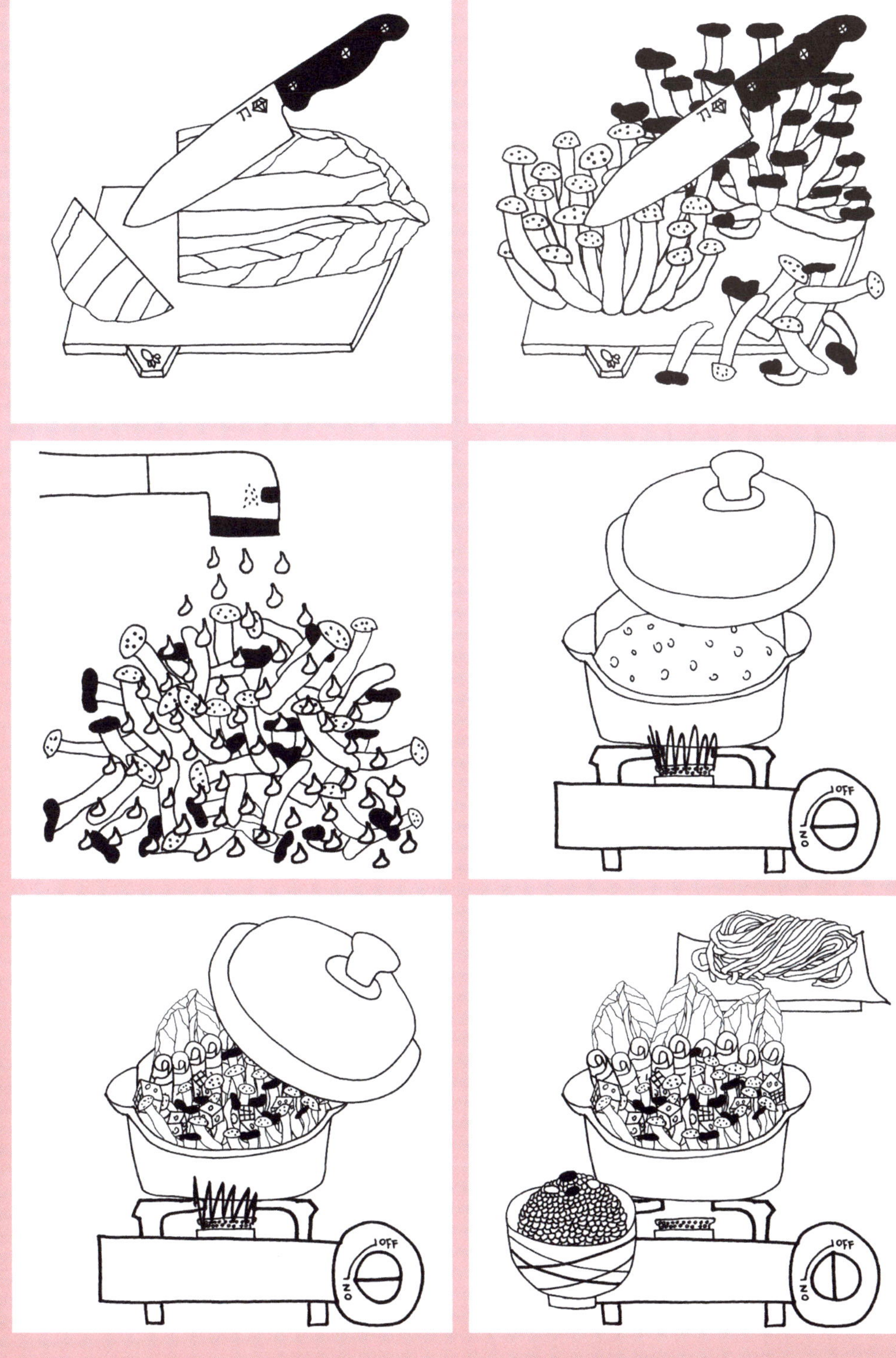

HAKYUNG

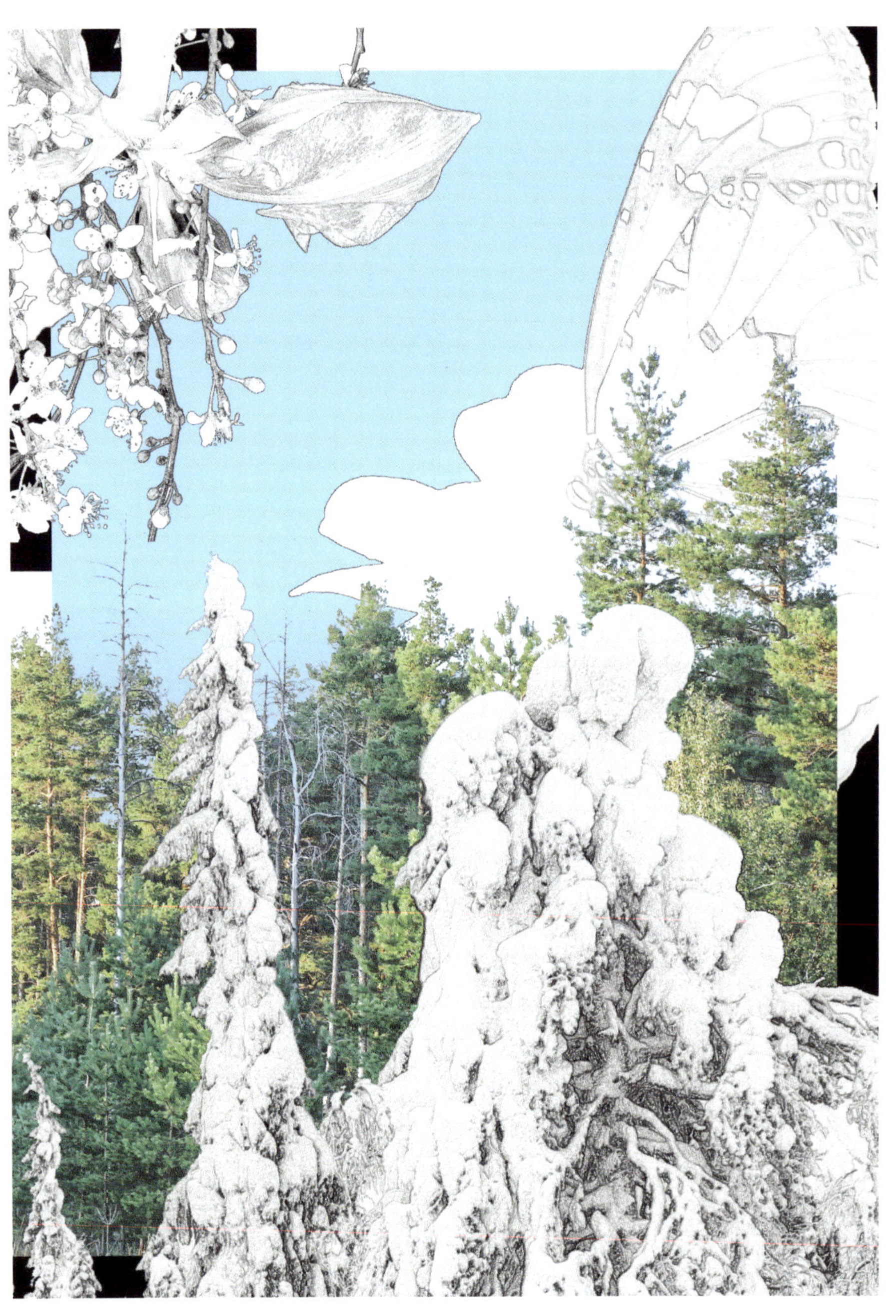

↑Four seasons
Poster, 2019.

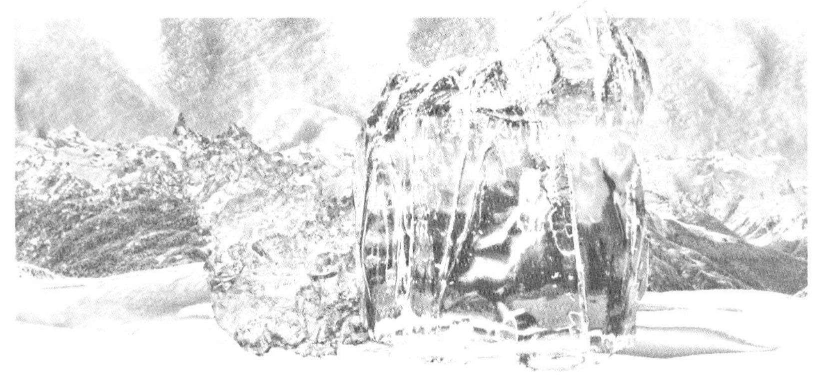

우린 봄이 오기 전에, Before Our Spring

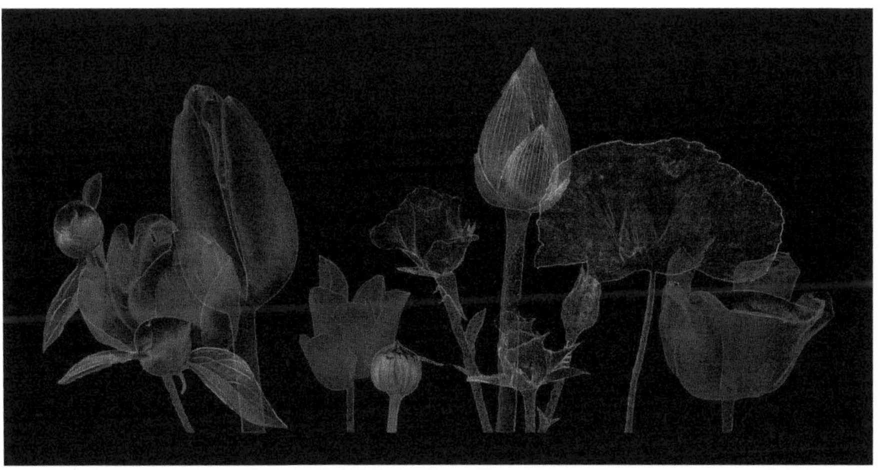

↑Before our spring
Poster for Weltformat Korea, 2019.

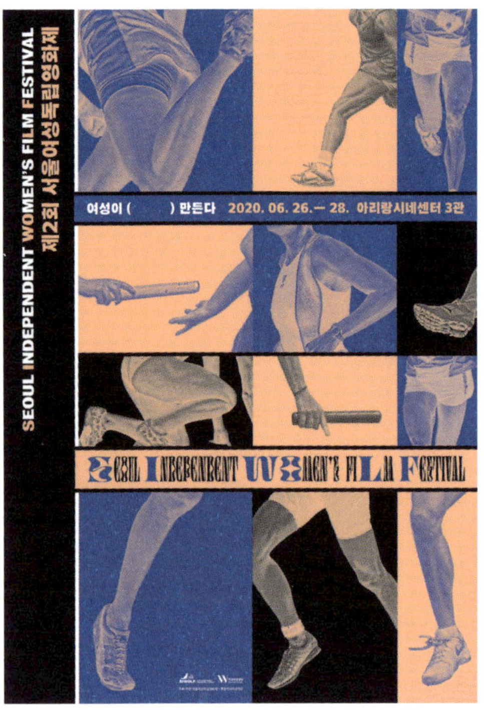

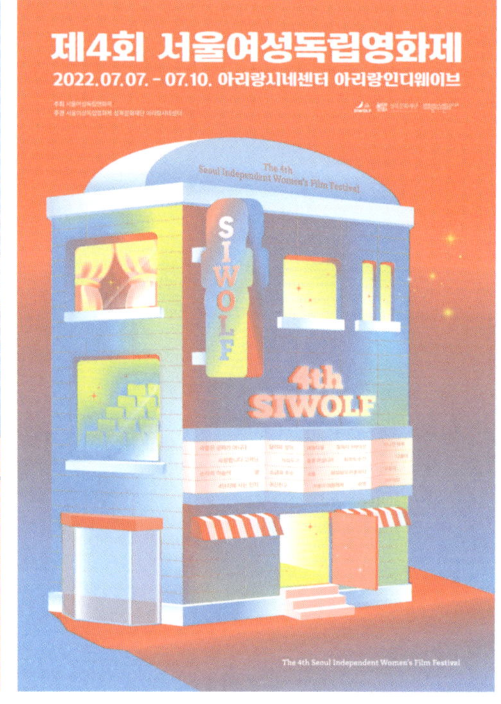

↑2nd SIWOLF
Poster for the 2nd Seoul Independent Women's
Film Festival, 2020.
↓Archive
Poster for Weltformat Korea, 2019.

↑4th SIWOLF
Poster for the 4th Seoul Independent Women's
Film Festival, 2022.
↓Cisgender Hetero Feminist Woman
Poster for Weltformat Korea, 2019.

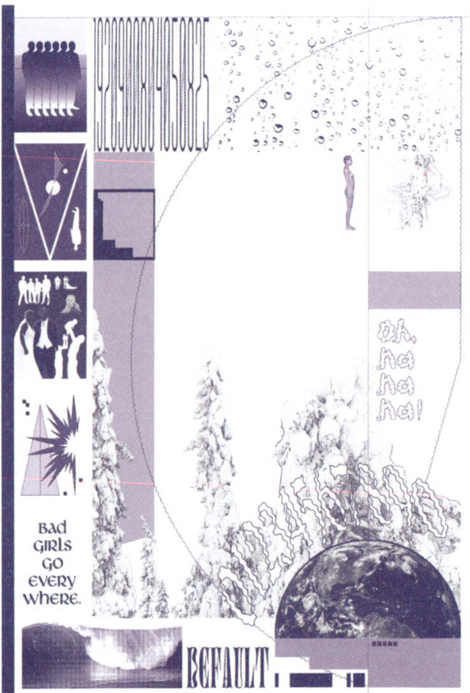

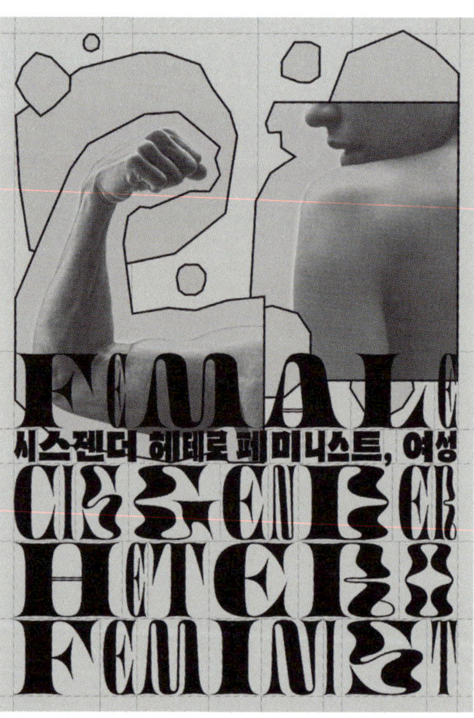

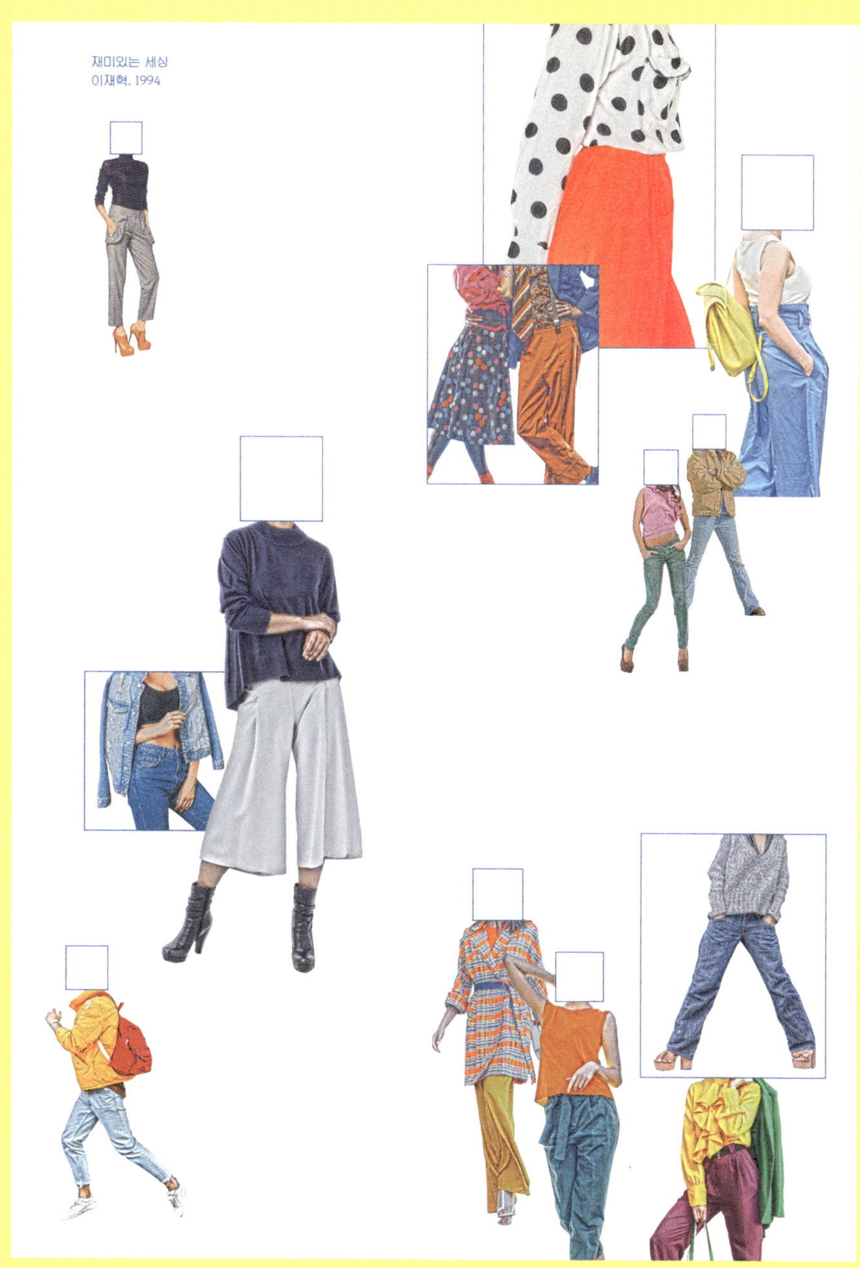

↑An Interesting World
Poster for Big River Poster Festival, 2019

HYOJEONG

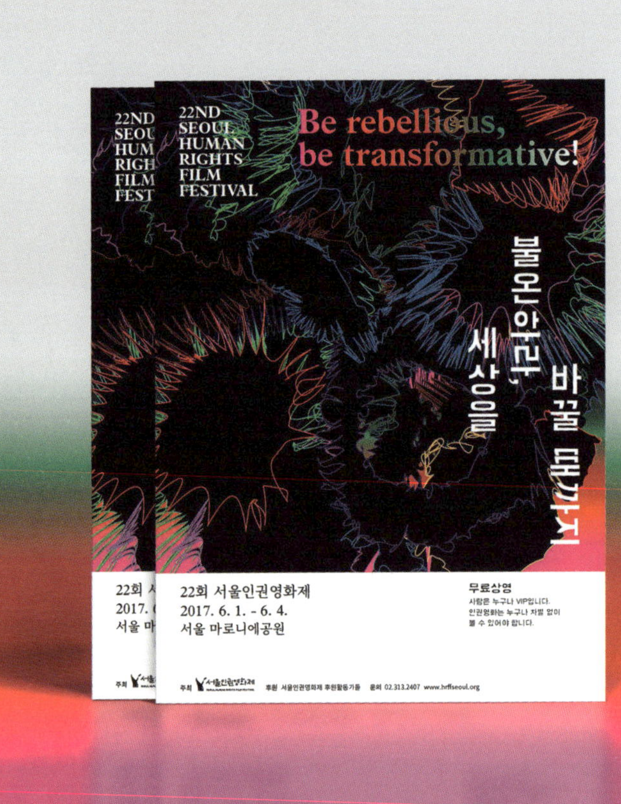

↑↗ Be rebellious, be transformative!
Poster for 22nd Seoul Human Rights Film Festival, 2017.

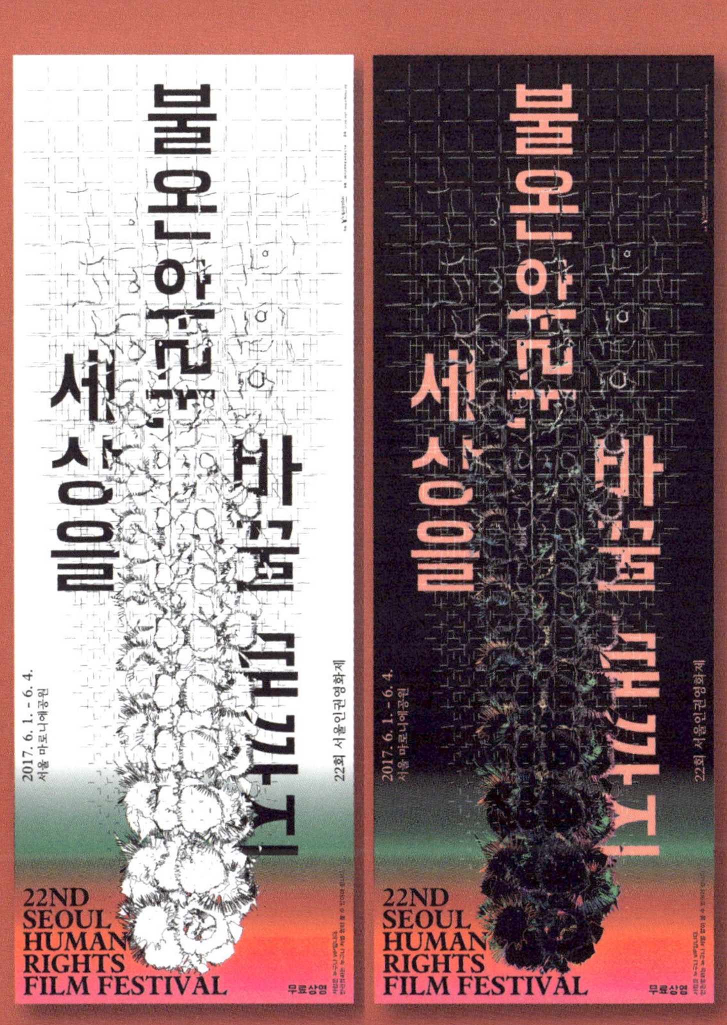
불온하라, 바꿔라 세상을
2017. 6. 1. - 6. 4.
서울 마로니에공원
22회 서울인권영화제
22ND
SEOUL
HUMAN
RIGHTS
FILM FESTIVAL
무료상영

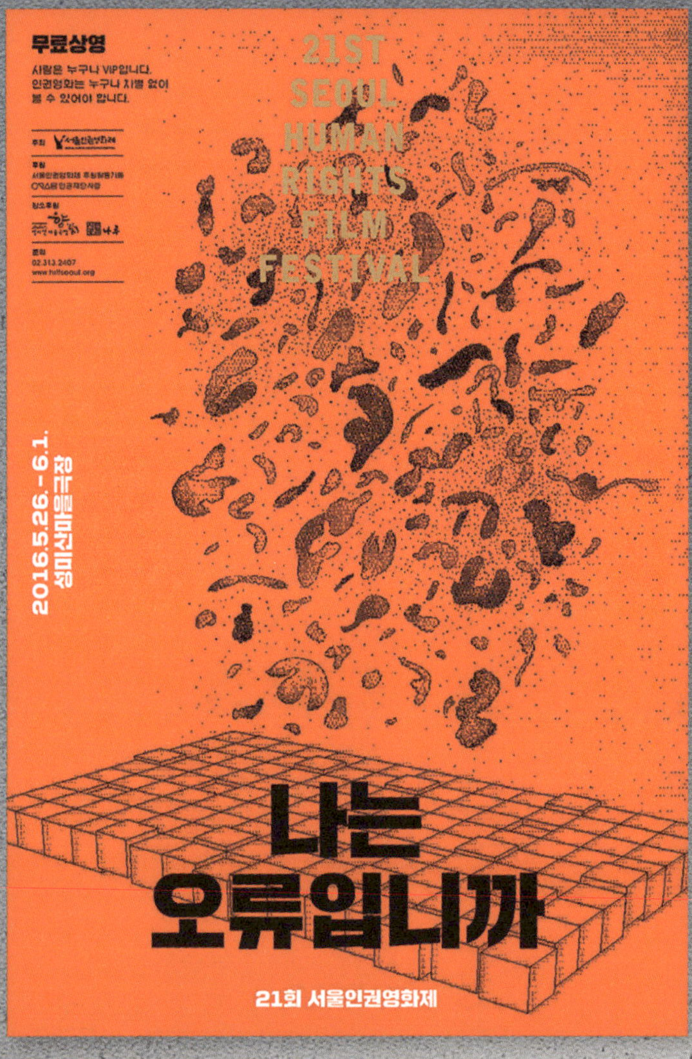

↑ Am I an error
Poster for 21st Seoul Human Rights Film Festival, 2016.
↗ Equality for all, a new year for all
Calendar that raises awareness on equality rights, 2016.

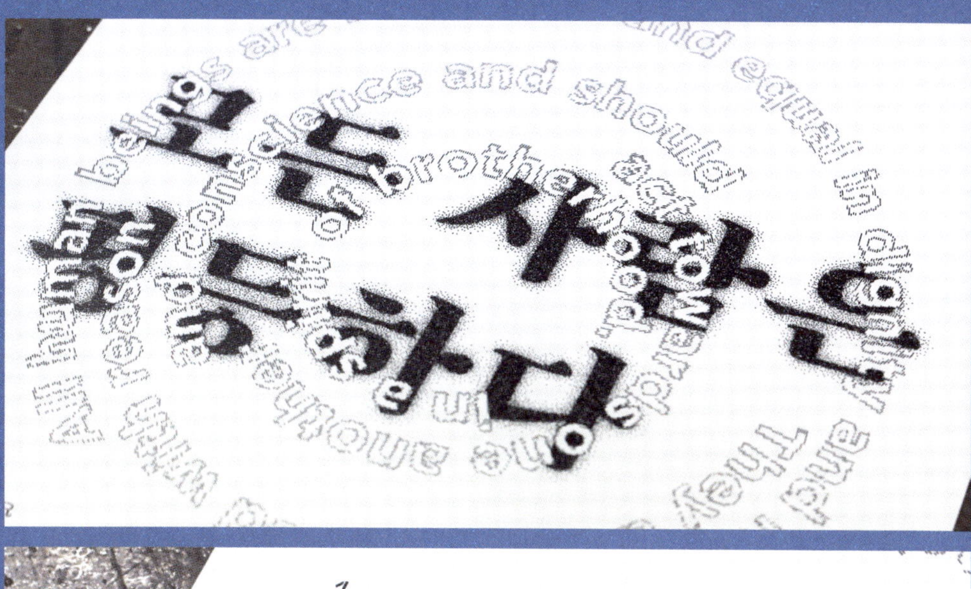
모든 사람은

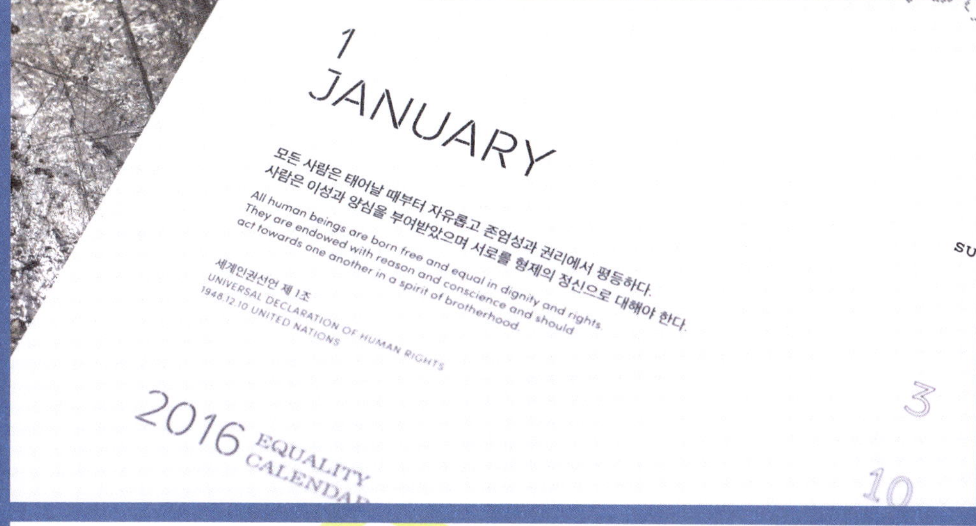
1
JANUARY

모든 사람은 태어날 때부터 자유롭고 존엄성과 권리에서 평등하다.
사람은 이성과 양심을 부여받았으며 서로를 형제의 정신으로 대해야 한다.
All human beings are born free and equal in dignity and rights.
They are endowed with reason and conscience and should
act towards one another in a spirit of brotherhood.

세계인권선언 제1조
UNIVERSAL DECLARATION OF HUMAN RIGHTS
1948.12.10 UNITED NATIONS

2016 EQUALITY CALENDAR

SU

3

10

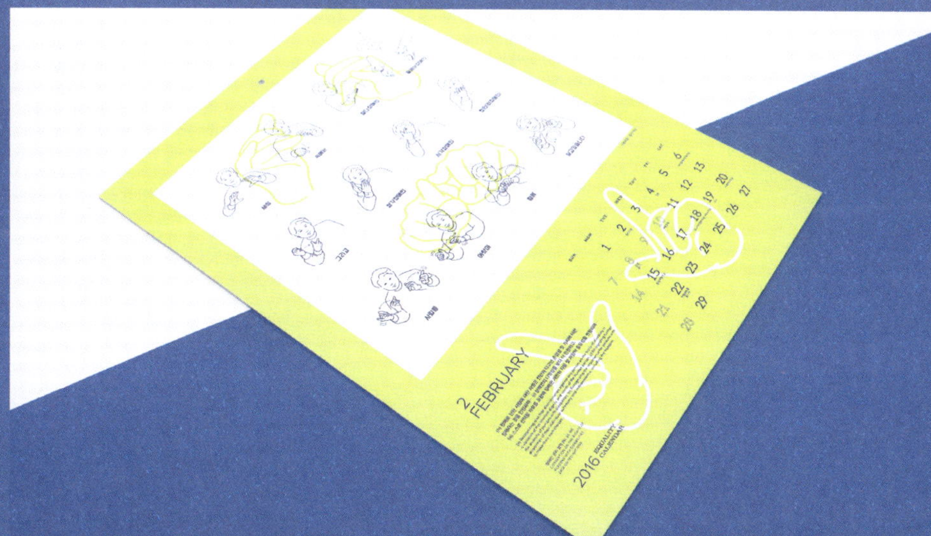
2 FEBRUARY
2016 EQUALITY CALENDAR

PAKDO

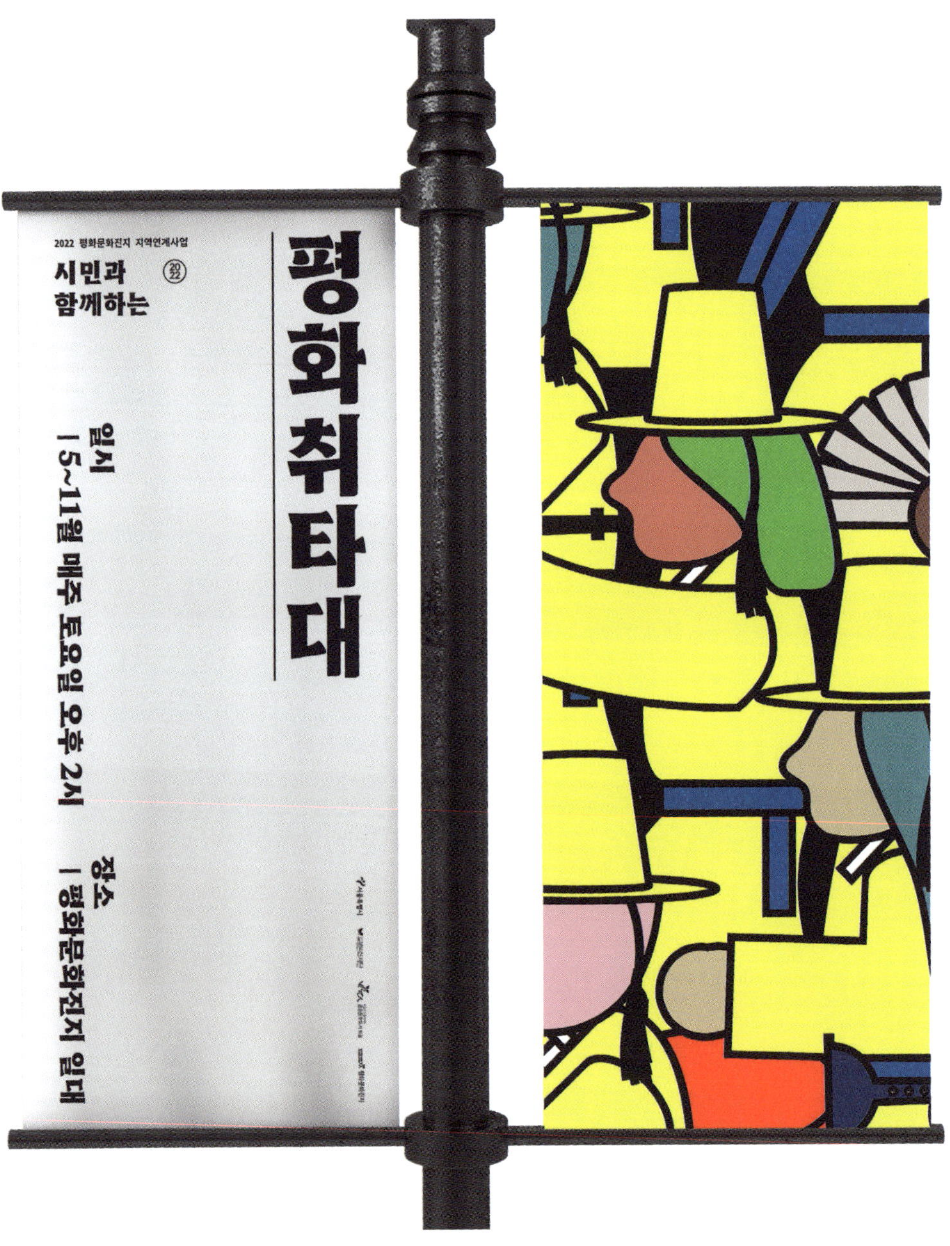

↑ ↗ Korean Music Parade
Poster and banners for the Korean
traditional music parade, 2022.

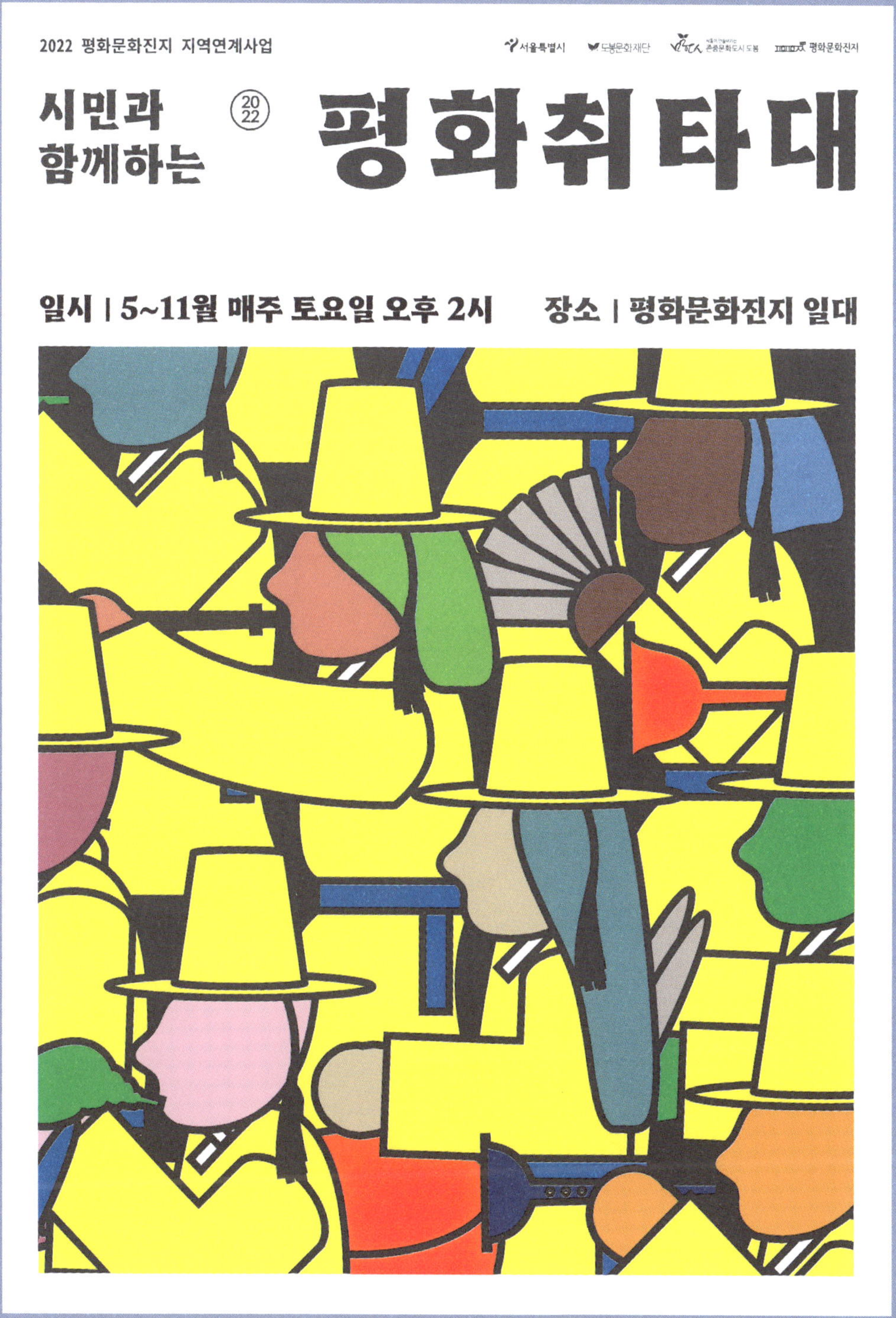

2022 평화문화진지 지역연계사업

서울특별시　도봉문화재단　존중문화도시 도봉　평화문화진지

시민과 함께하는  평화취타대

일시 | 5~11월 매주 토요일 오후 2시　　장소 | 평화문화진지 일대

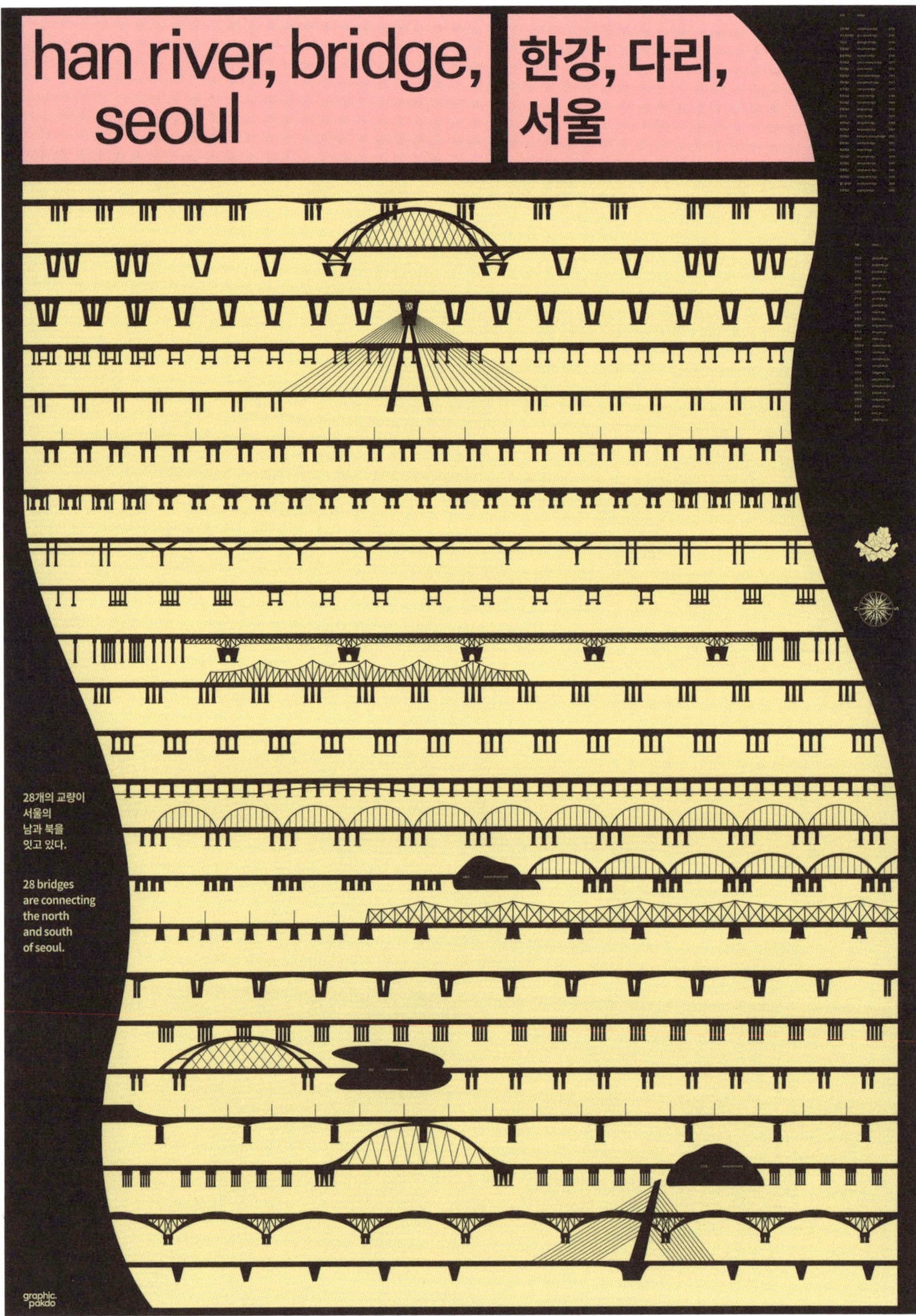

↑han river, bridge, seoul
Poster for the 24 bridges between South Seoul—
North Seoul. 841 × 1,189 mm, 2020.

→ Minor Infelicities
Catalog of Korea's first Asian queer exhibition
'Minor Infelicities,' 156 p., hardcover,
152 × 225 mm, Korean / English, 2022.

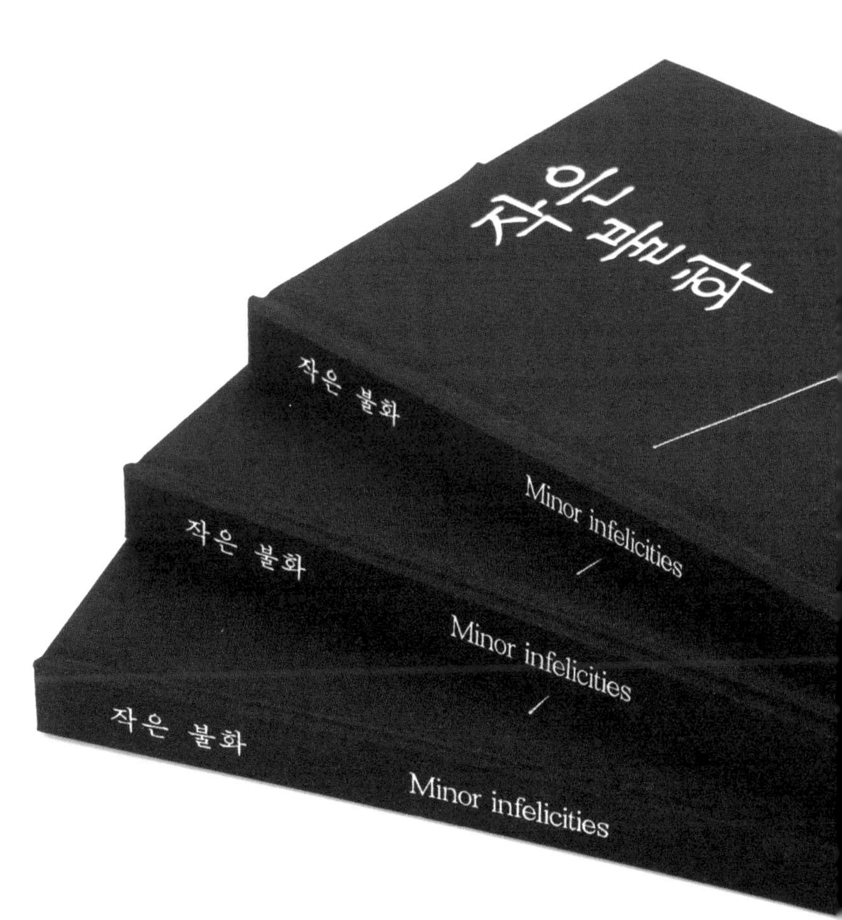
작은 불화
Minor infelicities
작은 불화
Minor infelicities
작은 불화
Minor infelicities

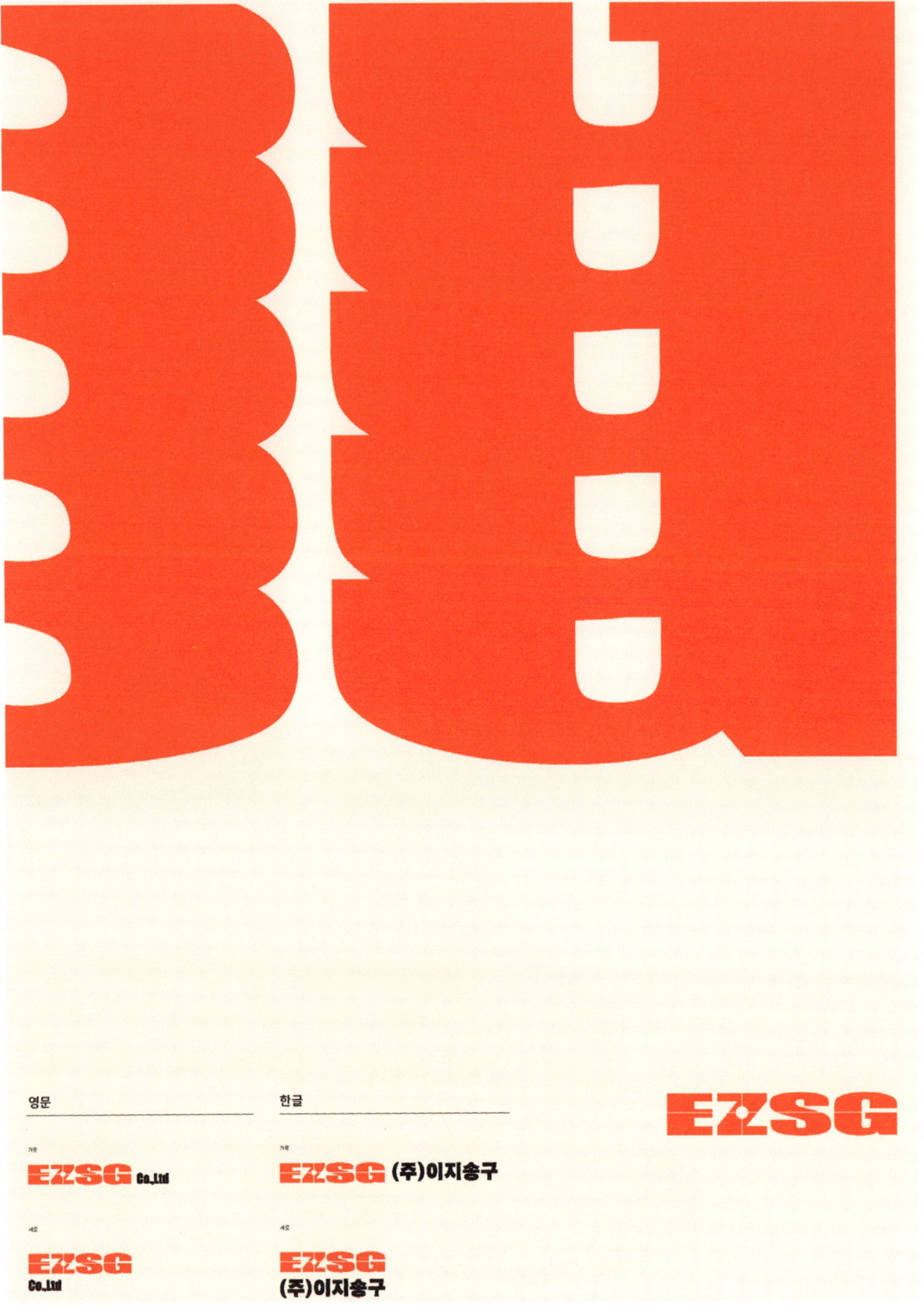

↑Songu
Poster for Songu's logo design, 2021.
↗Bankers
Poster for bankers stand lamps,
420 × 594 mm, 2020.

BANKERS STAND
뱅커스스탠드

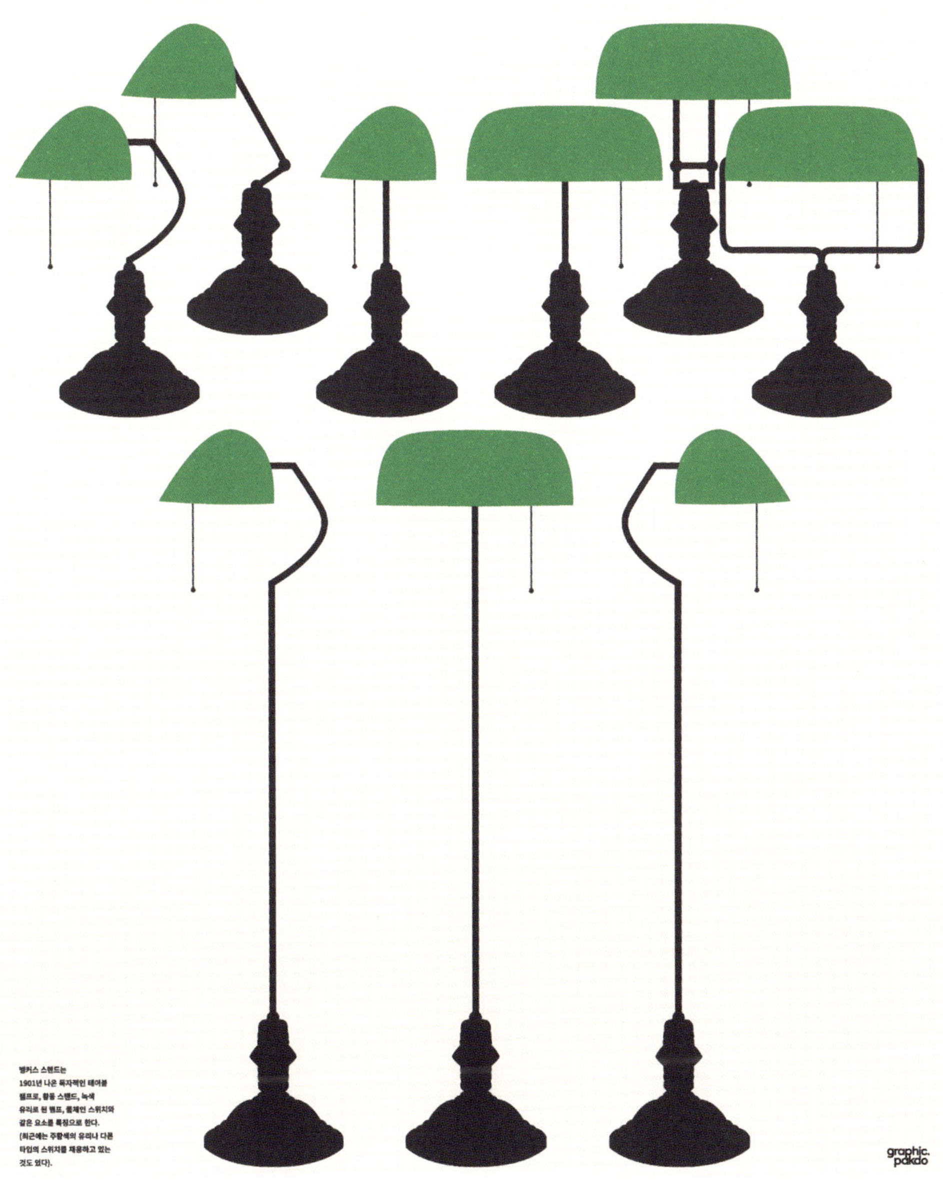

뱅커스 스탠드는
1901년 나온 독자적인 테이블
램프로, 활꼴 스탠드, 녹색
유리로 된 램프, 풀체인 스위치와
같은 요소를 특징으로 한다.
(최근에는 주황색의 유리나 다른
타입의 스위치를 채용하고 있는
것도 있다).

graphic.
pakdo

SEUNGHUN

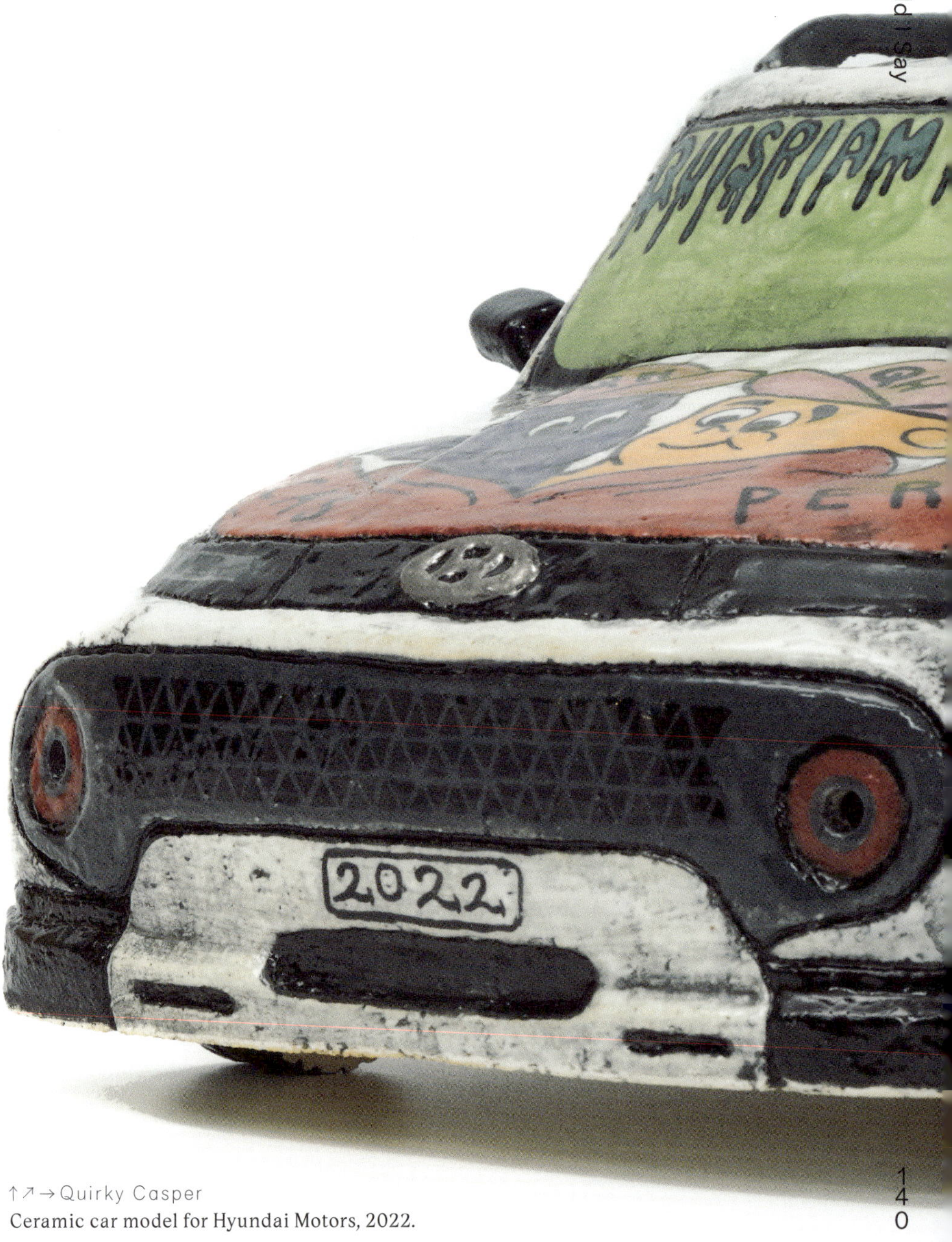

2022

↑↗→ Quirky Casper
Ceramic car model for Hyundai Motors, 2022.

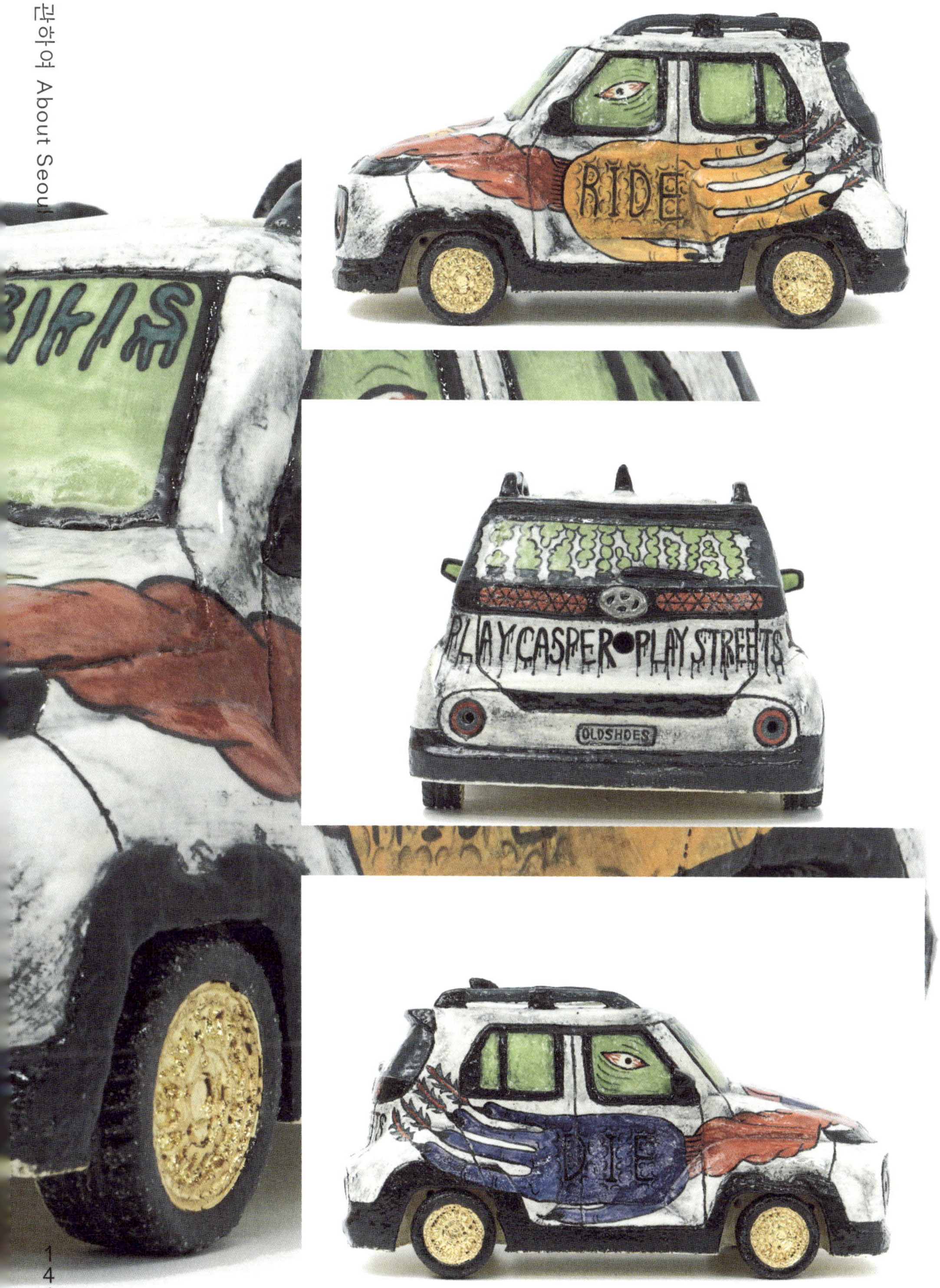

RIDE

PLAY CASPER•PLAY STREETS
OLDSHOES

DIE

JIWON

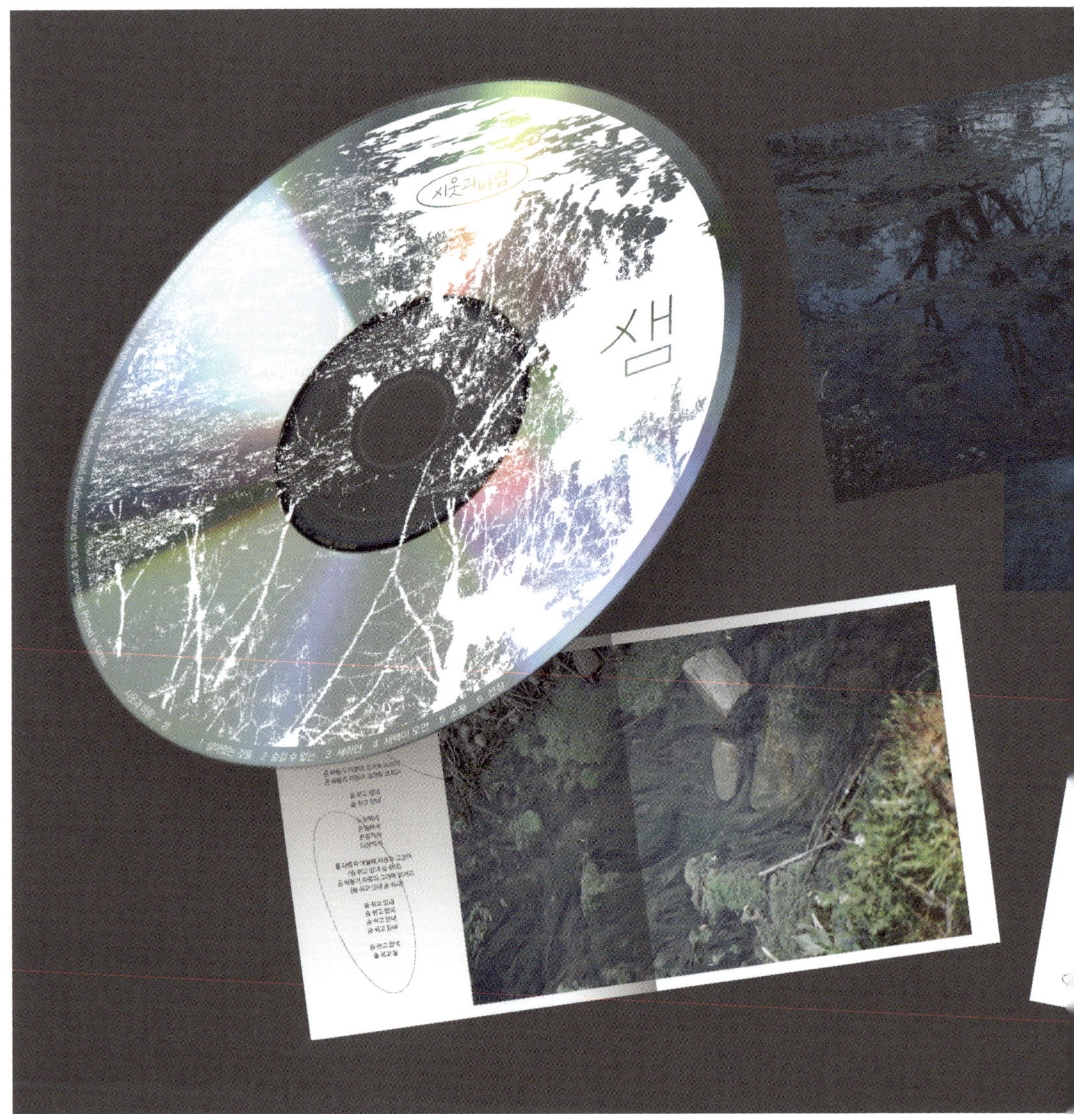

↙↓Spring
Album and poster design for the artist 'Siot and Breeze,' 2020.

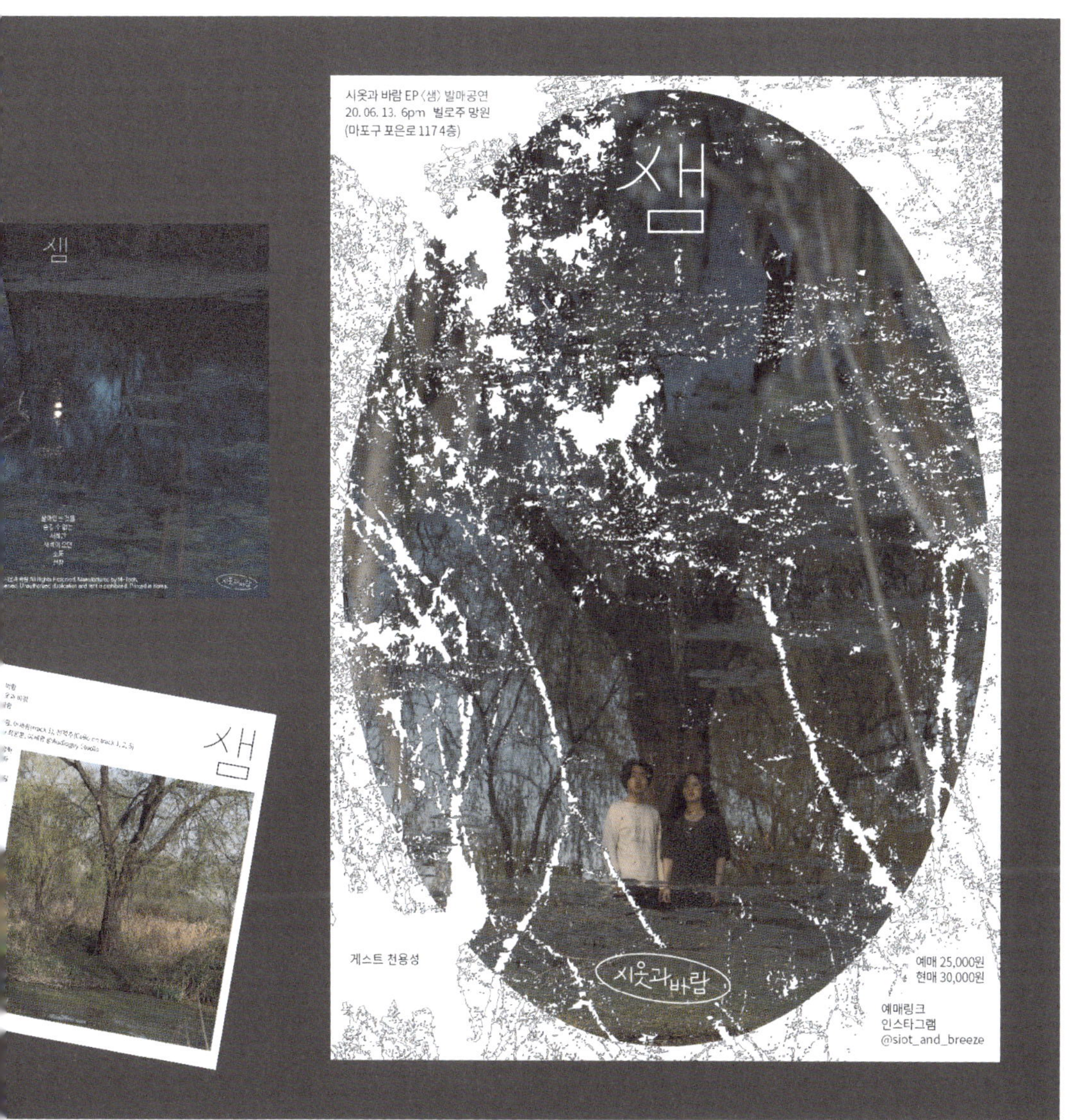

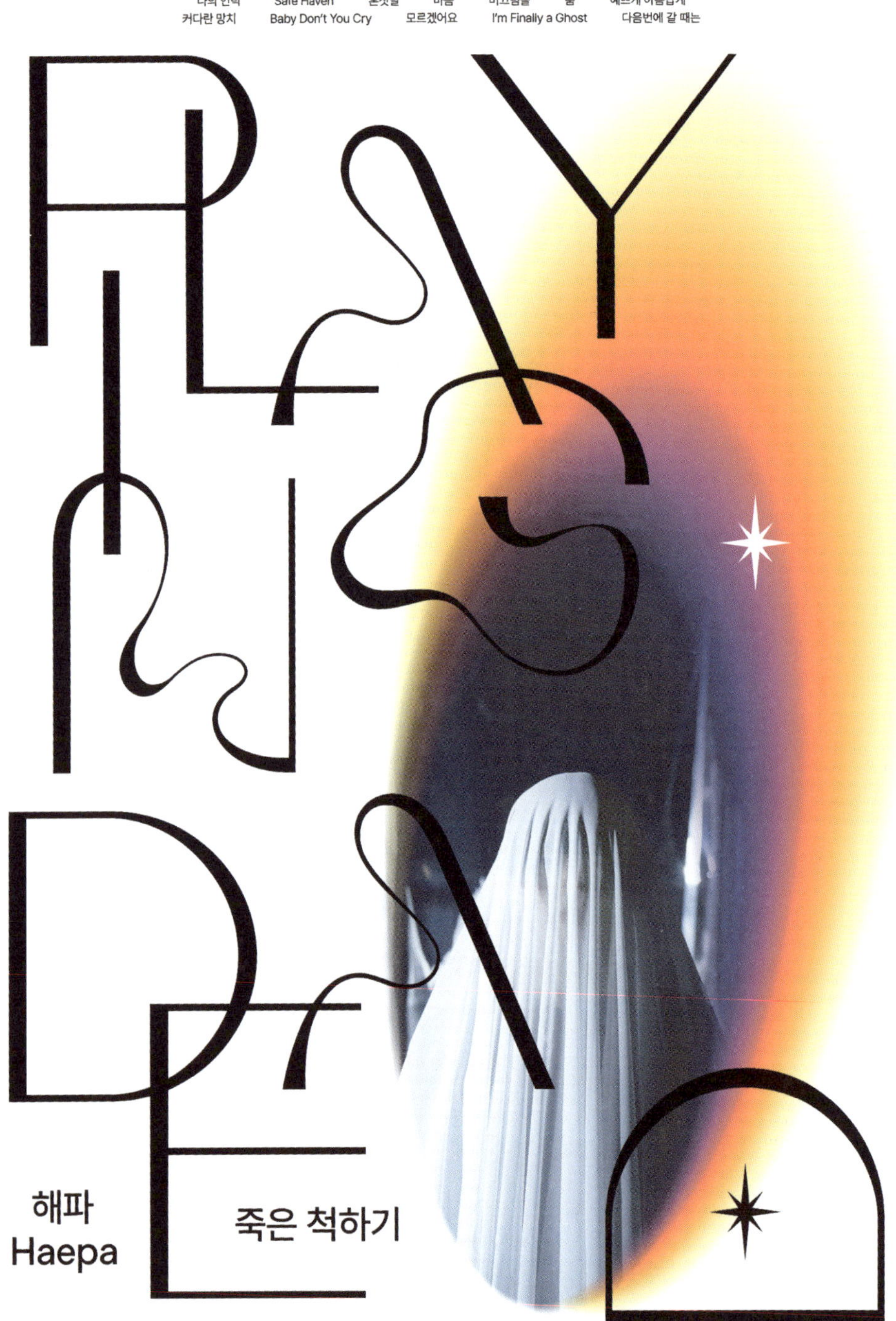

↖↗ Playing Dead
Album design for the artist 'Haepa' including poster
and custom type design, 2022.

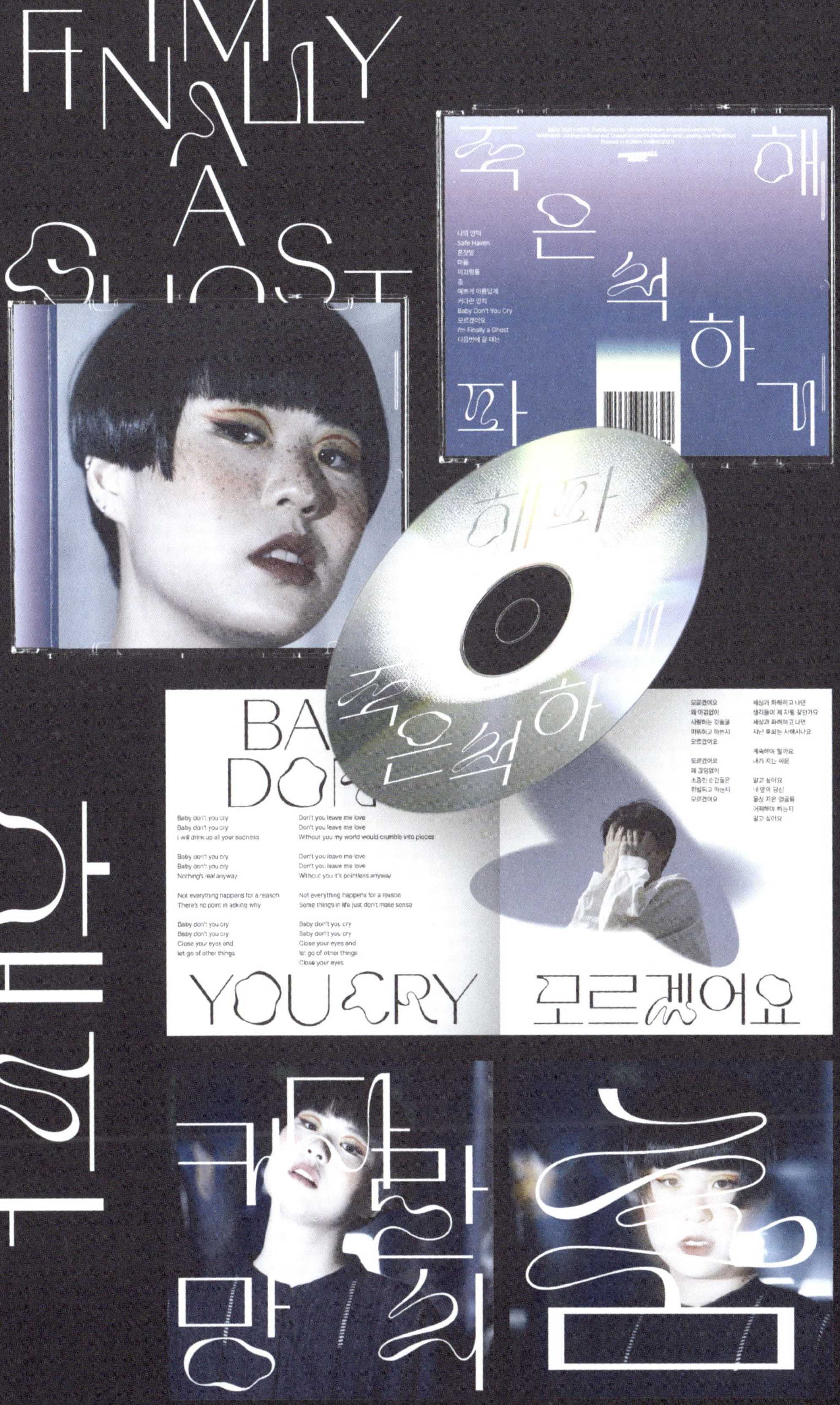

FINALLY A GHOST
I'M FINALLY A GHOST
죽은 석하기 해
파

나의 언덕
Safe Haven
혼잣말
이름
미끄럼틀
춤
예쁘게 아름답게
커다란 망치
Baby Don't You Cry
모르겠어요
I'm Finally a Ghost
다음번에 갈 때는

해파
죽은석하

BABY DON'T YOU CRY

Baby don't you cry
Baby don't you cry
I will drink up all your sadness

Baby don't you cry
Baby don't you cry
Nothing's real anyway

Not everything happens for a reason
There's no point in asking why

Baby don't you cry
Baby don't you cry
Close your eyes and
let go of other things

Don't you leave me love
Don't you leave me love
Without you my world would crumble into pieces

Don't you leave me love
Don't you leave me love
Without you it's pointless anyway

Not everything happens for a reason
Some things in life just don't make sense

Baby don't you cry
Baby don't you cry
Close your eyes and
let go of other things
Close your eyes

모르겠어요

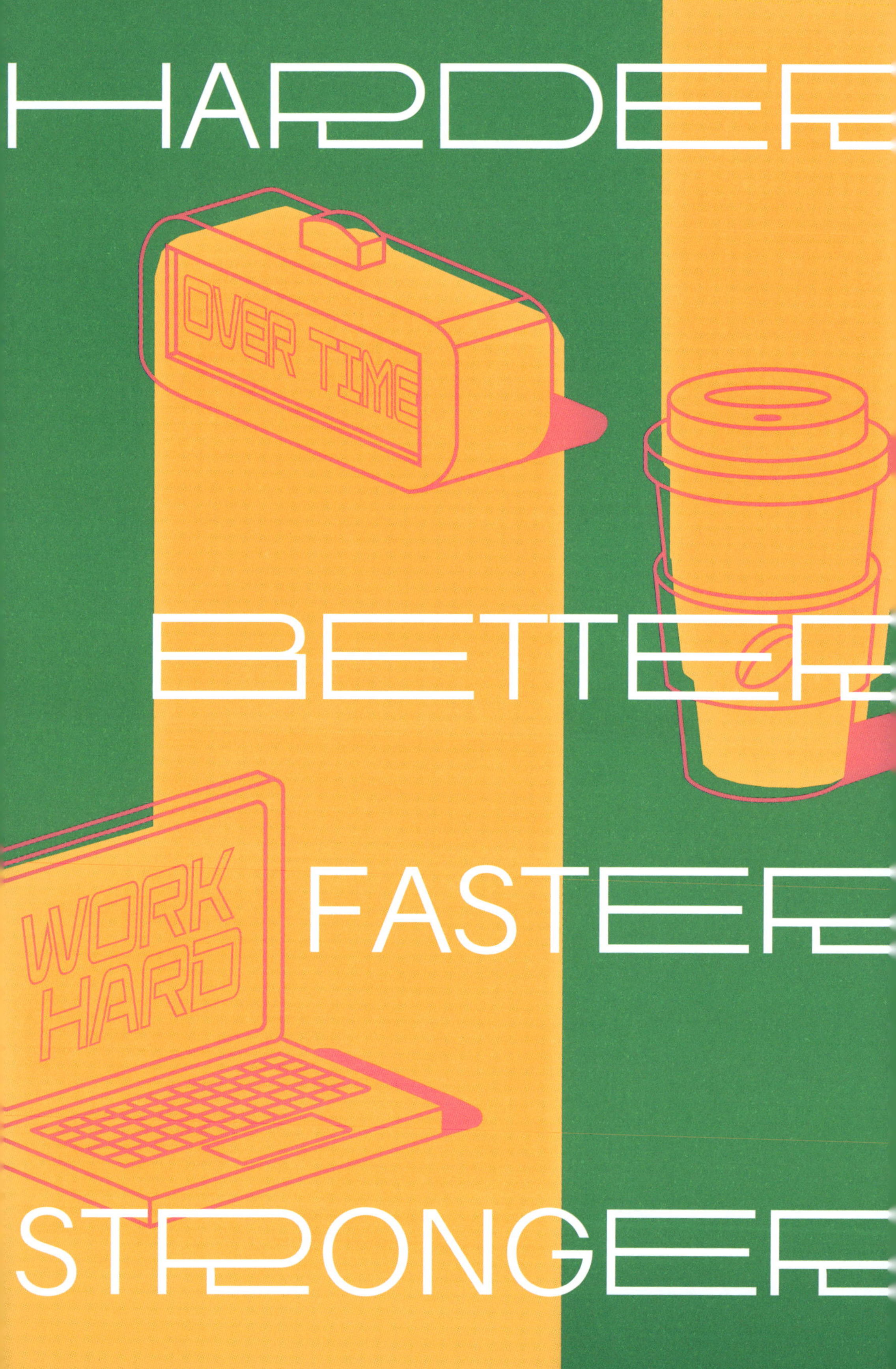

HARDER
OVER TIME
BETTER
WORK HARD
FASTER
STRONGER

REPUBLIC OF OVER-WORKING

Words & Illustrations: Youjin Kim

South Korea is one of the countries that have achieved rapid economic growth. And the 'Miracle on the Han River' is often referred to as the background of it.

The term 'Miracle on the Han River' was coined after the phrase 'Miracle on the Rhine' was used to refer to the economic rebirth of West Germany after World War II. This analogy was incorporated by Chang Myon, prime minister of the Second Republic of South Korea, in his New Year's address of 1961 in which he encouraged South Koreans to bear difficulties in the hope of achieving a similar economic upturn. The resulting growth has been attributed to the hard work of the labor force. Korean workers have been making sacrifices by working overtime with extremely low wages in order to aid the growth of the nation and major companies since that time.

And after 50 years, despite South Korea having achieved remarkable success in combining rapid economic growth with significant poverty reduction, many Korean workers are still required to work extortionate working hours.

I was one of them as a junior designer.

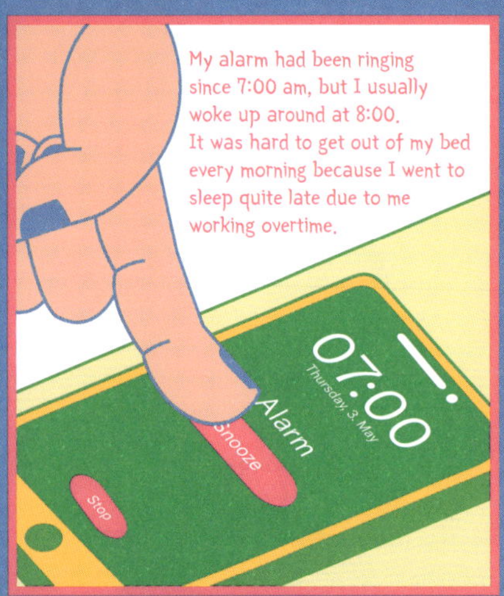
My alarm had been ringing since 7:00 am, but I usually woke up around at 8:00. It was hard to get out of my bed every morning because I went to sleep quite late due to me working overtime.
07:00
Thursday 3 May
Alarm
Snooze
Stop

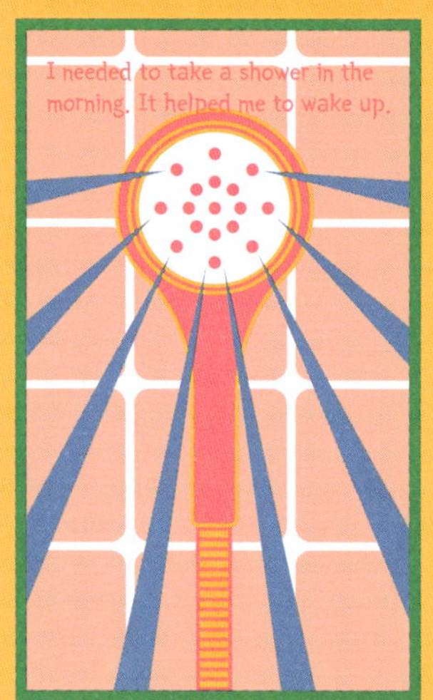
I needed to take a shower in the morning. It helped me to wake up.

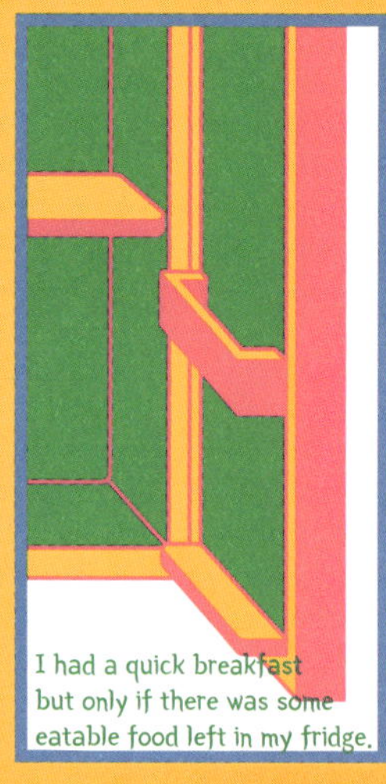
I had a quick breakfast but only if there was some eatable food left in my fridge.

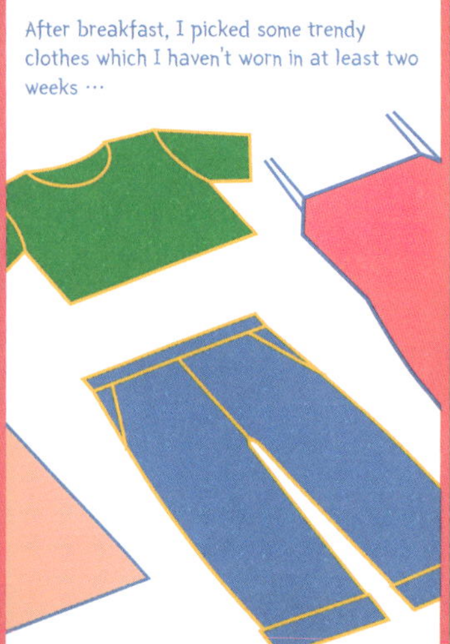
After breakfast, I picked some trendy clothes which I haven't worn in at least two weeks …

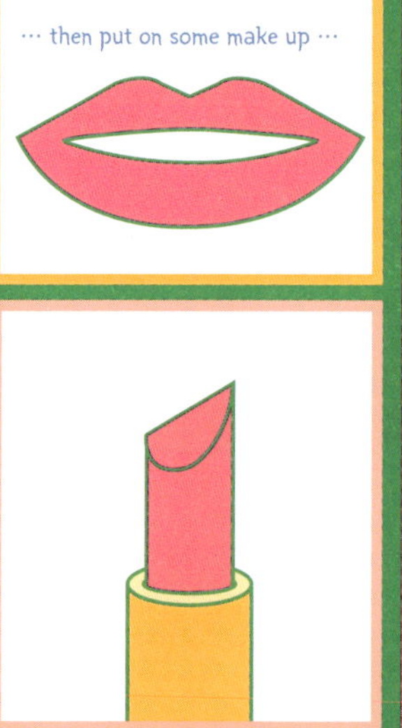
… then put on some make up …

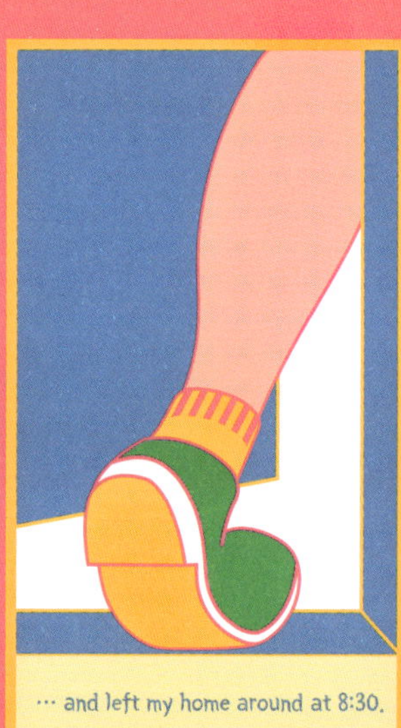
… and left my home around at 8:30.

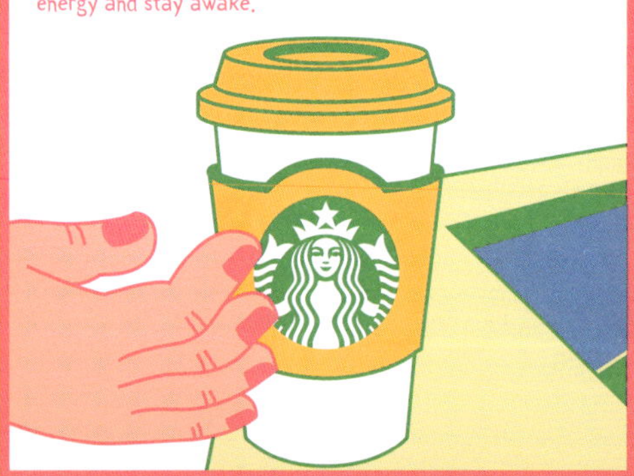
I always stopped by a cafe on my way for buying a cup of coffee with a double espresso. It helped me to boost my energy and stay awake.

I had to be at the office at least 20mins before my real working time. Otherwise I got scolded by my boss.
12 1 2 3 4 5 6 7 8 9 10 11
WORK FOR FREE

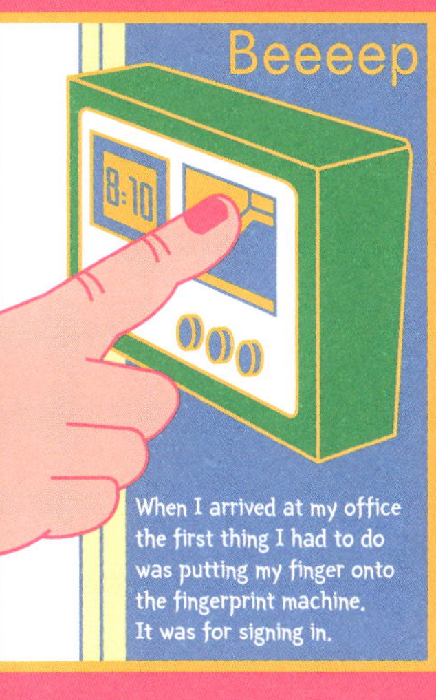

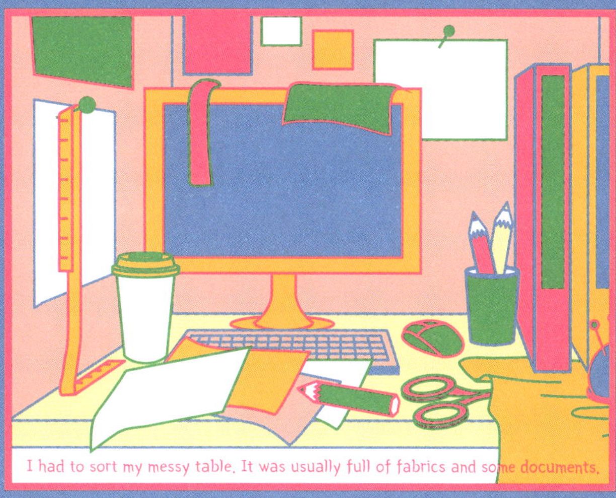

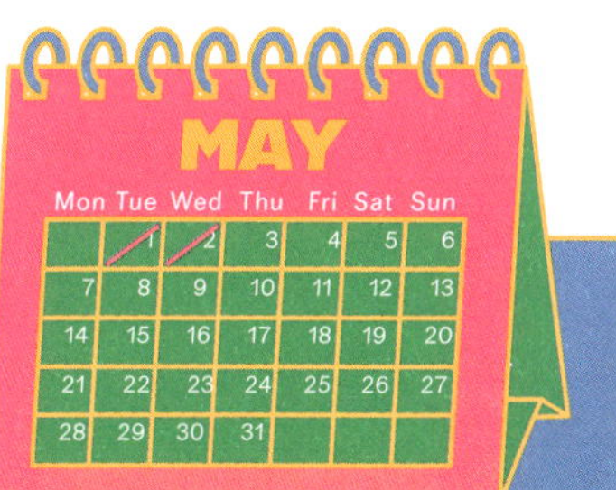

Sometimes, we had a morning meeting with all the designers and my boss.

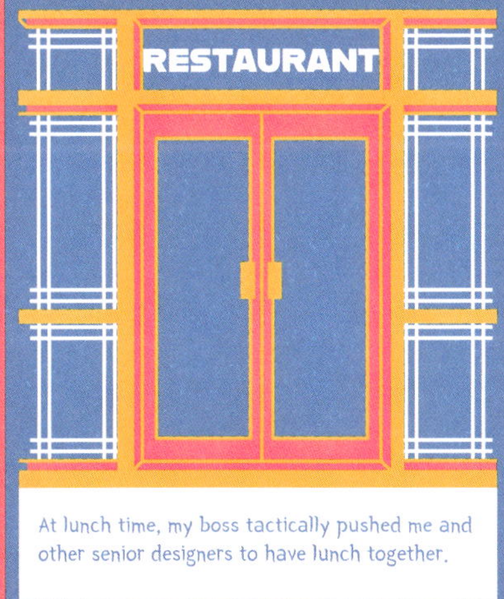

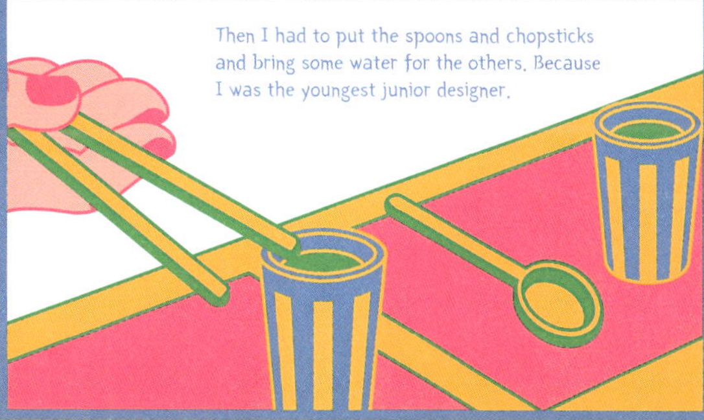

What it's like being a junior fashion designer in South Korea

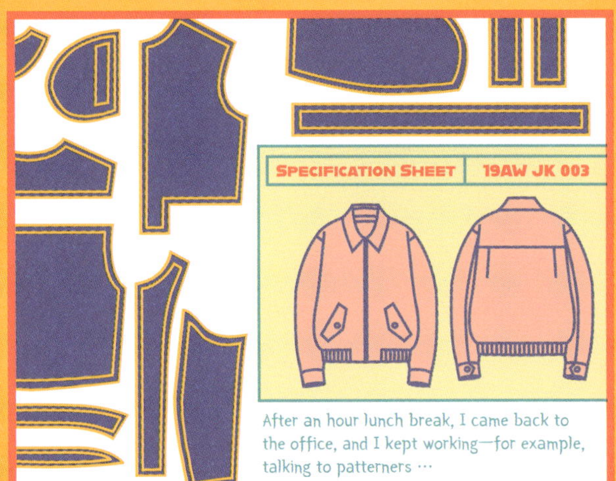

After an hour lunch break, I came back to the office, and I kept working—for example, talking to patterners …

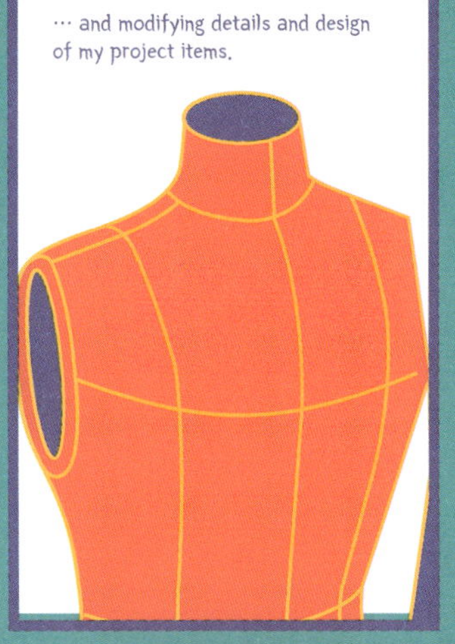

… and modifying details and design of my project items.

Almost everyday I needed to meet with outsource companies.

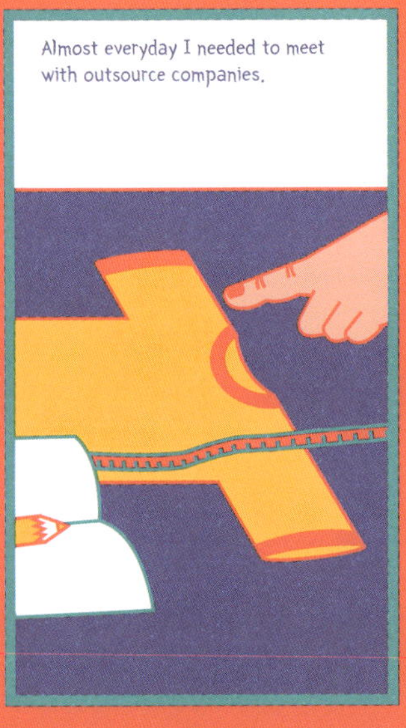

And we had to prepare our product show every two months.

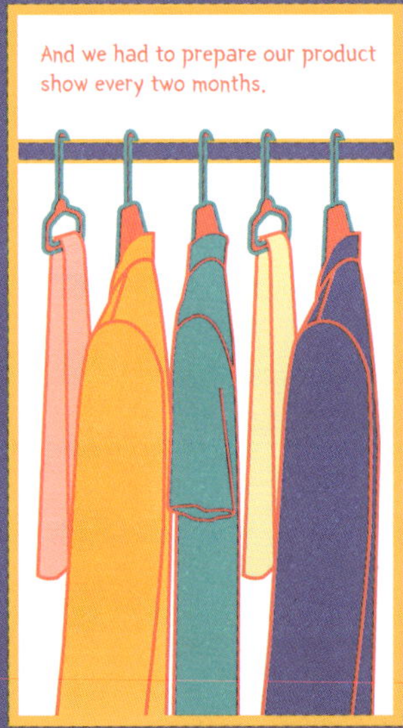

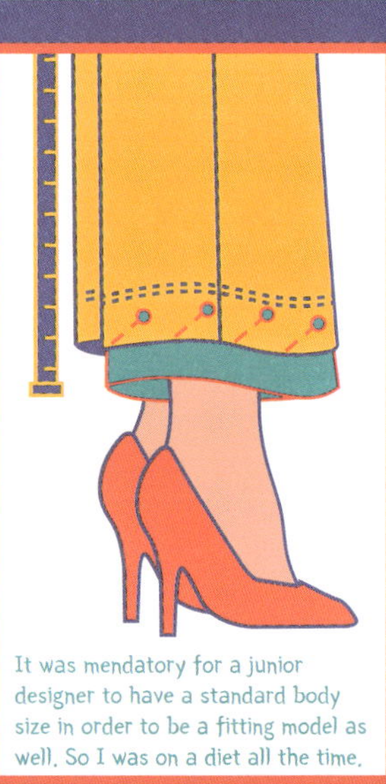

It was mendatory for a junior designer to have a standard body size in order to be a fitting model as well. So I was on a diet all the time.

Also I had worked like a secretary for my boss and the other senior designers. When they wanted to have some coffee, I brought it for them.

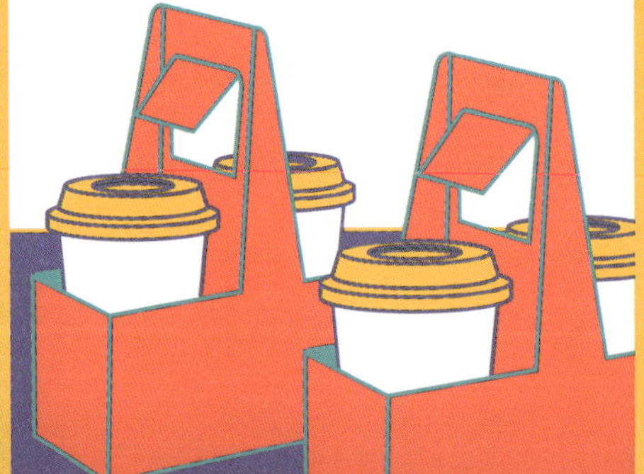

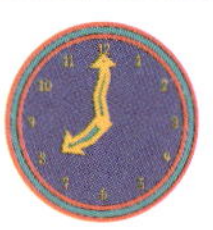

It was almost impossible to leave on time. The finishing time is officially at 6:30 pm but no one was able to leave at that time. And of course you wouldn't get paid for the overtime working, 'cause there is a fixed monthly salary defined by law.

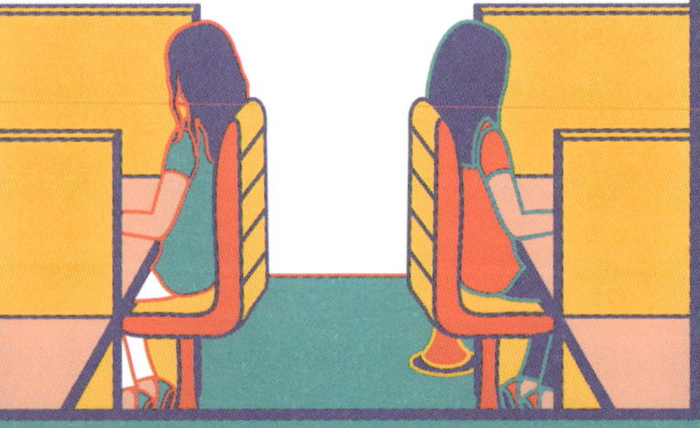

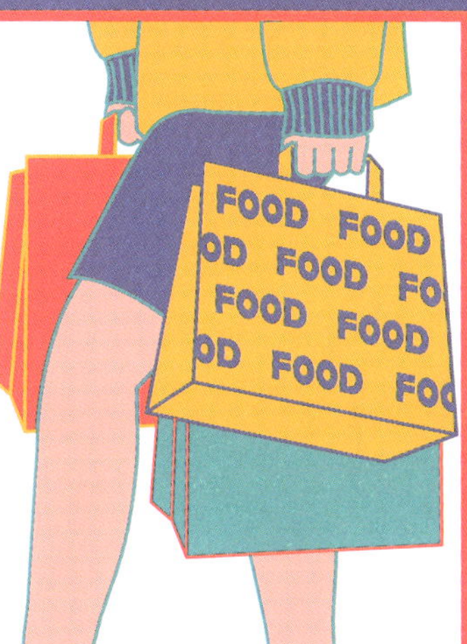

So when we had to work past 9pm, I had to pick some take out food from a restaurant for the senior designers and my boss. I actually liked this time because it was the only time that I could have my own free time while walking outside a bit and getting some fresh air.

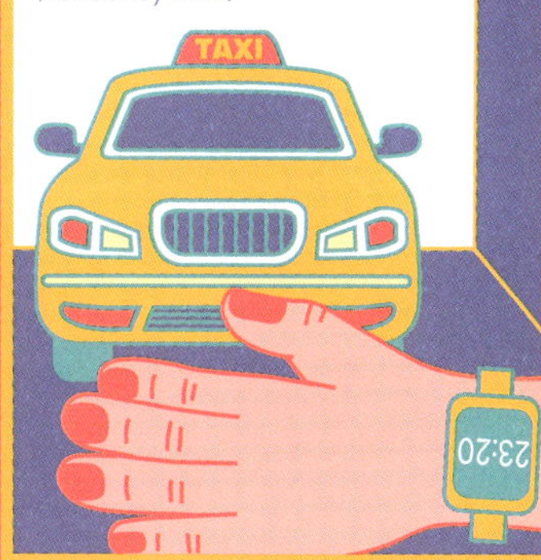

I usually left the office around 11 pm, because my boss wasn't leaving earlier. And I was not allowed to leave before him, even though I had already finished my work.

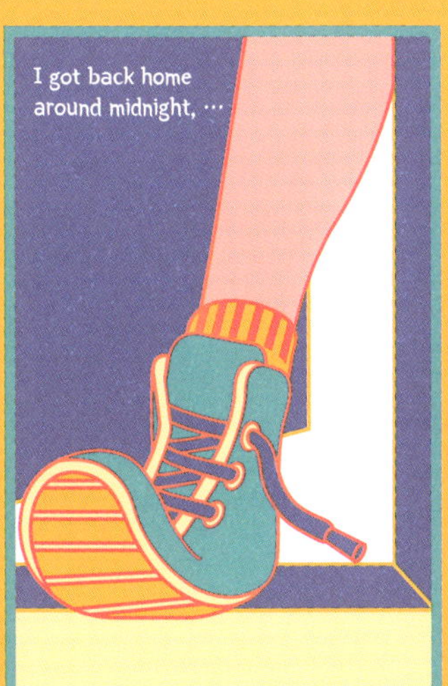

I got back home around midnight, ⋯

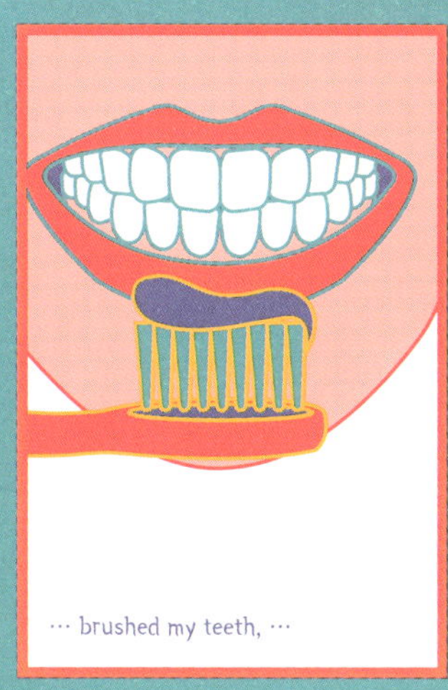

⋯ brushed my teeth, ⋯

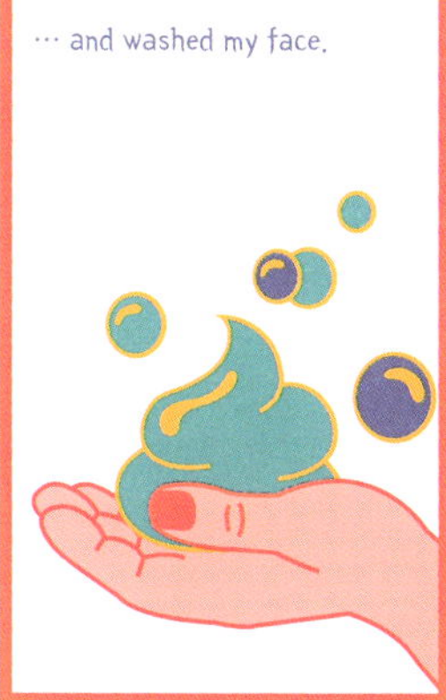

⋯ and washed my face.

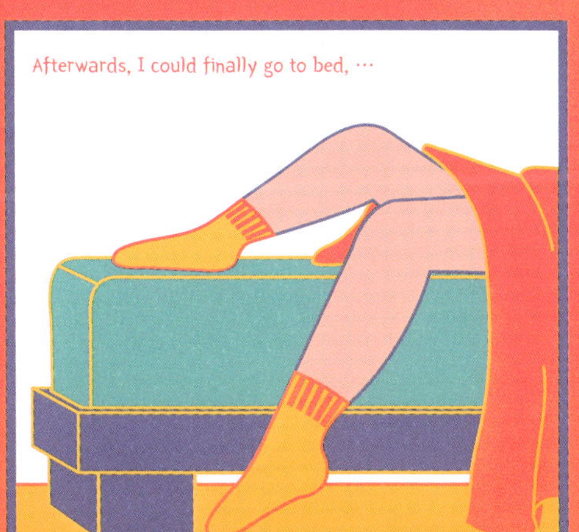

Afterwards, I could finally go to bed, ⋯

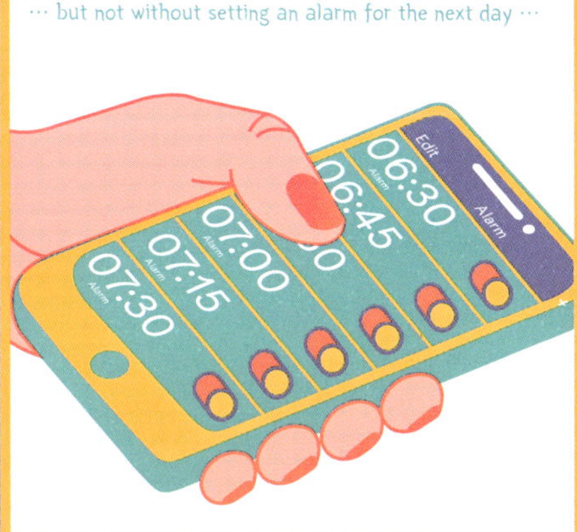

⋯ but not without setting an alarm for the next day ⋯

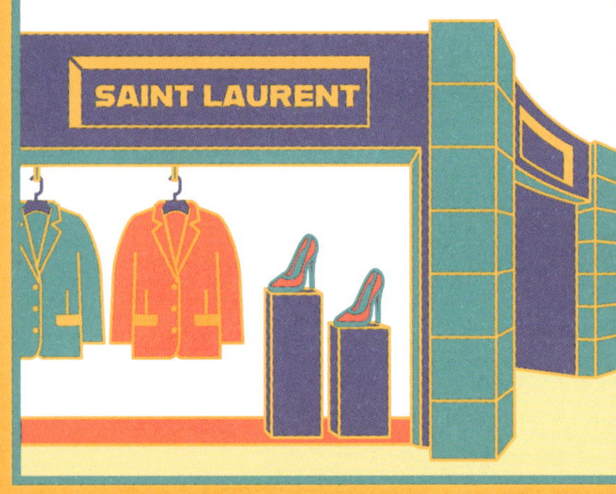

I had to do market research during the weekend as a "homework". So, I went to department stores with high fashion brands every two weeks …
SAINT LAURENT

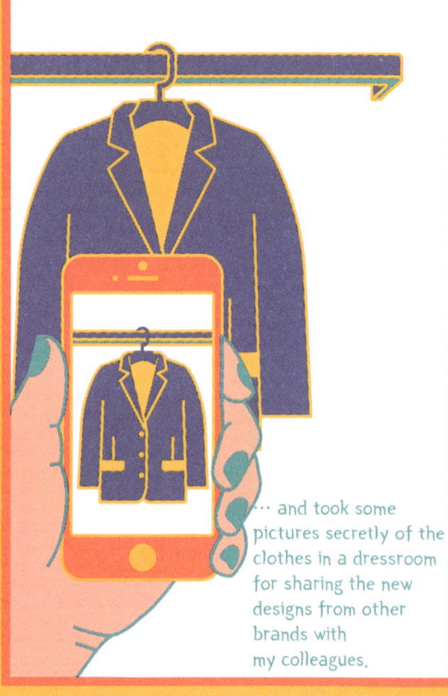

… and took some pictures secretly of the clothes in a dressroom for sharing the new designs from other brands with my colleagues.

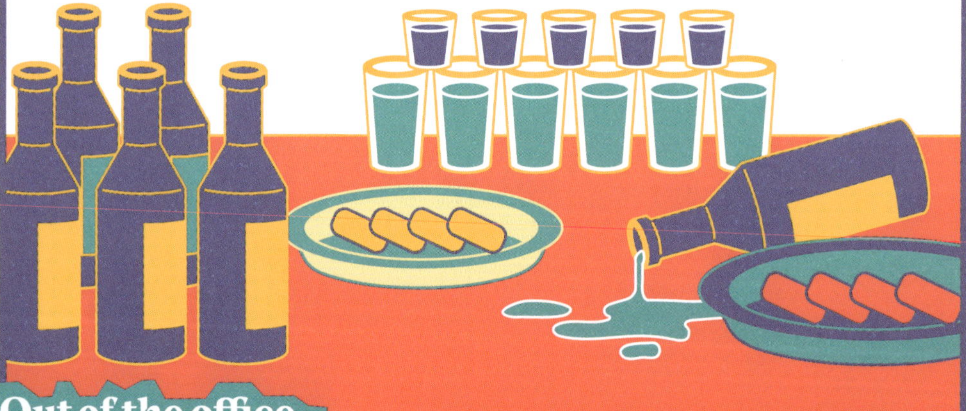

A company dinner, called "Hoesik", was also an extension of work. All the employees were expected to attend although their attendance was often passive and uncomfortable. My boss usually forced me to drink excessively and it was difficult to refuse the order.
Out of the office

I was really happy to be a fashion designer at first because it was my old dream. I was fully motivated and ambitious but the absurd working system took me down soon. It was one of the busiest, most stressful times of my life and I burnt out as a result.

Many Korean companies expect designers to come up with new and flashy ideas but they don't offer them any time to restore their energy and creativity. On top of that, the designers are demanded to show their passion and sacrifice for the company. It's quite ironic. But unfortunately, that is just the way it is in many Korean companies. One example of that is the overtime working culture which we call "Yegeun (야근)." Many employees in Korea are expected to work overtime regularly which is regarded as a sign of passion. Additionally, due to the hierarchy in the workplace, it's often frowned upon to leave the office before your boss has left——even though your tasks for the day are all done. On top of that, you don't get any compensation for those hours. It's definitely exploitation, but no one ever complains——they just conform to it.

We always had very tight deadlines and too few employees to handle it. It put the workers in a hysterical state all the time. I found it really hard to get out of my bed every morning and I often had this thought: "If I get into an accident on my way to the office, I wouldn't need to go to work."

South Korea has the disgrace of having the highest suicide rate among OECD countries. Many Korean media stations report about these issues regularly. But the laws for workers remain unchanged. Many Korean designers are still sacrificing their time, physical and mental health to create profits for their companies. When young Korean designers finally step into the workfield that they dreamed of, the first thing they are faced with are the absurd systems and practices of many Korean companies which makes them frustrated.

They are still dreaming about having work-life balance, but it is often far from being obtainable.

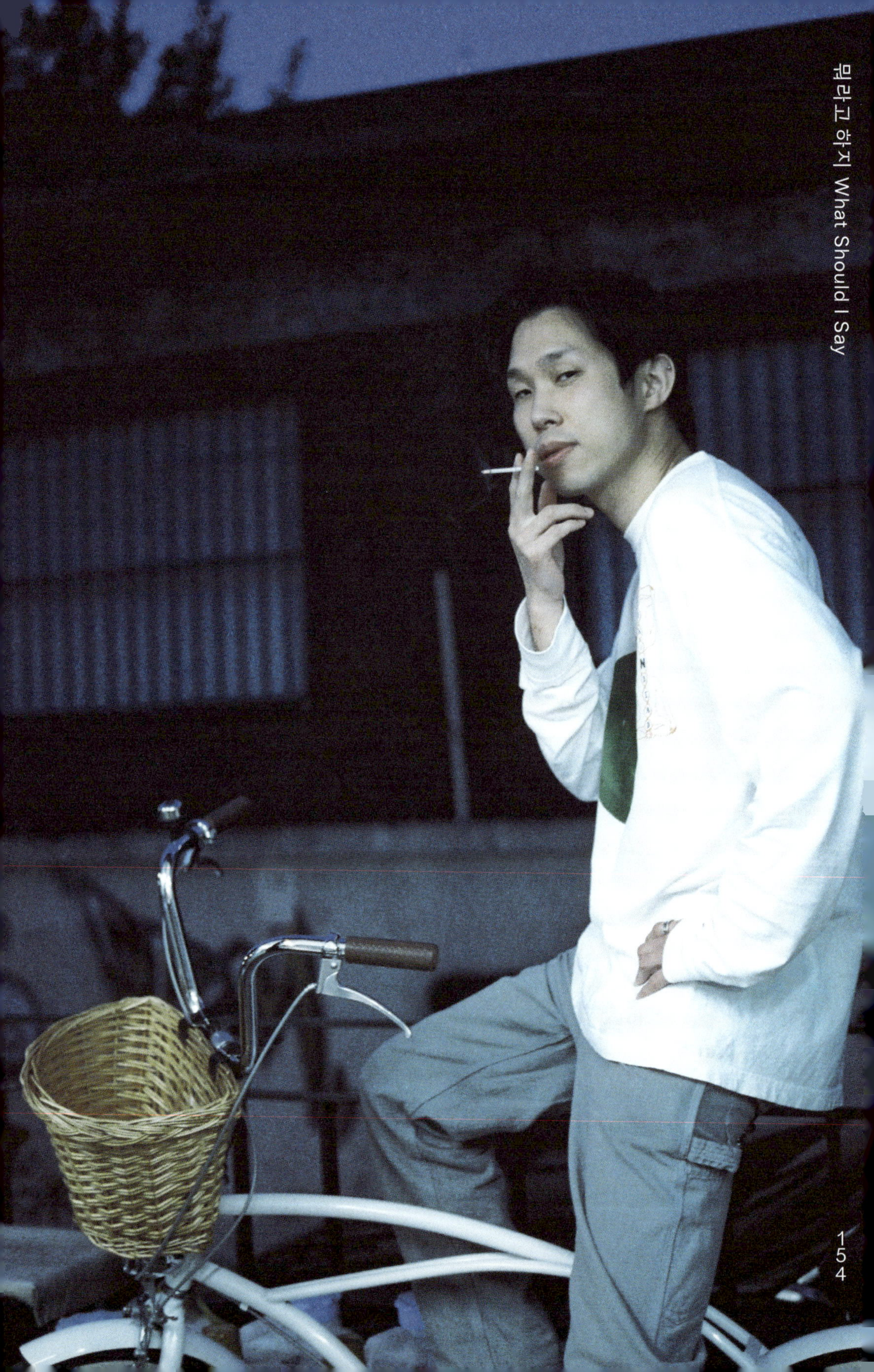
뭐라고 하지 What Should I Say

Working to survive

Interview with Woojae Lee

Interview | Pictures: Omid Fröhlich

CAN YOU TELL US A BIT ABOUT YOURSELF?

My name is Woojae. I'm 31 years old by the Korean age system and 29 years if you count via the international system. I'm a photographer and an illustrator. Therefore my main work is creating images. But it hasn't always been like that, I used to repair motorcycles for some time. Back then I didn't have any relation with the artistic scene, but I was already interested in visual media. That's why I went to the PaTI university (Paju Typography Institute). There I focused on photography and art, which I continued working in ever since.

WHO INSPIRED YOU LATELY?

The people who inspired me recently are Markus and Omid, as well as the studio members who I'm working with. I've been working here for six years now. I feel that six years is neither a short nor a long time. But I also think that there is still more for me to learn and stuff that I can get better at. When I look at how my superiors are constantly working and improving it also motivates me to develop my skills. I also gained some new insight on production methods and professionalization from you two (Markus and Omid). So all of these different people inspire me, to do my work well.

There is nothing in particular. Honestly, I didn't invest that much in studying the theory of photography or techniques during uni like reading some specialized books and applying that knowledge in my process. I don't have this kind of expertise. I'm just working in quite a simple way. Like, trying to capture the image that came to my mind, just drawing the idea that I had, or taking pictures of my favorite motives. I'm not charging my work with any special meaning, but just deal with what I like and what I'm interested in creating.

HOW DO YOU GET OVER OBSTACLES IN YOUR DESIGN PROCESS?

My main obstacle is often a lack of knowledge or if the work is not for myself but for a client. In the latter case the problem often boils down to miscommunication and misunderstanding of what the client really wants. It's kind of obvious but I would say, I'm only interested in what I feel interested in. Therefore I sometimes find it hard to get behind someone else's ideas. This often results an me being concerned during the process. But so far it worked out———me and my clients were both satisfied with the outcomes I produced. Even though I wrap up my work quite satisfyingly, I'm often worried. For example I worry that I have nothing in common with my clients or our ideas don't match up. Other times I can't come up with any fresh ideas due to my lack of knowledge. That's the thing: I have to google the fundamental things constantly in order to finish my work. When it comes to photography, there are some books about it, and they inspire me to get new ideas, by checking out the way the other photographers took their pictures. When it comes to drawing, I often get ideas by looking at art books. Luckily, it usually ends up the direction that I wanted to go, so it is fine. Anyway, reading a lot of books is my answer on how to overcome obstacles in my creative process.

WHAT DO YOU DO FOR RELAXATION?

Well, I do like drinking. I'm always up for drinking alcohol. I even started brewing my own beer. I've been doing that for six years by now. I also like to go to art museums, digging at record stores, or listening to music in a club is also great. And of course meeting friends. Overall nothing special. I usually spend my time with music, some visual works, and friends.

Because of my photography and art career I often draw satisfaction from my work. But next to the internal satisfaction there is also the external. As you know, people share their work through social media these days. So when people like my work on social media, it creates these short pleasure moments. I usually post my projects from work there. That creates the additional benefit that I can vibe-check if I'm going in the right direction. Trusting in my intuition is still the more important, but for additional feedback I find social media quite help-ful. That and of course asking for the opinion of my friends.

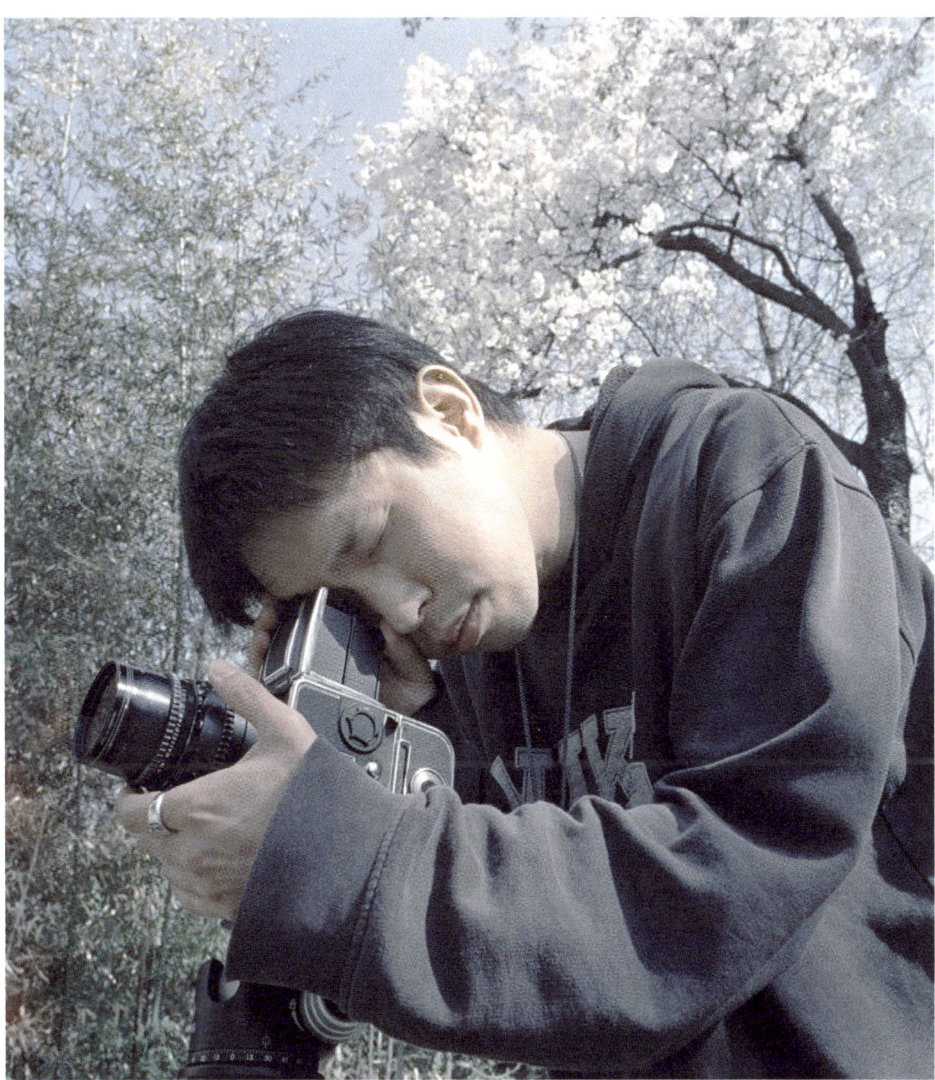

So when people like my work on social media, it creates these short pleasure moments

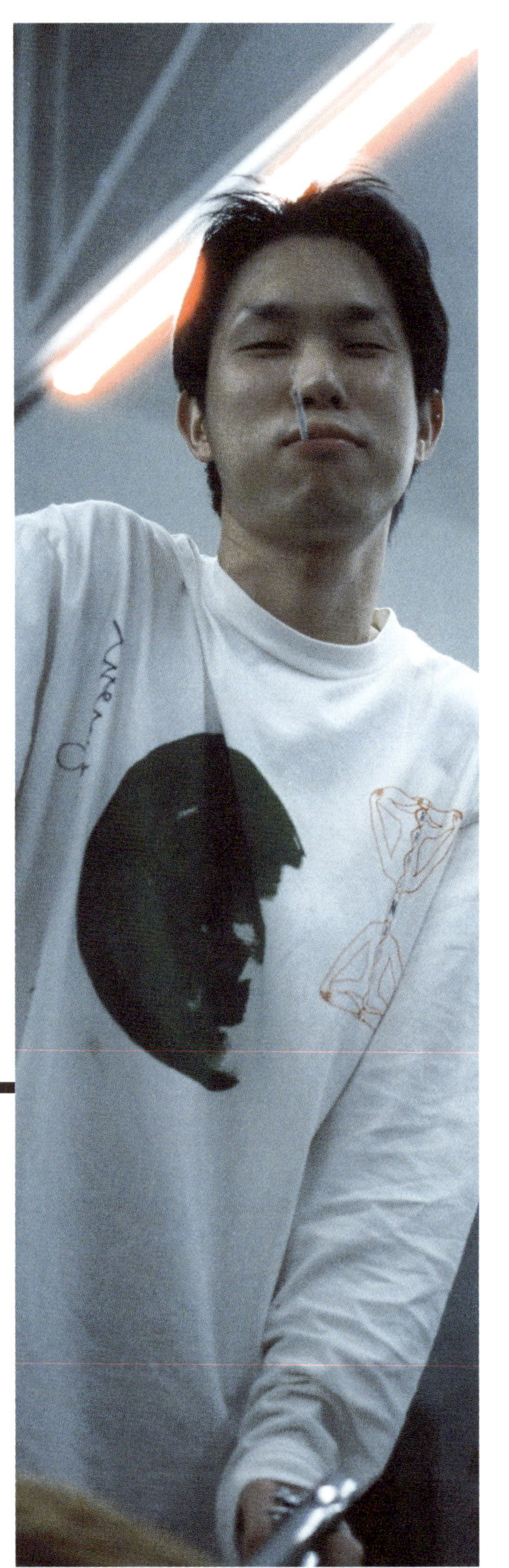

Building up confidence and faith in myself and my work is an issue. There are also other concerns like the 'fear-of-starving-to-death-due-to-my-drawings-being-bad.' Of course it would probably be better to not think about it and just focus on my art. But I wasn't born into a rich family, so I have to work hard to earn a living for myself. Of course even people that were born into rich families need to work from time to time. But the dangers and repercussions of failing in your job are a lot lower. So working to survive is basically why I work, and asking people if I go into the right direction with my work is how I do it. Anyway, I'm happy that I'm gaining more self-confidence recently.

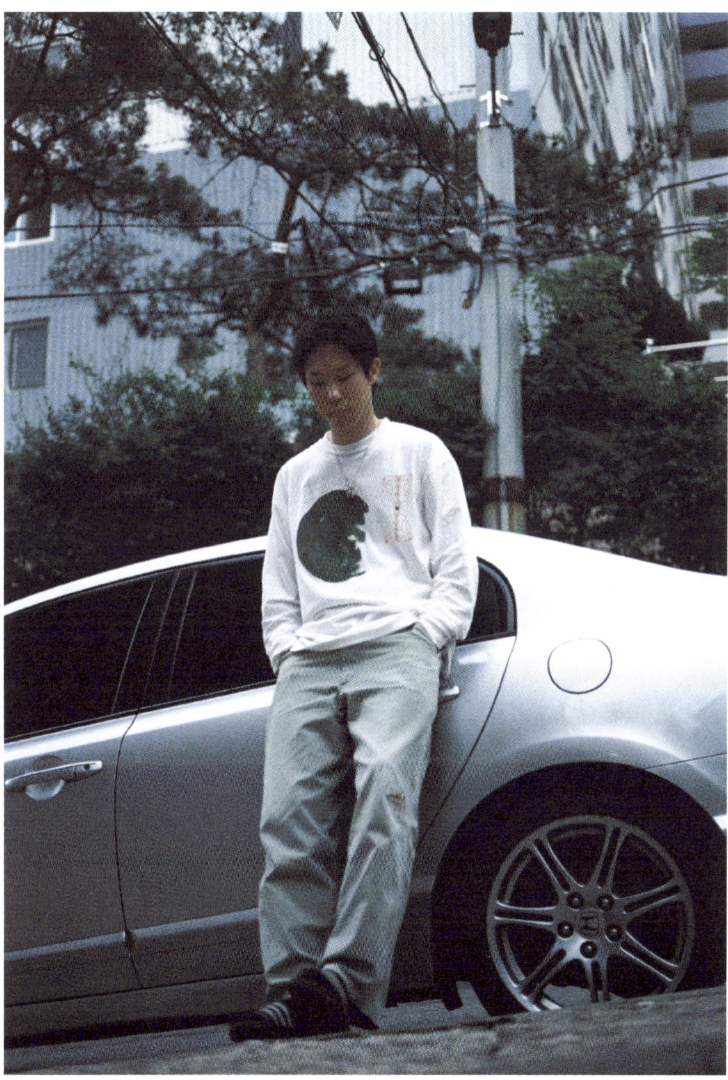

MY DESK IS

Designers and creatives about their workspace and their daily routines

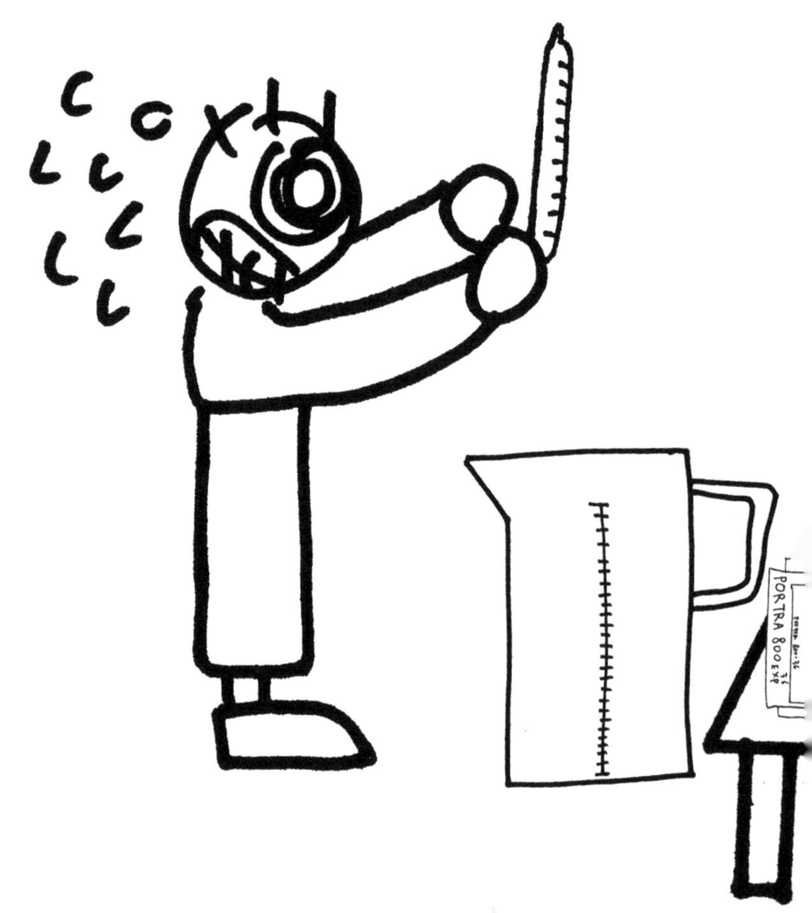

Pictures & Statements: by the respective designers themselves | Illustration: Woojae Lee

MY CASTLE

imacon
iso propanol
JOBO AUTOLAB 1500
MultiTank Tank system 1500
chemie/chemical
Rotation:
Film-kapazität
ILFORD MULTIGRADE
PAPER DEVELOPER
REVELATEUR PAPIER
PAPIERENTWICKLER
REVELADOR PARA PAPEL
1 LITRE
kodak Professional
Köln.
Juli 2005
S.F series
Dom!
kodak koda
E 100
120
ISO 100
11/2021
kodak kodak

SEUNGHUN

저는 밤에 일 하는 것을 좋아해서 보통 밤에 일 하고 아침 4~5시에 잠자리에 들어요 · 그런 다음 낮에는 회의를 하거나 주짓수를 해요 · 저는 딱히 정해진 스케줄이 없고 꽤 자유롭습니다 · 그래서 주말, 평일이든 상관 없어요 · 하지만 이게 건강에 좋지 않다고 생각해요 ·

I love to work at night, so I usually work during night-time. I go to bed at 4 or 5 in the morning. Then during the day I have meetings, doing Jujitsu etc. I really don't have a fixed schedule. I am available—it doesn't matter which day it is: weekend, weekdays—I don't care. But I think it is not good for my health.

Seunghun's pottery studio

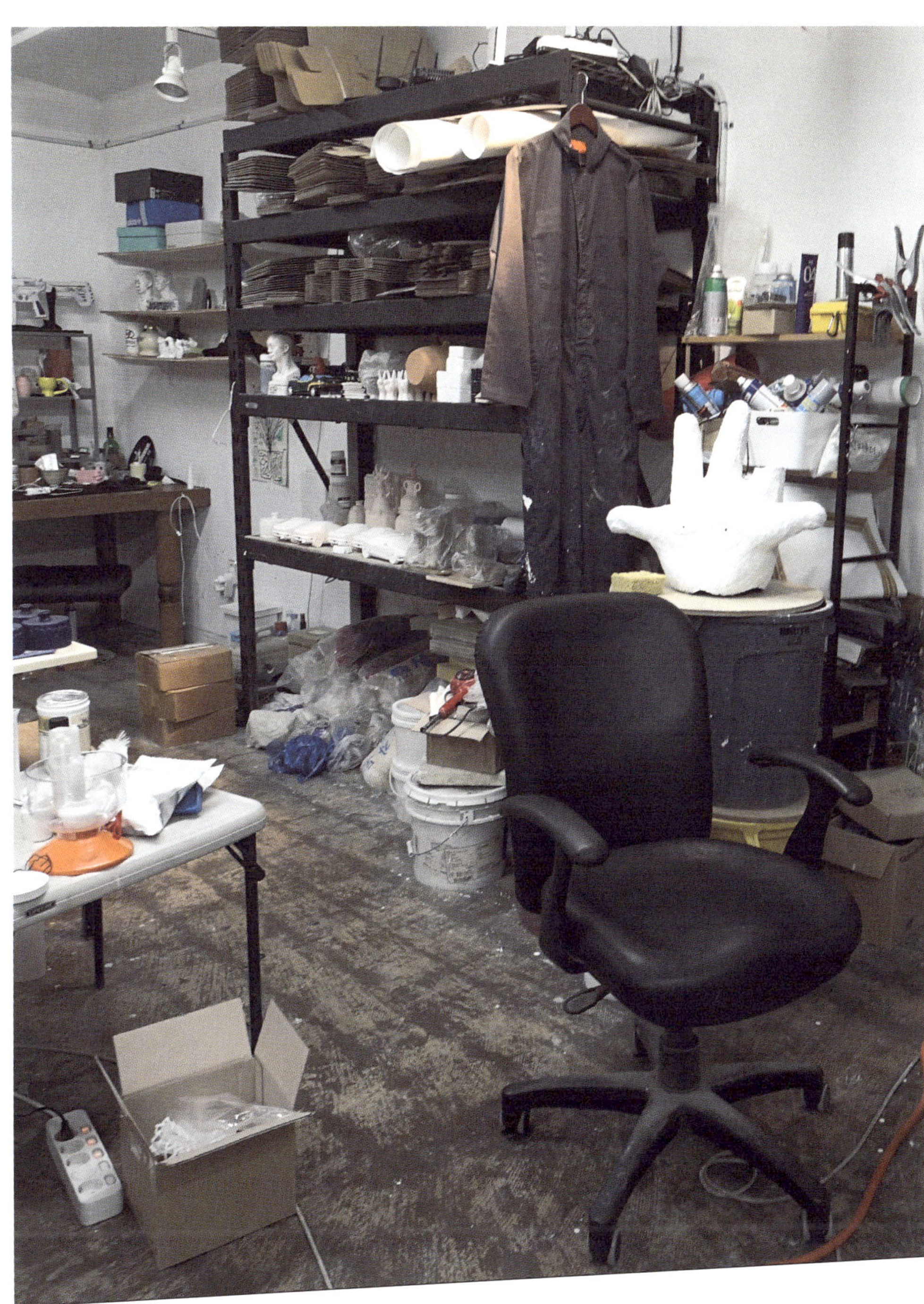

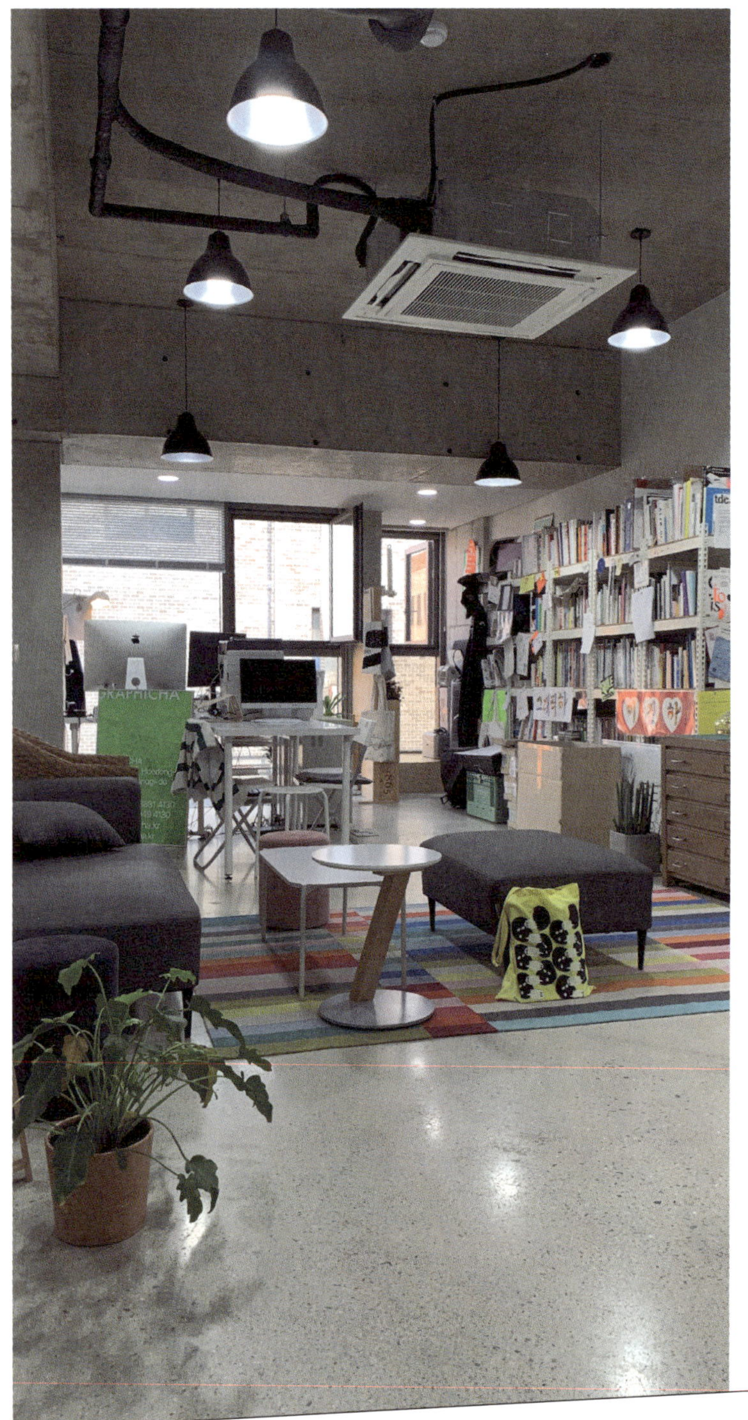

Kunha's office space

It's hard to go out and do something due to the pandemic, so I just spend my time working. Sometimes going for workout or taking a walk. That's all.

KUNHA

팬더믹으로 인해 밖에 나가서 뭔가를하기가 어려워서 주로 일을 하며 시간을 보내고있어요 . 그 외에는 가끔씩 운동을하러 나가거나 산책을합니다 . 그게 전부예요 .

평일에는 비비유 스튜디오에 일하러 가야해서 일어나서 샤워를하고
서울에서 파주로 운전하고 가요 . 거기가 제가 일 하는 곳입니다 . 보통 일이
끝나면 집으로 돌아가서 저녁을 먹고 집을 청소합니다 . 그렇지 않으면 제
작업과 외주작업을 합니다 . 그리고 자유 시간이 나면 운동을해요 . 그 뒤
저녁을 먹은 후에는 잠을 자러 가요 . 흔하진 않지만 가끔 주말에도 할 일이
많으면 계속 일을 할때도 있어요 . 그렇지 않은 주말엔 친구들과 음악을
듣습니다 . 왜냐하면 제 주변에 디제이인 친구들이 꽤 많아서요 . 그래서인지
저희는 자주 파티에 가곤 해요 . 그 외에도 재밌는곳은 많아요 . 친구의
스튜디오나 집 , 혹은 클럽 , 아니면 레코드가게에 가서 디깅하는 것 . 그게
다예요 .

WOOJAE

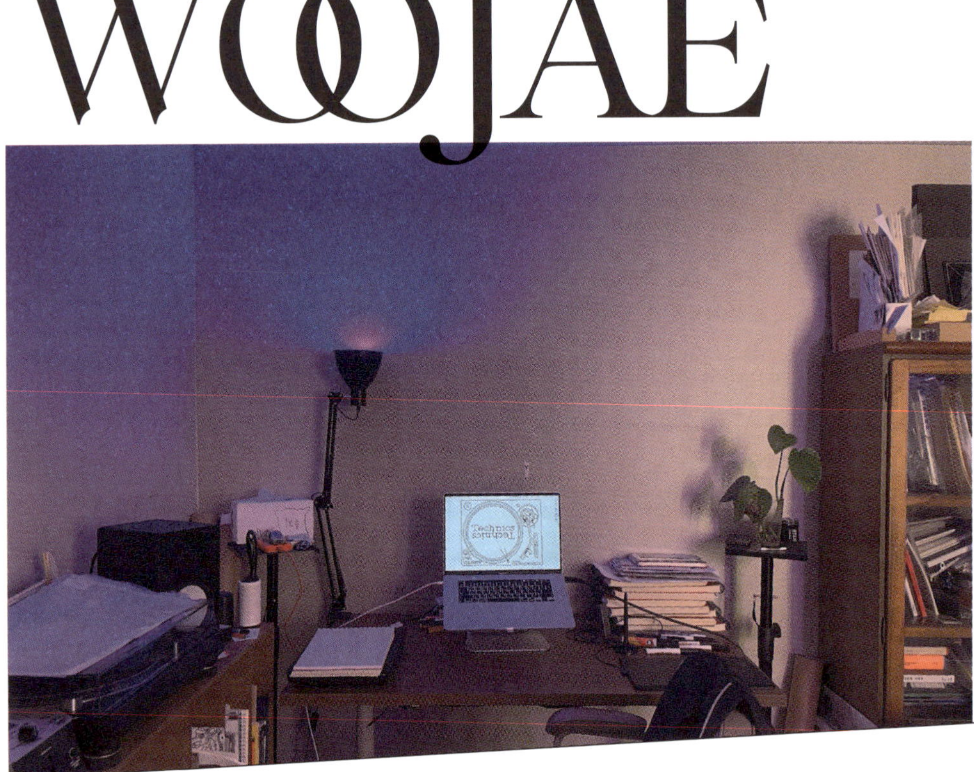

Woojae's desk

I have to travel to the studio during weekdays. I wake up, shower, and drive from Seoul to Paju. After my work is done, I drive back home usually. I have dinner at home and clean my house. In addition I do my own projects and contract work. During my spare time I workout as well. During the weekend I sometimes have to keep working—it's not often, only when I have a lot of work to do. Otherwise I listen to music with friends of mine—because I have quite a lot of friends who are DJs. That way there are often parties that I can join. In general there are many places to go to for having fun. Either going to a friend's studio or house, going to a club, or digging through records in a record store. That's it.

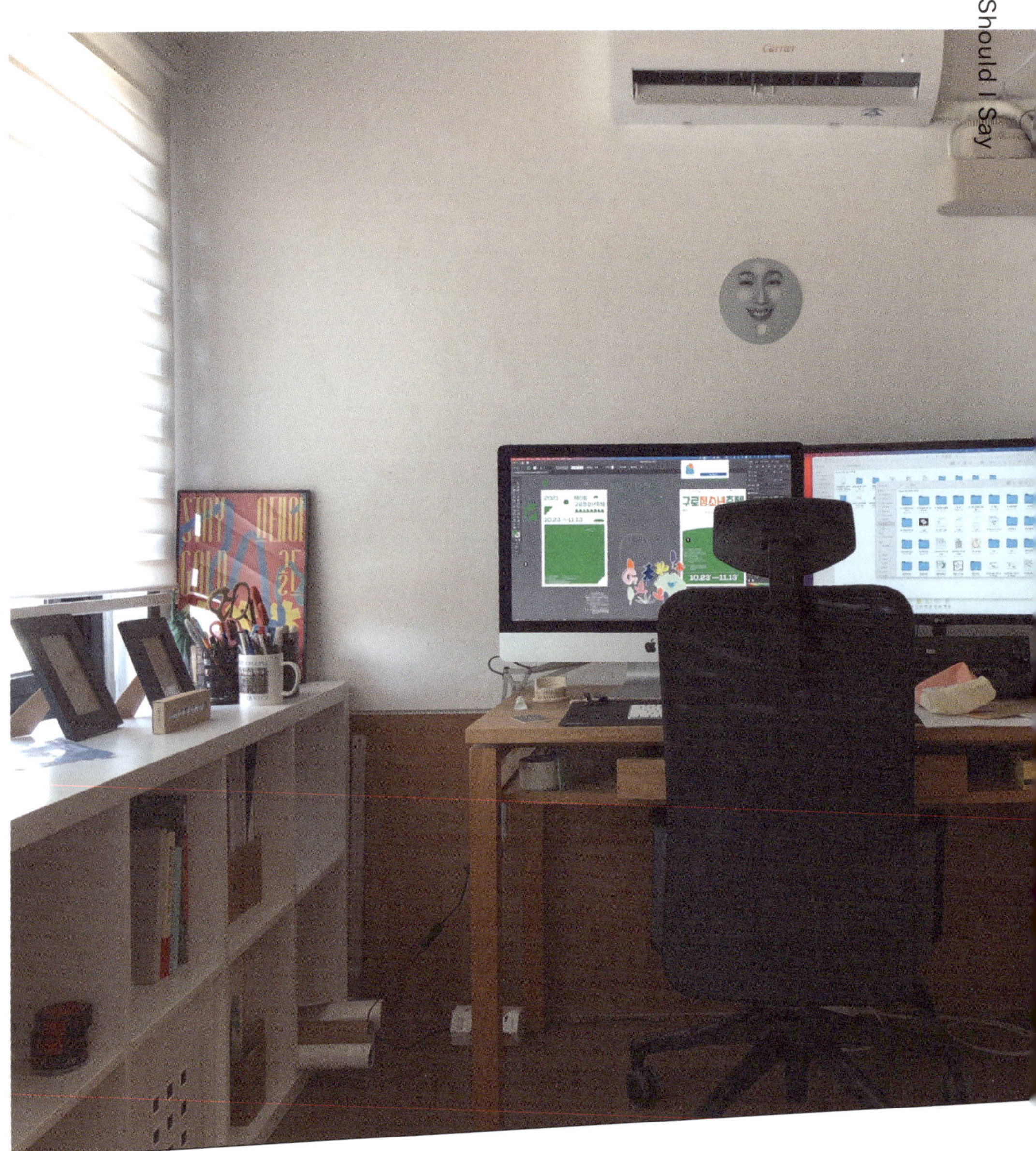

Pakdo's workspace

PAKDO

프리랜서로서 일 하는 것은 일상적인 루틴을 갖는걸 어렵게 합니다 · 하지만 더 많은 경험들은 당신이 그 일들을 잘 처리할수 있는 방법을 배울 수 있게해요 ·

Working, as a freelancer it is hard to have routines because the work doesn't rest. But with more and more experience you learn more and more to deal with it.

My life before the Corona? I think it was pretty similar. The only difference is, that now I'm not able to go to a party after work. Otherwise it is pretty much the same. Because I work until late during the week I don't really have that much personal life since I've moved to Korea due to work. I go to work, and than I come back home—that became my routine here. On weekends I try to see some friends of mine and try to have a good time with them. Or I read a book. I think that's it. A very normal and unremarkable routine.

JIEUN

제생각엔 코로나 이전의 제삶은 지금과 꽤 비슷한거 같아요 . 유일한 차이점은 지금은 퇴근후 파티에 갈수 없다는것 . 그것빼곤 그전 생활과 거의 동일해요 . 왜냐하면 주중에는 보통 늦게까지 일하다 보니 제 개인생활이 거의 없어요 . 출근하고 퇴근하는것 , 한국에서 직장을 다니면서부터 그게 여기서의 제 평일 동안의 일상 전부가 되었어요 . 그래도 주말에는 친구들을 만나려하고 또 그들과 좋은시간을 보내려 해요 , 아니면 책을 읽거나 . 하지만 그게 전부예요 . 특별할것도 없는 아주 평범한 일상이죠 .

Jieun's desk at her office

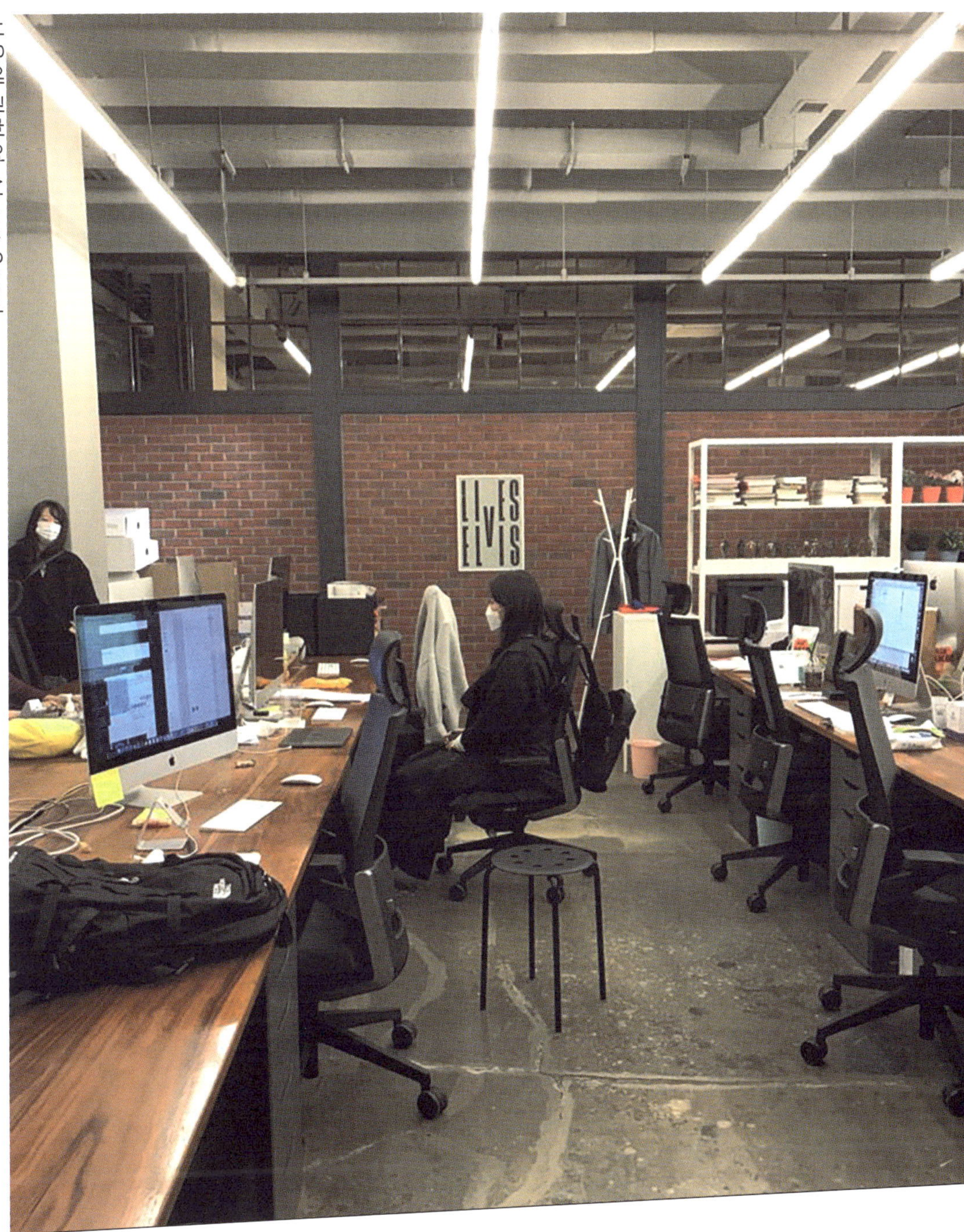

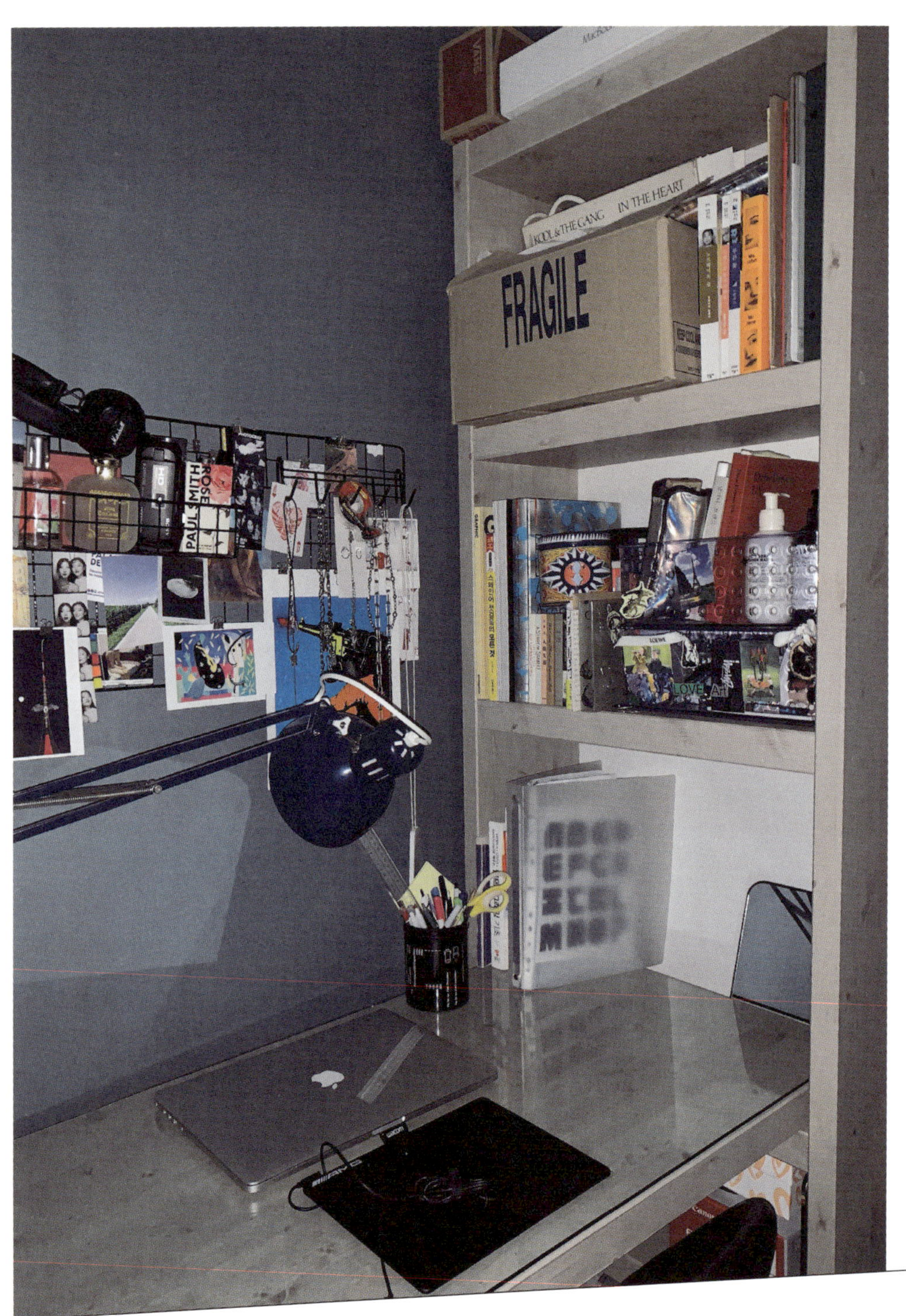

Yuri's desk and the desk lamp that plays a crucial role in her daily routine.

YURI

밤이든 낮이든, 저는 일할 때마다 내 방 천장의 불을 끄는 걸 선호해요 · 대신에, 항상 책상 조명을 켜놓아요 · (책상 조명은 이케아에서 샀어요) 믿거나 말거나, 이게 저를 더 자신감있게 해주기도 하고, 또 집중할 수 있게 도와주거든요 · 제 생각엔 이건 그냥 제 일상루틴을 넘어서 일종의 의식같아요 ·

Doesn't matter if it's day or night: I prefer turning off the ceiling light in my room whenever I'm working. Instead, I always turn on the desk lamp—which I bought at IKEA.

Believe it or not: It makes me more confident and helps me to concentrate better on work. It is a kind of ritual—I think—beyond just being a daily routine.

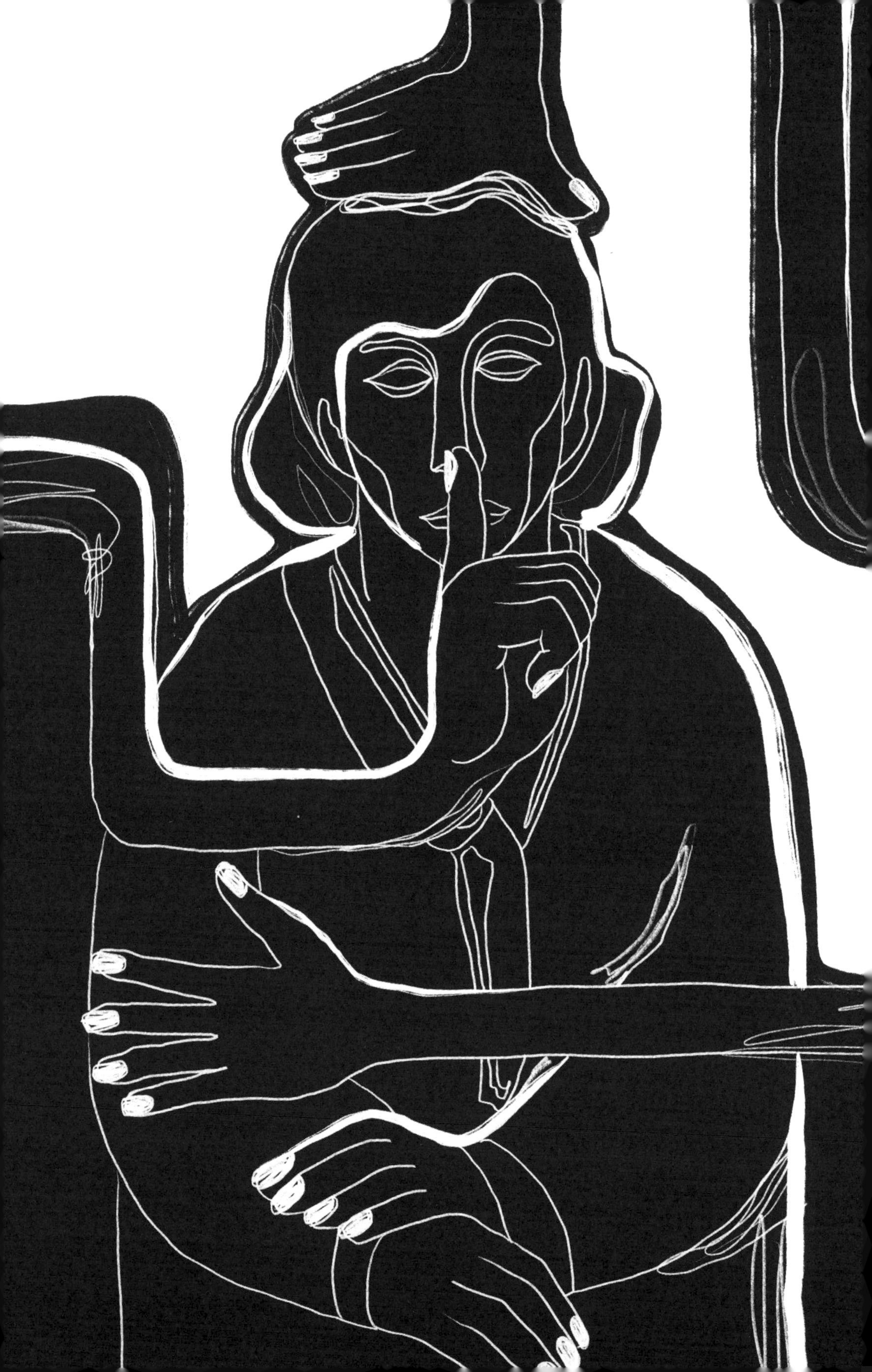

FEMINISTS WHO MUST NOT BE NAMED

Words: Youjin Kim & David Wiesner (Co-Writer) | Illustrations: Youjin Kim

Feminism refers to a theory or movement that should strengthen women's rights and identity in society. It aims for gender-equality which is not a given in most (if not all) countries where a male-centered ideology is still predominant in defining the role of men and women. In a broader sense, feminism fights against societal and personal discrimination based on gender in its many forms and intersectional appearances.

However, feminism in South Korea has a very negative reputation. The movement is often perceived as a "female chauvinism," the rejection of men in general or even hatred against men. This position is widespread and can be found especially amongst young Korean men. As a result, anti-feminist rhetoric and behavior is on the rise. Patriarchy is deeply engrained into Korean tradition and influences many everyday interactions. Because these minor and major discriminations seem to be the norm, many Koreans are reluctant towards change—if it's normal, it must be so for a reason, and therefore be correct. Additionally patriarchy is anchored and legitimized through Confucianism—the predominant philosophy in South Korea for centuries. Confucianism aimed to order the whole universe and determine a place for every member in society. In this system, women are assumed to be inferior to men. This world view created many tangible barriers for women. In my parents' generation, most women didn't have the opportunity to get higher education. Their duty as women was to stay home, do the housework, and take care of their children.

These days women can work and earn money just like men. But this state is far from equality. It's more like additional duties have been piled on top, with the patriarchal hierarchy still intact: Women have to work while still being solely responsible for doing the housework. Additionally, women are skipped over for job promotions—those still go mostly to men. To dissolve this schizophrenic situation, wherein women are simultaneously expected to do more and less than men, they are pushed to choose between either following a career or having children—practically forcing them back into the established roles. With many women now receiving the same education as men, the validity of the old claims of inequal capability becomes harder to believe. As a result, more and more women become aware and dissatisfied with such discrimination.

One source for the increasing awareness for feminist issues came through the inception of the radical feminist website called 'Megalia.' Many young women who experienced misogyny and discrimination at home, work, and in public learned to frame their experiences through the lens of feminism—all through 'Megalia.' Before, feminism was not a well known term in Korea. But the more women pointed out the unfair conditions caused by the patriarchy, the more backlash they received by men. These men labeled themselves as anti-feminists. They managed to change the discourse in such a way, that 'feminism' is perceived negative. The anti-feminists claim that men are at a disadvantage compared to women because of the mandatory military service and competitive job market. They also insist that they do not benefit from the patriarchal structures like their parents did. But instead of rejecting the patriarchal structures altogether, they just want to go back to an imagined better past. Feminist achievements towards more equality stand in the way of that goal. And as the actual reasons for the decreased quality of life are far more difficult to tackle, these men resort to cowardly harassing women Online as well as offline.

One prominent example was the treatment of three-times gold medal winner An San. An anti-feminist mob accused her of being a feminist (used here in a derogative way) based on her short hair cut and the trivia that she went to a women's university. For archery, there are no regulations on haircuts. Practical concerns are probably the only ones influencing how an athlete wears their hair. An San herself never stated being a feminist publicly, it was just assumed because some feminists wear short hair, but it is not an identity marker. More likely, is was because long hair is expected for women based on a certain femininity performed in Korean media. This goes to show how dangerous it still is to stray from the norm. Women get attacked by anti-feminists just by a perceived proximity to feminism. On top of the Online harassment she was met with, the mob went as far as demanding her gold medals should be revoked. So aside from the psychological damage this causes women, there can be tangible career consequences as well (In An San's case luckily her medals were not revoked): Some women have been fired from their jobs based on them having a "feminist look." This to me bears a stark resemblance of a witch hunt. The volatile mix of collectivist thinking and conservatism have created an atmosphere in which women have to be afraid to be associated to feminism. If there is a danger of being ostracized for looking like a feminist, just imagine the repercussions if you actually are a feminist. This effectively hinders long-term improvements true gender equality brings as they are overshadowed by the overwhelming backlash caused by men desperately clinging to their puny privileges.

Living in Germany now, I can tell that people's perception of feminism is very different in Korea compared to Germany. To me this stark difference is baffling and I wonder how it's possible to come to such a diverging understandings of one term. Of course, gender inequality also still remains in Germany, but at least being a feminist publicly does not entail being personally dismissed or judged negatively by others. Moreover, many German women continue raising their voices against discrimination even though much has already been achieved, considering that Germany is one of the more gender equal countries.

Since I moved to Germany, I encountered a lot less discrimination based on my gender. Unfortunately gender discrimination for me was replaced by racism. This form of discrimination was multiplied during Corona. I was given the feeling that I'm just an Asian alien, who isn't welcome in Germany. I sometimes hear insulting words directed towards me when I walk alone in the street. Some people covered their nose in a very obvious manner and bluntly stare at me right after they notice me in the subway. These micro-aggressions over time destroyed me mentally. At first I was just furious about their absurd behavior. I thought I just have to push through, that it would stop some-day. But over time I became lethargic and developed social anxiety—I simply couldn't leave my house for a while.

What really helped me during that time—next to friends and family—where activists who bravely stood up against racism. Were I lacked the strength to leave my house, they confronted discrimination. To me, they were strangers, but their actions still encouraged me. I think that is an inherent power social movements have. They not only advocate for change in a direct way, but they also give confirmation to those affected by discrimination, in a way telling them: "You are not crazy. This is absurd and wrong. You do not deserve this."

The pain discrimination causes is invisible. You can be together in a group, and a certain form of discrimination only hits you. The others won't understand what happened or why you become so outraged. It is an experience that is hard to translate if you have never been con-fronted with it. I think for that reason people not affected sometimes deny the existence of discrimination—either flat out or by saying things like "It wasn't that bad. Don't make such a fuss."

A society will always be confronted with weaker members. There is the saying that you should measure the quality of a society by how they treat their weak. Not only because the likelihood of becoming weak at some point is high. But also because humans are very depended beings to begin with. Instead of denying that fact, we should embrace it and care for each other. Humanity didn't get to the point it is at without cooperation. We should build a society wherein being weak is not a detriment. At least raising one's voice against discrimination shouldn't be met with anger, but with attention.

Inequality is a stable in human society and all the social movements looking for serious change have caused discomfort for privileged. Nothing can be achieved without struggle and therefore the fight against misogyny and patriarchal structures in South Korea continues. Korean feminists stand together in solidarity in order to build a better society. Contrary to what anti-feminists claim, those changes would ben-efit the whole society—men included. A gender war or a simple role-switch is no feminist goal.

Solidarity is the most powerful weapon for those without power. In the Korean society where feminists are not welcomed for the most part, communities of those affected start to form in order to help each other. One such group is the Feminist Designer Social Club (FDSC). The club was found by Inah Shin, Somi Kim, Yuni Ooh, and Meanyoung Yang. The four women all work in graphic design and proudly call themselves feminists. The initial reason to start this community was to address the lack of opportunities for female designers. They wanted to build the network to share information and console each other. With the community growing, a set of principles were established. Those are:

"To respect each other and pursue equal relationships no matter the age, gender identity, gender orientation, disability, nationality, color, origin, educational background, etc."
"Questions and suggestions, mistakes and failures are all welcome."

With these two simple principles, the FDSC tries to create a culture wherein women can confidently talk about their work. Allowing for questions establishes that no one has all the answers and every question is sure to help someone. To include mistakes and failures into their credo was a deliberate choice, because the pressure of leading the charge on feminism in the graphic design industry can be crushing. The more so because people that point out the need for change are often held to a higher standard (often unrealistic).

> Learning about gender-based institutionalized discrimination and the goals of feminism helped me to sort many of my own professional experiences. It means so much to hear that the discrimination one received is not just imagined. Getting outside confirmation that you were treated wrong goes a long way.

Therefore I'm very glad to have found out about this community of designers that strive towards solidarity and change.

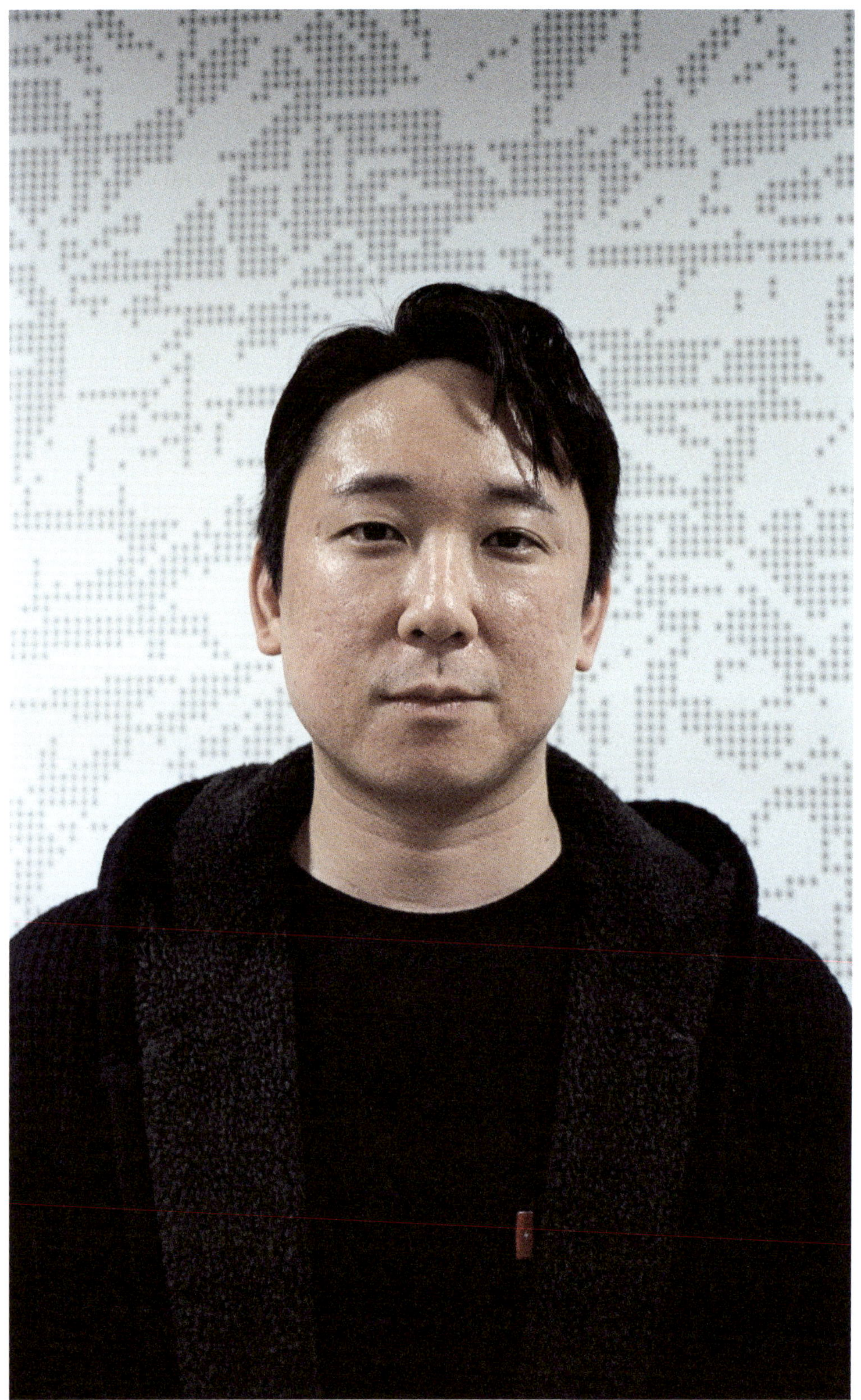

Keep going on

Interview with Kunha Lee

Interview | Pictures: Omid Fröhlich

Q: **Can you tell us a bit about yourself?**

A: My name is Kunha Lee Lee, I'm 35 years old in Korean age. I'm a graphic designer and professor for typography.

Q: **How did you end up doing what you do?**

A: I became interested in design after I visited the paper-road exhibition in Korea 2012. It was a typography exhibition about analog methods and media in the digital age. A Bunch of type designers from East Asia —— each representing a different country —— were showing ways to communicate through the medium paper. I was very impressed and since then embargoed on my way to become a graphic designer. Part of this process was acquiring a master's degree.

Q: **What inspired you lately?**

A: I can't think of anything recent. But I was influenced a lot by one of my professor, who taught me a certain attitude and way of thinking as a designer.

Q: **Can you show me some of your work that you are especially fond of, and tell me what makes it special to you?**

A: I have an affection for the graduation work of my master's degree. It was about three different fields: 'book & paper, graphic, and literature.' I did a lot of experiments with different book features at that time and I was able to figure out my own style that I wanted to pursue in the future.

Q: **How do you start your designing process (for a new design)?**

A: I don't follow a systematic approach. I prefer developing an idea fast, and fine-tune the visual outcome while talking to my clients rather than researching and collecting data.

Q: **How do you get over obstacles in your design process?**

A: I don't think there is any specific way to overcome obstacles. Just agonizing over it the whole time to find a solution is the answer. When I can't find any solution, I politely refuse to take the work from the client.

Q: **What are your daily routines?**

A: It's hard to go out and do something due to the pandemic right now. So I just spend my time working, sometimes taking a walk or working out. That's all.

Q: **What do you do for relaxation?**

A: I don't have any specific relaxation ritual. Maybe going out to drink is my way to relax. But due to the Corona regulations all bars are closing at 10 p.m.. I usually come to the workplace and drink here at the moment. Also, working on my own projects relaxes me. They are like a hobby of mine, as ideas come easy because I can do whatever I want. So when I do my own work, I try to do something that I've never done before. For example, designing a new typeface —— even though I'm not a type designer, or making a book that's related to photography. I'm trying to work in other design fields in my free time to spice things up. Because my business work is normally not broadening my horizon.

Q: **Can you tell me of something that gave you joy recently?**

A: Magazine QT —— I'm making this magazine together with my students. Because of it they asked us to design posters to celebrate a new publication of some Korean designers. I also contributed a poster design and was so happy with it, that I submitted this poster to the Tokyo TC award. Seemingly the people at Tokyo TC were also quite happy with it, so received the award. So now this poster will also be published in the accompanying book.

Q: **Can you give me some recommendations on designers?**

A: That's a hard question to answer. Well, there are a lot of different criteria depending on a chosen perspective. But I'd like to choose Jiseung Ahn who worked several years in PaTI's (Paju Typography Institute) design studio named '멋진공작소' (Meotjin Gongjakso). All the design work from PaTI goes through his hand. So I recommend him when talking about design work. One of the reasons I recommend him is, that he stays true to his own style. You see, there is this recent trend to use these strong and overemphasized visuals. But his designs are quite different to that —— maybe understated, keeping in line with PaTI's motto. I'm not saying that I don't like this recent trend —— I'm just impressed that Jiseung doesn't follow the trend and keeps going with his own style.

Q: **What do you think is a general strength of graphic designers?**

A: The strength as a graphic designer is to be able to reach into any field. It might sound cliché but design is everywhere. Even just color or

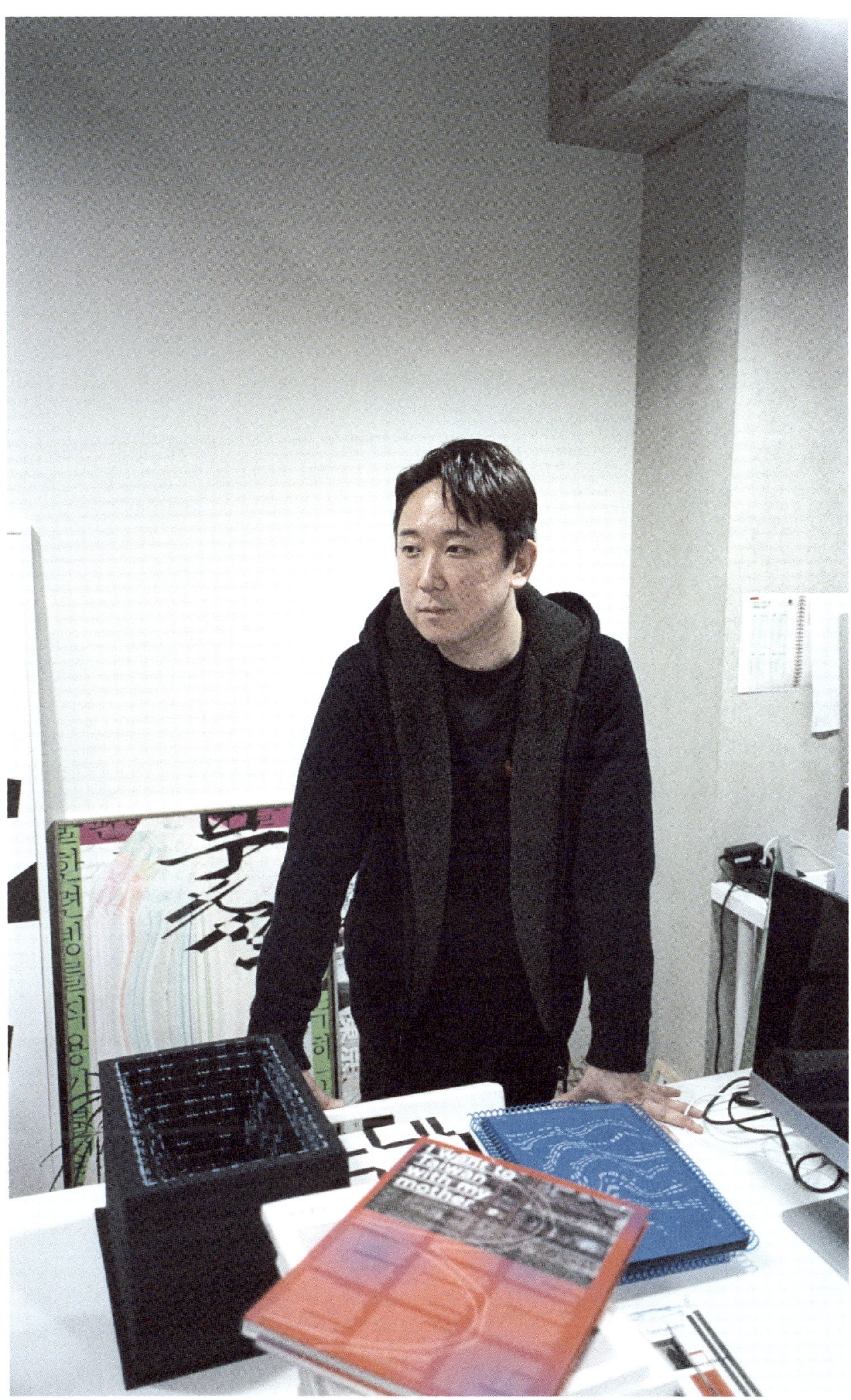
I want to
Taiwan
with my
mother

typefaces that we can see everyday are actually designed. And there is no design border which means graphic designers can design other fields too. That's why I'm designing graphic art, typefaces, and branding at the same time.

Q: **What is your biggest concern these days?**

A: I'm getting old and a lot of young people are becoming designers. They are really good and creative. In the 2000s, designers were simply categorized into good or bad, but not anymore. Contemporary design works are evaluated by how fresh or distinct they are. As a designer that is between the old and the young generation I'm concerned with how I can make use of my special position. I want to create something of my own —— something distinct. Because it would allow me to work independently as long as I want —— just by having a unique style that is tied to my name. I focus on printed books, and studied old fashioned type design, so I try to uphold the good craftsmanship that is present in these old designs. Honestly, the work of young designers nowadays is astounding and I find it hard to keep up with them. So, for a while I thought: "Do I have to pick up these trends as well in order to be compatible? Or do I just continue with what I'm already familiar with?" Neither of those options seemed like a good solution to me. So I decided to come up with my own style —— something that is neither just trendy nor traditionalistic. I think mixing these influences is good, because I noticed that sometimes the graphic designers that create these fabulous visuals don't have a good sense for picking fonts. With everything focused on expressive visuals I feel the basics get lost. I think designers should learn design principles and develop new forms by deconstructing those. However many young designers don't start with the basics, and instead build from the already deconstructed forms without understanding them.

Q: **Is there anything you want to do or try as a designer in the future?**

A: I'd like to keep going on with the analog way: Publish design books and bring these publications to bigger business.

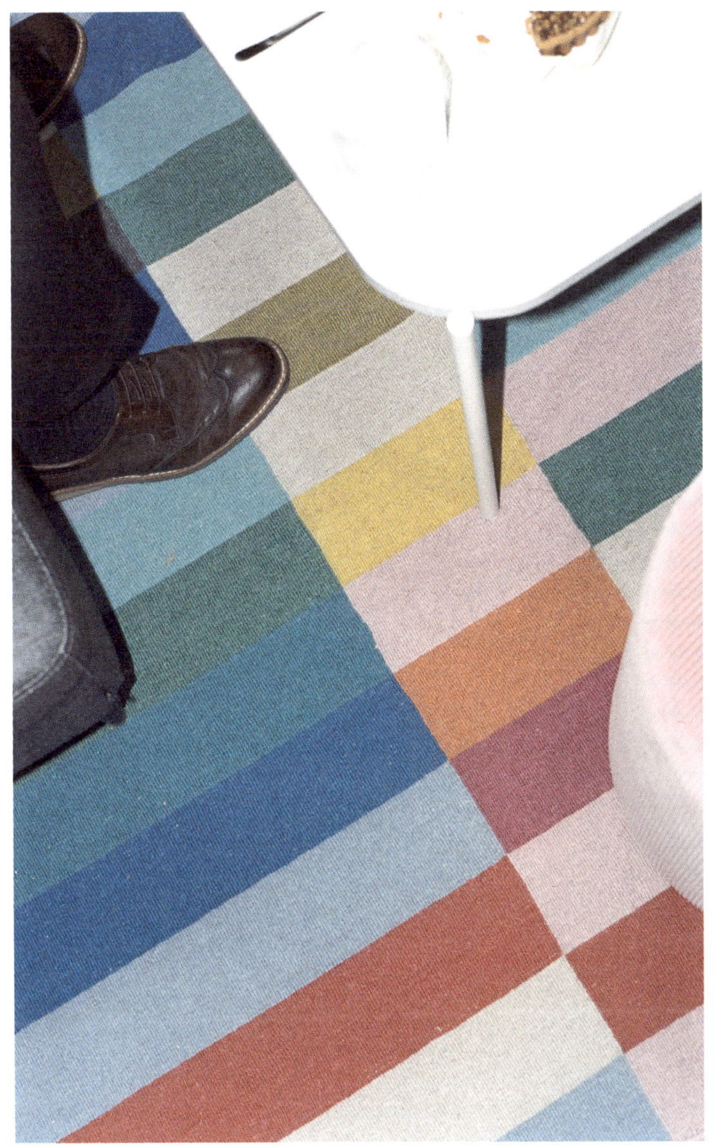

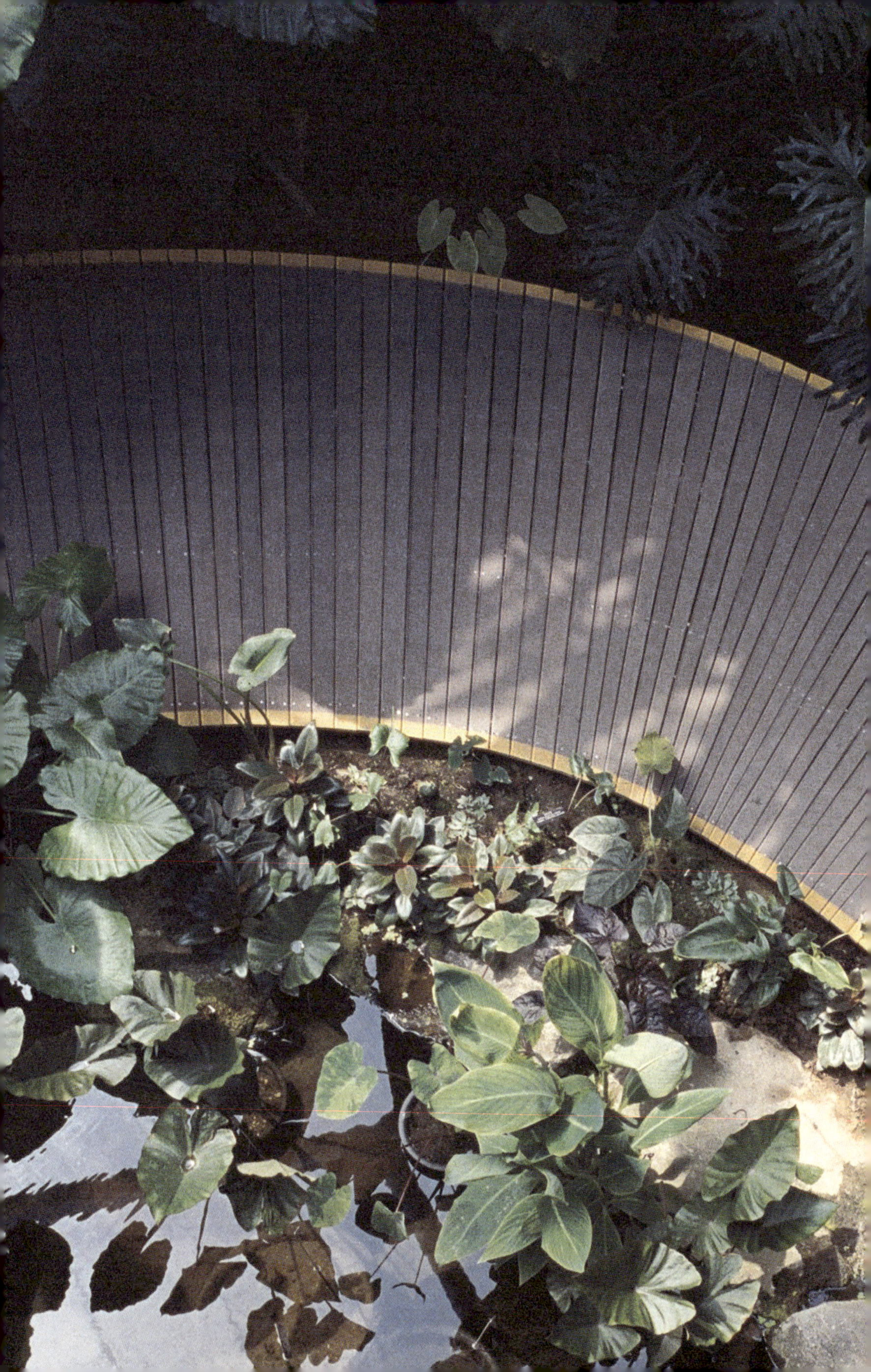

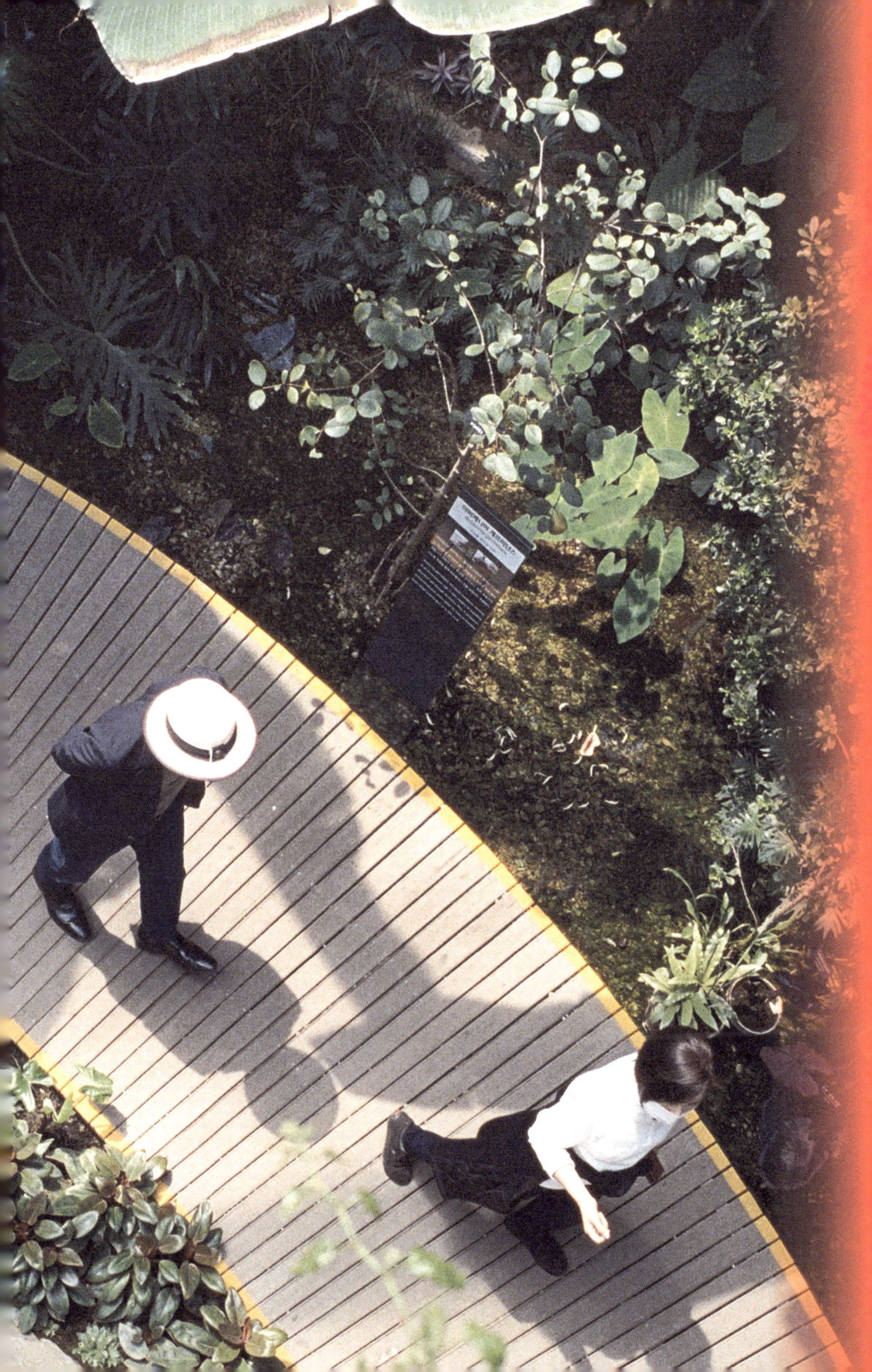

Alphabetical Index

Imprint

WHAT SHOULD I SAY—
ABOUT SEOUL

PUBLISHER

Slanted Publishers (UG)
(haftungsbeschränkt)
Nördliche Uferstraße 4–6
76189 Karlsruhe
Germany
T +49 (0) 721 85148268
info@slanted.de
slanted.de
@slanted_publishers

© Slanted Publishers, Karlsruhe, 2023
Nördliche Uferstraße 4–6,
76189 Karlsruhe, Germany

© Design by Omid Fröhlich, Youjin Kim,
David Wiesner

All rights reserved.

ISBN: 978-3-948440-45-9

2nd edition 2023

TEAM

EDITORIAL & ARTISTIC LEAD
  Omid Fröhlich
  Youjin Kim
  David Wiesner
PHOTOGRAPHY
  Omid Fröhlich
LAYOUT & EDITING
  David Wiesner
PUBLISHING DIRECTION
  Lars Harmsen, Julia Kahl
PRODUCTION MANAGEMENT
  Julia Kahl
PROOFREADING
  Jürgen Fröhlich, Natascha Fröhlich,
  Anne Wiesner
FINAL DESIGN
  Clara Weinreich

PRODUCTION

PRINTING
  Balto Print
TYPEFACES
  Fritzi Sans & Serif
by David Wiesner
  Happiness Sans
by AG Typography Institute
  Nanum Myeongjo
by Fontrix & Sandoll
  Futtenach Transitional
by David Wiesner
  Gimpel
by David Wiesner

DISCLAIMER

The publisher assumes no responsibility for the accuracy of all information. Publisher and editor assume that material that was made available for publishing, is free of third party rights. Reproduction and storage require the per mission of the publisher. Photos and texts are welcome, but there is no liability. Signed contributions do not necessarily represent the opinion of the publisher or the editor. The German National Library lists this publication in the German National Bibliography; detailed bibliographic data is available on the Internet at 'dnb.d-nb.de.'

ABOUT SLANTED PUBLISHERS

Slanted Publishers is an internationally active publishing and media house founded in 2014 by Lars Harmsen and Julia Kahl. They publish the award-winning print magazine Slanted, covering international developments in design and culture twice a year. Since its establishment in 2004, the daily Slanted blog highlights events and news from an international design scene and showcases inspiring portfolios from all over the world. In addition, Slanted Publishers initiates and creates publications, focusing on contemporary design and culture, working closely with editors and authors to produce outstanding publications with meaningful content and high quality. Slanted was born from great passion and has made a name for itself across the globe. Its design is vibrant and inspiring—its philosophy open-minded, tolerant, and curious.

ACKNOWLEDGEMENT

Thank you to all the people that took time off in their busy schedules to give us interviews or shared their stories, works, and research. This book would not have been possible without you.

Thanks to Youngji and Markus for making the trip to Seoul possible. Thanks to Prof. Iris Utikal for her feedback and support during the creation of the book as well as Kölner International School of Design (KISD) for giving us the opportunity to start this book as part of our curriculum.

A special thank you to Natascha and Jürgen Fröhlich, as well as Anne Wiesner for proofreading. Another special thanks to Dohwan Park, Johannes Mechler, Olga Funk, Henk Szanto, Katharina Reusteck, Jule Arden, Leonard Irtel von Brenndorff, and Bessie Norman for their feedback and input. Thanks to Julia Kahl and Slanted Publishers for taking good care of us during the publication process, as well as bringing these stories to a wider audience. Thanks as well to Tim Ahrens and Shoko Mugikura for their 'Kern On' plugin that was used to optimize the kerning of 'Fritzi' and 'Futtenach Transitional.'

And thank You for taking time to read this book.

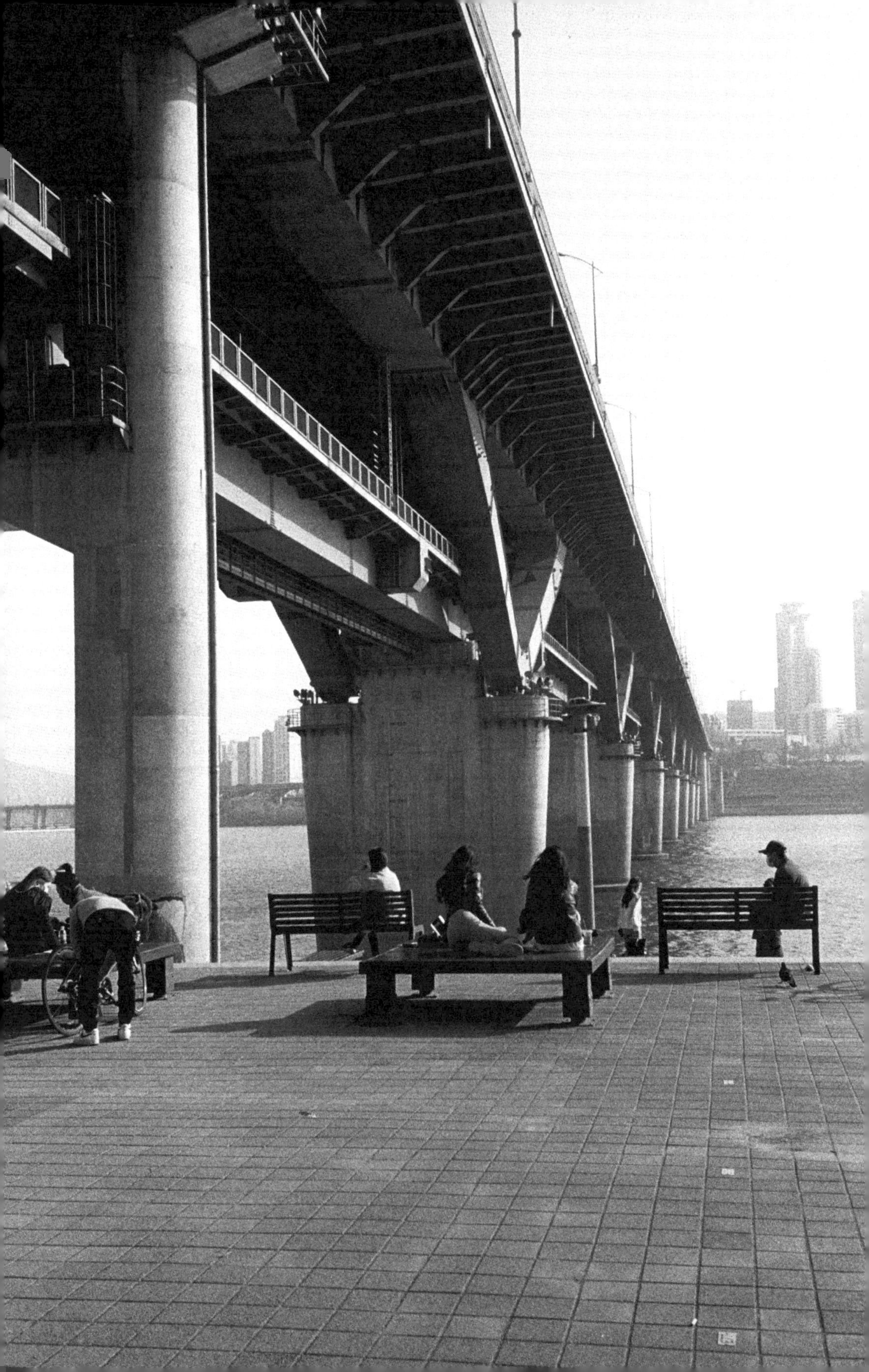